IDENTIFICATION EVIDENCE

David Deutscher
B.A., LL.B., LL.M.

Heather Leonoff
B.Sc., LL.B., LL.M.

A Carswell Publication

Canadian Cataloguing in Publication Data

Deutscher, David, 1948-
  Identification evidence

Includes index.
ISBN 0-459-35621-6

1. Criminals – Canada – Identification.
2. Evidence, Criminal – Canada.   I. Leonoff,
Heather, 1953-   II. Title.

KE9312.D48 1991   345.71'064   C91-093839-3
KF9660.D48 1991

for
H.E.W.

ACKNOWLEDGMENTS

We would like to take this opportunity to thank those who have made working on this book such a pleasure.

Many thanks to the Faculty and Staff at the Law School, University of Auckland, New Zealand, for making our stay with them so enjoyable. We would especially like to mention the efforts of the librarians who made sure that the materials we required were always accessible in the midst of extensive library renovations.

Thanks as well to the Legal Research Institute of the University of Manitoba for its most generous financial contribution. We would like to acknowledge the assistance of our three research students: Cathy Kelly, who assisted with much of the primary research, and Karen Beattie and Jonathan Penner, who have checked and rechecked our footnotes and have seen the manuscript through to its final revision.

Chapter 5 could not have been written without the assistance of Barry Gaudette of the Royal Canadian Mounted Police, Forensic Laboratory, and without the help of the librarians at the R.C.M.P. Forensic Laboratories in both Winnipeg and Ottawa. We are very appreciative of the fact that their collections were made available to us.

Last, but certainly not least, we would like to express our sincere thanks to the Partners of Wolch, Pinx, Tapper, Scurfield, for their unending support, encouragement and friendship. We would like to mention specially John Scurfield, Q.C., who first suggested this book and encouraged us to write it. We hope it meets his expectations. Our acknowledgments would not be complete without mentioning the contribution of Hersh Wolch, Q.C., whose friendship recognizes no limits and whose thoughtful advice is always appreciated.

D.B.D.
H.S.L.

TABLE OF CONTENTS

TABLE OF CASES

Chapter One

The Psychological Framework

1. THE IMPACT OF IDENTIFICATION EVIDENCE

In April 1974, the Home Secretary announced to the British House of Commons his decision to form a special committee to investigate the issue of identification in criminal cases. The inquiry was necessitated after two unrelated convictions based solely on eyewitness identification had both been shown to be wrong.[1] In both cases, witnesses had come forward and, with the best of intentions, had identified the accused as the person responsible for the crime they had observed. In both cases, the accused had proffered alibi witnesses to show he had not been at the scene. However, the visual identification of the accused by the prosecution witnesses could not be overcome despite the contrary evidence. One accused was later pardoned, the other acquitted by the Court of Appeal, but not before both had served many months of incarceration.

The special committee, under the chairmanship of Lord Devlin, reported in 1976. The *Devlin Report*[2] showed that 347 persons whose files were reviewed by the committee were prosecuted when the only evidence implicating the accused was identification by one (169 cases) or more (178 cases) eyewitnesses.[3] Seventy-four per cent of these people were convicted. This statistic indicates that the testimony of one or more eyewitnesses can be highly persuasive.

---

1   The cases involved the accused Doughtery and Virag. Details of the cases are reviewed in *Report to the Secretary of State for the Home Department of the Departmental Committee on Evidence of Identification in Criminal Cases (Devlin Report)*, (London: H.M.S.O., 1976).

2   *Ibid.*

3   *Ibid.*, Appendix B, Table 1.

1

There have been several attempts to establish the impact of identification evidence on jurors in an experimental setting. Dr. Elizabeth Loftus demonstrated the effect of eyewitness testimony on the verdicts of simulated jurors.[4] Subjects were presented with a description of a crime and a summary of the evidence and arguments presented at trial. One third of the jurors read only circumstantial evidence implicating the accused. Another third were told that in addition to the circumstantial evidence there was an eyewitness who could identify the accused. The remaining third were told that the eyewitness had been discredited in cross-examination where it was revealed that he had not been wearing his glasses at the time of the crime. The results of the study offer compelling evidence of the importance of eyewitness testimony and its impact on jurors. Only 18% of the jurors who read the circumstantial case would have convicted as compared to 72% of those who read the eyewitness testimony. A rather disturbing finding was that 68% of the group that had read of the discredited eyewitness still returned guilty verdicts. Dr. Loftus concluded from this experiment that jurors place a great deal of weight on eyewitness testimony.[5]

Researchers at the University of Alberta have also shown that jurors in an experimental setting tend to "overbelieve" identification witnesses.[6] Unsuspecting students viewed a staged theft. In some of the experimental situations the opportunity to view the "thief" was good, in others it was poor. An equal number of students who had made correct and incorrect identifications of the culprit were then cross-examined. Even in a situation where the opportunity to view the perpetrator was very poor, there was an overwhelming tendency to believe and accept the witness. Sixty-two per cent of the subjects believed the eyewitnesses even though only 50% were in fact correct. When viewing conditions were good, 77% believed the eyewitnesses against an expected rate of 50%. The researchers concluded that the subject-jurors were "overbelieving" of eyewitness testimony regardless of the witnesses' original viewing conditions.[7]

---

4   E.F. Loftus, "Reconstructing Memory: The Incredible Eyewitness" (1974), 8 Psychology Today 116.

5   E.F. Loftus, *Eyewitness Testimony* (Cambridge, Mass.: Harvard Univ. Press, 1979), at 10.

6   R.C.L. Lindsay, G.L. Wells & C.M. Rumpel, "Can People Detect Eyewitness-Identification Accuracy Within and Across Situations?" (1981), 66 J. Applied Psychology 79.

7   *Ibid.*, at 86, 87. See also, G.L. Wells, "A Reanalysis of the Expert Testimony Issue", as found in G.L. Wells & E.F. Loftus (eds.), *Eyewitness Testimony: Psychological Perspec-*

These studies suggest that eyewitness testimony has a profound impact on the outcome of a trial. There is no accurate way to estimate how often people are wrongly convicted on the uncorroborated evidence of one or more eyewitnesses. Commentators in Britain, the United States and Australia have documented many cases of false identification that have led to wrongful convictions.[8] The reason for this is that not only does this type of evidence have a profound impact but it is also inherently unreliable. The human mind is not a camera, accurately recording on film a series of events for play-back at a latter time. The human observer, unlike a mechanical device, is influenced by a variety of environmental stimuli and, because of this, accurate recall can be distorted at the time of perception, during retention and during retrieval. Without an appreciation of this, one cannot fully understand the fallibility of eyewitness identification.

2. PERCEPTION

When we see an event we do not merely record it, but consciously and unconsciously screen the event, selecting only a minimal number of environmental stimuli. The human brain is limited in what can go into it at any given time.[9] We therefore learn to concentrate on a finite number of factors and ignore others. This methodology works well in our daily living but may lead to inaccuracies when fine details such as facial features are to be observed. The optical illusion is an example of a situation where visual perception is inaccurate.[10]

There are numerous factors that affect perception. Some are related to the event itself, such as the length of time of the event or

---

tives (New York: Cambridge Univ. Press, 1984), at 306.

8   See, for example, R. Brandon & C. Davies, *Wrongful Imprisonment: Mistaken Convictions and Their Consequences* (Hamden, Conn.: Archon Books, 1973); F. Frankfurter, *The Case of Sacco and Vanzetti: A Critical Analysis for Lawyers and Laymen* (Boston: Little, Brown & Co., 1927); P. Hain, *Mistaken Identity: The Wrong Face of Law* (London: Quartet Books, 1976); Australian Law Reform Commission, Report No. 26, *Evidence*, Vol. 1 (Canberra: A.G.P.S., 1985), at 228-49; and, in general, Law Reform Commission of Canada, *Pretrial Eyewitness Identification Procedures: Police Guidelines*, by N. Brooks (Ottawa: Law Reform Commission of Canada, 1983).

9   For example, in one tenth of a second the human brain can absorb four or five digits but not nine. See H.E. Burtt, *Applied Psychology* (New York: Prentice-Hall, 1948), at 292-301; see also G.A. Miller, "The Magic Number Seven, Plus or Minus Two: Some Limits on Our Capacity for Processing Information" (1956), 63 Psychological Rev. 81.

10   R.L. Gregory, *Eye and Brain*, 3rd ed. (London: Weindenfeld and Nicholson, 1979), at 138*ff*.

the lighting conditions. Others are related to the witness, such as the age of the witness or the stress level experienced during the event. The effects of some of the factors, such as lighting, are intuitively obvious.[11] Other factors run counter to intuition. An understanding of the effect of these factors is important in order to assess the quality of the eyewitness identification.

(1) Event Factors

(a) Exposure Time

It is obvious that the longer one has to observe an event the more details one can remember. This was confirmed by psychologist Laughery and colleagues[12] in an experiment where subjects viewed a particular face for either 10 or 32 seconds. The subjects then searched for the individual among 50 slides. Not surprisingly the results indicated that the longer the exposure time the greater the probability of correct identification (58% to 47%).

Since exposure time is a relevant factor, it is important to understand our ability to estimate the length of time of an event. The duration of an event is routinely canvassed in a trial setting. Studies have established that people tend to overestimate the length of time if there is great activity and underestimate it if there is little action.[13] In an anxiety-producing situation, time is perceived to pass slowly and a stress situation appears longer than it actually is.[14] In one study into this phenomenon, psychologist Loftus showed subjects a 32-second videotape of a simulated bank

---

11   It may not, however, be obvious that there is a loss of colour perception in dim light. See E.F. Loftus & J.M. Doyle, *Eyewitness Testimony: Civil and Criminal* (New York: Kluwer, 1978), at 42.

12   K.R. Laughery, J.I. Alexander & A.B. Lane, "Recognition of Human Faces: Effects of Target Exposure Time, Target Position, Pose Position and Type of Photograph" (1971), 55 J. Applied Psychology 477.

13   R.J. Filer & D.W. Meals, "The Effect of Motivating Conditions on the Estimation of Time" (1949), 39 J. Experimental Psychology 327; R.A. Block, "Memory and the Experience of Duration in Retrospect" (1974), 2 Memory and Cognition 153; D.G. Doehring, "Accuracy and Consistency of Time Estimation by Four Methods of Reproduction" (1961), 74 Amer. J. Psychology 27.

14   J. Langer, S. Wapner & H. Werner, "The Effect of Danger Upon the Experience of Time" (1961), 74 Amer. J. Psychology 94. In this experiment subjects were blindfolded and placed on a cart moving towards a staircase. Time and distance were both overestimated in this stressful situation.

robbery.[15] The average estimation of time was 2 minutes and 32 seconds. Six per cent of the males and less than 1% of the females underestimated the time. A few people (3% of the females) provided gross overestimations, exceeding 15 minutes.

(b) Crime Seriousness

Which statement is true: a crime that appears serious will result in greater motivation to attend to the physical appearance of the criminal; or, serious crimes are more emotionally arousing than trivial ones and this arousal interferes with perception? The answer to the question is that both are true to a point. If an individual knows that he or she is witnessing a serious event then accuracy increases to a point through greater attention.[16] However once an event creates a significant level of arousal, for example through violence, perception performance begins to decline.[17] The relationship between seriousness and accuracy would appear to be an inverted "U". Seriousness will increase accuracy to a point through greater attention and then will decrease it due to arousal and avoidance properties.[18] The difficulty with this relationship is that there is no way to determine after the fact if the witness observer was at an optimum level of arousal to ensure good observation, or was on the downside of the curve, where stress would impede accuracy.[19] If a witness testifies to a high level of fear or anxiety, it is probable that stress has begun to impede perception accuracy. The statement, "I was so frightened I will

---

15   E.F. Loftus, J.W. Schooler, S.M. Boone & D. Kline, "Time Went By So Slowly: Overestimation of Event Duration by Males and Females" (1987), 1 Applied Cognitive Psychology 3. See also, B.L. Cutler, S.D. Penrod & T.K. Martens, "The Reliability of Eyewitness Identification. The Role of System and Estimator Variables" (1987), 11 Law and Human Behaviour 233.

16   M.R. Leippe, G.L. Wells & T.M. Ostrom, "Crime Seriousness as a Determinant of Accuracy in Eyewitness Identification" (1978), 63 J. Applied Psychology 345. The subjects viewed the theft of an expensive object (high seriousness) or an inexpensive object (low seriousness). When witnesses had prior knowledge of the article's value, accurate identification of the thief was more likely when the theft was of the high value goods as opposed to the low value goods (56% to 18%). When knowledge of the crime seriousness was gained after the theft, seriousness did not affect identification accuracy.

17   B.R. Clifford & J. Scott, "Individual and Situational Factors in Eyewitness Testimony" (1978), 63 J. Applied Psychology 352; E.F. Loftus & T.E. Burns, "Mental Shock Can Produce Retrograde Amnesia" (1982), 10 Memory and Cognition 318.

18   *Supra*, note 16 at 350; see also, M. McClosky, H. Egeth & J. McKenna, "The Experimental Psychologist in Court" (1986), 10 Law and Human Behaviour 1.

19   McCloskey *et al., ibid.*

never forget that face", may impress judges and juries but it is contrary to scientific research.[20]

(2) Witness Factors

(a) Stress

The effect of stress on perception is closely related to the topic of crime seriousness described above. In most cases, the more serious the crime, the more the stress that will be experienced by both victim and bystander.[21] Researchers Clifford and Hollin[22] had subjects view either a violent videotape of a mugging or a non-violent tape where street directions were sought. Subjects were then asked questions concerning age, height, weight and clothing as well as being asked to select the photograph of the male depicted in the tape from an array of ten photographs. The researchers found that the testimony of the witnesses to the non-violent event was significantly better than that of the witnesses to the violent event. Of interest was that only 27% of all the subjects were able to correctly identify the photograph. The non-violent group did slightly better than the violent group, but in general the researchers concluded that, regardless of the nature of the event, face identification is inherently unreliable.[23]

The reason stress interferes with perception is that stress leads to a narrowing of attention.[24] In the experiment discussed above, Clifford and Hollin added an additional two, then an additional four, men to the videotape.[25] In the non-violent scenario the additional perpetrators did not significantly affect overall ac-

---

20   See, for example, the words of the trial judge in *R. v. Dunlop* (1976), 33 C.C.C. (2d) 342 at 348 (Man. C.A.).

21   There is little empirical data on whether bystanders or victims differ in their ability to perceive detail. One hypothesis would suggest that the victim is unifocused on the perpetrator, thus improving performance. The other hypothesis is that stress reduces performance, thus aiding the bystander. For some preliminary studies into this issue see S.M. Kassin, "Eyewitness Identification: Victims versus Bystanders" (1984), 14 J. Applied Social Psychology 519; H. Hosch *et al.*, "Victimization, Self-Monitoring, and Eyewitness Identification" (1984), 69 J. Applied Psychology 280.

22   B.R. Clifford & C.R. Hollin, "Effects of the Type of Incident and the Number of Perpetrators on Eyewitness Memory" (1981), 66 J. Applied Psychology 364.

23   *Ibid.*, at 368.

24   J.A. Easterbrook, "The Effect of Emotion on Cue Utilization and the Organization of Behaviour" (1959), 66 Psychological Rev. 183; Ellis, "Practical Aspects of Face Memory", as found in Wells & Loftus, *supra*, note 7 at 20.

25   *Supra*, note 22.

curacy. However, in the violent scenario the loss of accuracy was pronounced as the number of perpetrators increased. The researchers concluded that in a non-violent situation witnesses can cope with the extra demands on attention and memory, but in time of stress the brain's ability to encode is reduced and thus memory is impaired.[26]

(b) Eye Fixation

Well-known effects of stress are increases in heart rate and breathing rate, but another phenomenon produced by stress is fixation of the eyes.[27] There are a multitude of stimuli that one can focus on at any given moment. In times of stress there is a tendency to block out any external stimuli and concentrate on that which causes the greatest amount of stress.[28] The term "weapon fixation" or "weapon focus" has been coined by psychologists to describe the natural tendency of an observer to focus on a weapon and ignore other details in the environment.[29] A cross-examination at trial may yield a vivid description of the weapon involved to the detriment of the witnesses' ability to identify the assailant. The eyes have focused on the most visible element of danger to the virtual exclusion of all else.

Eye fixation may come into play in other ways. For example, if a victim is seeking an escape route, he or she might concentrate on the door. Or the victim of a crime might focus on the criminal's hands if these represent the greatest threat. An experiment conducted by Professor Kassin gives some support for this proposition.[30] He showed that victims of a staged theft were entirely unable to identify the perpetrator because they appeared to concentrate on the hands that were grabbing at their money. Half of the bystanders were able to make a correct identification because their gaze had been directed to the perpetrator's face. Our eyes therefore, do not act as a wide-angle lens capturing a maze of detail. Rather, the brain has limited capacity and if it fixates on one object there may be little room left for the detailed processing involved in face recognition.[31]

---

26   *Supra*, note 22 at 368.
27   F.D. Woocher, "Did Your Eyes Deceive You? Expert Psychological Testimony on the Unreliability of Eyewitness Identification" (1977), 29 Stan. L. Rev. 969 at 979.
28   *Ibid.*
29   E.F. Loftus, G.R. Loftus & J. Messo, "Some Facts About Weapon Focus" (1987), 11 Law and Human Behaviour 55.
30   Kassin, *supra*, note 21.
31   G.L. Wells, *Eyewitness Identification*, (Agincourt: Carswell, 1988), at 18.

(c) Expectations

Perception is also affected by personal needs and biases. In essence, we see what we want to see. This was well illustrated by a 1954 study by Hastorf and Cantrill,[32] where groups of students from two universities watched a replay of a very dirty football game between their respective university teams. The two groups seemed to watch different games; each seeing more infractions and more violent infractions by the other team.

We are familiar with this phenomenon in our ordinary life. Recall how difficult it is to proofread your own written material. Our eyes tend to correct the spelling. In fact, in scientific experiments where subjects are asked to write down the words flashed on a screen, there is an overwhelming tendency to see a properly spelled English word. For example, in a 1935 study, 80% of the study group shown the word "dack" reported it as "duck" when told they would see words associated with animals.[33]

In a 1982 Manitoba murder trial,[34] the Crown proved that the accused had shot through a glass window which had light-weight curtains on it, killing his wife's lover. The issue was whether the accused could see the man inside and therefore had meant to kill, or whether, as he testified, he did not realize the deceased was there and had discharged the gun in an attempt to frighten his wife. He testified he could not see through the window, but police officers who conducted experiments under the same lighting conditions testified that they could see a man inside the room. The accused was convicted of manslaughter. The case is an excellent example of how expectations influence perception. The accused, in a high state of stress and wanting to frighten, failed to see the deceased; police officers conducting the experiments in a controlled environment and concentrating on seeing a man, were able to. Both parties were influenced by their expectations.

(d) Age

The issue of how memory is affected by age is not fully understood. The reliability of children's testimony is particularly salient as society becomes more aware that children are extremely vulnerable and are often the victims of crime.

---

32   A.H. Hastorf & H. Cantrill, "They Saw A Game: A Case Study" (1954), 49 J. Abnormal and Social Psychology 129.
33   Siipola, "A Group Study of Some Effects of Preparatory Set" (1935), 46 Psychological Monographs 27.
34   *R. v. Langlois* (1983), 20 Man. R. (2d) 396 (C.A.).

One of the findings concerning children's testimony that has been replicated consistently is that spontaneous recall increases with age.[35] The amount of information reported through free narrative increases steadily from ages 6 through 12 and then levels out, children over the age of 12 performing equally to adults.[36] What is of particular interest, however, is that although young children recall less detail, the information they do recall is no less accurate than that of adults.[37] As well, research has shown that if children do innocently add wrong information it is often exaggerated or blatantly contradictory and thus easier to detect as false.[38] Adults, on the other hand, also innocently incorporate information into their recall, but it is logical and plausible and therefore difficult to detect.[39]

Other research into children's testimony shows that children are better able to describe actions than they are at giving descriptions.[40] This is relevant in the courtroom setting, where children are often asked questions concerning clothing or facial features. Preliminary research suggests that children may perform poorly at this task but may be very able to describe activities they witnessed.

Face recognition of familiar faces is good in children as young as 6.[41] However, at age 6 the ability to recognize a previously unfamiliar face is only slightly above chance. As age increases to 12, performance improves. Past the age of 12, children perform equally to adults.[42] Of concern to the criminal justice system is that research suggests that children under the age of 13 are significantly more likely than adults to report false identifications; that is, make a wrong identification as opposed to refusing to identify.[43] This would imply a tendency on the part of young children to guess

---

35   G.S. Goodman, C. Aman & J. Hirschman, "Child Sexual and Physical Abuse: Children's Testimony", as found in S.J. Ceci, M.P. Toglia & D.F. Ross (eds.), *Children's Eyewitness Memory* (New York: Springer-Verlag, 1987), at 1; M.A. King & J.C. Yuille, "Suggestibility and the Child Witness", as found in Ceci, Toglia & Ross, *supra*, at 24; K.J. Saywitz, "Children's Testimony: Age Related Patterns of Memory Errors", as found in Ceci, Toglia & Ross, *supra*, at 36.

36   C.B. Cole & E.F. Loftus, "The Memory of Children", as found in Ceci, Toglia & Ross, *ibid.*, at 183.

37   *Supra*, notes 35 and 36.

38   Saywitz, *supra*, note 35 at 46, 47.

39   *Ibid.*

40   Cole & Loftus, *supra*, note 36 at 185.

41   J.E. Chance & A.G. Goldstein, "Face Recognition Memory: Implications for Children's Eyewitness Testimony" (1984), 40, No.2, J. Social Issues 69 at 71, 72.

42   *Ibid.*

43   *Ibid.*, and Cole & Loftus, *supra*, note 36 at 199-205.

rather than admit to a lack of knowledge.[44] The implication of this for law enforcement officers is to ensure that children are cautioned against guessing and that they feel no pressure to answer a question or make an identification.

The psychological research into this area is far from complete. It would appear, however, that children 6 years of age and over are able to make a contribution to the justice system. The exact limits of that contribution are still to be determined.

At the other end of the spectrum are the elderly. The natural aging process also has an effect on aspects of memory. Though elderly people may have excellent memories for events of many years ago,[45] aging appears to interfere with the input processing of both verbal and visual material.[46] Statistical studies involving the elderly can only provide information on the average older person. Individual differences will be of prime importance.[47] With this caution in mind, it may be noted that memory decline is not statistically noticeable until after the age of 60.[48] Face identification is somewhat poorer for the elderly than for the younger population.[49] However, studies have also shown that the elderly are cautious, declining to make an identification without a high degree of confidence.[50] The elderly may be more affected by some of the factors that generally influence perception, such as stress or limited exposure time, but research into these variables is not complete.[51]

(e) Sex

Studies on whether males or females make better identification witnesses are contradictory.[52] The bulk of research suggests

---

44   Saywitz, *supra*, note 35 at 47, 48; Cole & Loftus, *supra*, note 36 at 207.
45   H.P. Bahrick, P.O. Bahrick & R.P. Wittlinger, "Fifty Years of Memory for Names and Faces: A Cross Sectional Approach" (1975), 104 J. Experimental Psychology: General 54.
46   A.D. Yarmey, "Age as a Factor in Eyewitness Memory", in Wells & Loftus, *supra*, note 7 at 150.
47   Loftus & Doyle, *supra*, note 11 at 59, 60.
48   *Ibid.*, at 59.
49   A.D. Yarmey & J. Kent, "Eyewitness Identification by Elderly and Young Adults" (1980), 4 Law and Human Behaviour 359; and, *supra*, note 46.
50   *Ibid.*
51   *Supra*, note 46.
52   See, in general, P.A. Powers, J.L. Andriks & E.F. Loftus, "Eyewitness Accounts of Females and Males" (1979), 64 J. Applied Psychology 339; Loftus & Doyle, *supra*, note 11 at 60-62; A.D. Yarmey, *The Psychology of Eyewitness Testimony* (New York: Free Press, 1979), at 127.

that women are slightly better than men in face recognition.[53] Sexual socialization would appear to play a minor role in perception; that is, males tending to focus on male-relevant stimuli and *vice versa*. A 1979 study showed that men were better able to describe a car than women. However, the women outperformed the men in describing the female subject.[54] This finding would be consistent with the studies suggesting slightly better face identification by females over males, if one assumes that female socialization has tended to direct women's attention to the human form. In a practical sense, knowledge of this phenomenon may be important in assessing witness credibility. The ability of a witness to describe certain elements of a scene to the exclusion of others may possibly be explained by sex related aspects of perception.

(f) Alcohol and Drugs

It is beyond the scope of this book to discuss in detail the effects of alcohol or other drugs on the human memory.[55] Individual drugs will act in specific ways with particular results. However, a few general comments may be made.

Alcohol appears to interfere with the acquisition stage of memory.[56] The hypothesis is that alcohol reduces the processing resources.[57] Marijuana has been shown to impair memory after a delay of four to six seconds.[58] The viewed material is not passed along from short term memory into long term memory. Time perception is also impaired by marijuana. Marijuana, as well as amphetamines and L.S.D., lengthens perceived duration.[59] There is of course a plethora of other drugs, with individual properties. If drug ingestion by a witness is in issue, a pharmacologist may be able to provide valuable information.

---

53   Yarmey, *ibid.*
54   Powers, Andriks & Loftus, *supra*, note 52.
55   See, in general, Loftus & Doyle, *supra*, note 11 at 65.
56   I.M. Birnbaum & E.S. Parker, "Acute Effects of Alcohol on Storage and Retrieval", in I.M. Birnbaum & E.S. Parker (eds.), *Alcohol and Human Memory* (Lawrence Erlbaum, 1977), at 99.
57   *Ibid.* See also, F. Craik, "Similarities Between the Effects of Aging and Alcoholic Intoxication on Memory Performance, Construed Within a Levels of Processing Framework", in Birnbaum & Parker, *ibid.*, at 9.
58   National Institute on Drug Abuse, *Marijuana Research Findings: 1980* (U.S. Dept. of Health and Human Services); E.L. Abel, "Marijuana, Learning and Memory" (1975), 18 Int. Rev. Neurobiology 329.
59   Yarmey, *supra*, note 52 at 43.

3. RETENTION AND RETRIEVAL

Once an event has been coded into memory, the process of forgetting begins. Simply put, as time passes and new events occur that must be stored in memory, older events become interfered with or obliterated.[60]

The classic experiment on retention is the Ebbinghaus Nonsense Syllable Test which gave rise to the "forgetting curve". Forgetting is initially rapid and then becomes more and more gradual as time passes.[61] This general theory has been confirmed in several subsequent experiments both of a general nature[62] and specifically on face recognition.[63] The "forgetting curve" is a well accepted principle indicating that identification procedures held several days, weeks or even months after a crime are of suspect validity. Further, if a witness becomes more detailed at trial than he or she was at an earlier stage, the additional details must be considered suspect. It is likely the additional details have been added unconsciously, either from another source or through the brain's own unconscious modification of memory.

(1) Post-Event Information

Time is not the only factor that causes memory to decay. Memory, like perception, is an active process and memories can be altered or replaced by the introduction of new material.[64] Once altered, the original memory is lost, or at least very difficult to locate.[65]

---

60   This is deliberately oversimplified. The study of memory is complex. For greater detail see J.A. Adams, *Human Memory* (New York: McGraw Hill, 1967); A.D. Baddeley, *The Psychology of Memory* (New York: Basic Books, 1976); L.S. Cermak & F. Craik, *Levels of Processing in Human Memory* (New York: John Wiley and Sons, 1979); J.M. Gardiner (ed.), *Readings in Human Memory* (Methuen & Co., 1976); Loftus, *supra*, note 5.

61   The Ebbinghaus experiments and the forgetting curve are discussed in Baddeley, *ibid.*, at 3-15. See also, Loftus & Doyle, *supra*, note 11 at 70-72.

62   Loftus, *supra*, note 5 at 53, 54; J.P. Lipton, "On the Psychology of Eyewitness Testimony" (1977), 62 J. Applied Psychology 90.

63   J.W. Shepherd & H.D. Ellis, "The Effect of Attractiveness on Recognition Memory for Faces" (1973), 86 Amer. J. Psychology 627.

64   Wells, *supra*, note 31 at 5-7; D.F. Hall, E.F. Loftus & J.P. Tousignant, "Postevent Information and Changes in Recollection for a Natural Event", in Wells & Loftus, *supra*, note 7 at 124.

65   There is controversy over whether the original memory is entirely lost (see Hall, Loftus & Tousignant, *ibid.*; Loftus & Doyle, *supra*, note 11 at 79, 80), or whether it is buried in favour of the new information (see M. McCloskey & M. Zaragoza, "Misleading Postevent Information and Memory for Events: Arguments and Evidence

Many experiments have been done to show the effect of post-event information on memory. In one such experiment[66] researchers had subjects view a group of people. In one part of the experiment subjects were even told to pay careful attention as they would be required to make a photographic face identification later in the experiment. After an interval ranging from $1^1/2$ hours up to three days, the participants viewed a photographic array and were asked to identify the targets. Finally four days to a week later the subjects viewed a live lineup and were asked to make an identification. The results indicated that the subjects were quite able to distinguish faces of individuals never encountered. However, after having seen a photograph the subjects were equally likely to identify a person seen in a photograph as they were to identify the live target. The faces viewed in the photographs had supplanted the original observation, presumably erasing for all time that originally seen.[67]

It is not uncommon for a witness to state during an identification procedure (a lineup or photo array for example) words to the effect that the subject "looks like" or is "closest to" or "may be" the perpetrator. Shortly thereafter, sometimes within seconds, sometimes by trial, the guess has become a certainty. Researchers have hypothesized that this rapid transformation from uncertainty to certainty is another example of one memory supplanting another. The memory is rapidly adjusted and the new stimulus is implanted. Subsequent identification at lineups or in a courtroom are then of no use. If a lineup is subsequently conducted containing both the actual criminal and the wrongly identified individual, there is an overwhelming tendency to reconfirm the wrong identification.[68]

Numerous studies over the past decade have also shown that witnesses will incorporate new, often false, information into their reports of events if the information is introduced through a credible source.[69] The typical study has subjects view an event and then

---

Against Memory Impairment Hypotheses" (1985), 114 J. Experimental Psychology: General 1). There is probably little practical significance. If lost, it is lost for good. If buried, it is buried so deep as to be indistinguishable from the new memory.

66   E. Brown, K. Deffenbacher & W. Sturgill, "Memory for Faces and the Circumstances of Encounter" (1977), 62 J. Applied Psychology 311. See also, *infra*, note 68.

67   Hall, Loftus & Tousignant, *supra*, note 64 at 128.

68   G.W. Gorenstein & P.C. Ellsworth, "Effect of Choosing an Incorrect Photograph on a Later Identification by an Eyewitness" (1980), 65 J. Applied Psychology 616.

69   D.A. Bekerian & J.M. Bower, "Eyewitness Testimony: Were We Misled?" (1983), 9 J. Experimental Psychology: Learning Memory and Cognition 139; J.M. Bower & D.A. Bekerian, "When Will Post-event Information Distort Eyewitness Testimony?"

misleading information is introduced through leading questions or an erroneous written summary. The person's memory of the original event is then tested. The studies have shown that the subjects will incorporate the false information into their final reports. For example, Loftus[70] showed subjects slides of a traffic accident where a car failed to stop at a stop sign. Afterwards viewers were asked a question concerning a yield sign. On a subsequent memory test, subjects exposed to the misleading information were more likely than control subjects to report seeing a yield sign in the original film sequence. Even very small and subtle changes in language may influence the memory of a witness. For example, asking the age of the "young man" as opposed to the "man" results in significant differences as to age estimation.[71]

The hypothesis surrounding this observed phenomenon is that the subjects doubt their own memory and therefore accept the superior knowledge of the experimenter, or, alternatively, they have no memory of the original fact and are quick to accept additional information from a credible source.[72] Whatever the reason, it is clear that post-event information can alter the person's report of the memory. Witnesses can obtain post-event information from a variety of sources; other witnesses, police and prosecutors, media reports. Once altered, the witness quite honestly will be unable to distinguish the originally perceived material from that which has been gleaned from other sources.

Finally it should be noted that if witnesses are warned in advance to watch out for false or misleading information, they are better able to resist suggestion.[73] The implication for law enforce-

---

(1984), 69 J. Applied Psychology 466; R.E. Christiaansen & K. Ochalek, "Editing Misleading Information From Memory: Evidence for the Co-existence of Original and Postevent Information" (1983), 11 Memory and Cognition 467; E.F. Loftus, "Leading Questions and the Eyewitness Report" (1975), 7 Cognitive Psychology 560; McCloskey & Zaragoza, *supra*, note 65; H. Weinberg, J. Wadsworth & R. Baron, "Demand and the Impact of Leading Questions on Eyewitness Testimony" (1983), 11 Memory and Cognition 101.

70   Loftus & Doyle, *supra*, note 11 at 76.
71   R.E. Christiaansen, J.D. Sweeney & K. Ochalek, "Influencing Eyewitness Descriptions" (1983), 7 Law and Human Behaviour 59.
72   McCloskey & Zaragoza, *supra*, note 65; M. Zaragoza, "Memory, Suggestibility, and Eyewitness Testimony in Children and Adults" in Ceci, Toglia & Ross, *supra*, note 35 at 61.
73   J.D. Read & D. Bruce, "On the External Validity of Questioning Effects in Eyewitness Testimony" (1984), 33 Int. Rev. Applied Psychology 33; D.H. Dodd & J.M. Bradshaw, "Leading Questions and Memory: Pragmatic Constraints" (1980), 19 J. Verbal Learning & Verbal Behaviour 695. This study is extremely interesting to lawyers. The

ment officers is that not only should questions be neutral, but witnesses should be specifically warned in advance to watch out for and resist suggestion.[74]

Of particular concern to the legal system at the present time is the issue of the suggestibility of children. It would appear to be a widely held belief that children are highly suggestible, much more so than adults. The empirical research into this issue is still in its infancy and no definitive response can be given.[75] However, some preliminary findings suggest that preschoolers are highly suggestible, the hypothesis being that their mental functions are not sufficiently developed to be able to detect the false information or to take the necessary actions to reject the false information if they detect it.[76] With respect to slightly older children (ages 6 to 9), the research shows that they tend to "go along" with post-event information to please the experimenter.[77] Since children of this age group provide less information through free recall,[78] they are extremely vulnerable to post-event suggestion through later questioning. The experiments with older children indicate that, by the age of 10 or 11, they are no more vulnerable to suggestion than are adults.[79] When dealing with children extra care should be taken to ensure neutral, unbiased questioning, but beyond this general caution there is nothing in the literature at present which would suggest that children over the age of 10, and perhaps as young as 6, cannot provide evidence that is of value to the system.

(2) Unconscious Modification

Not only is memory affected by the receiving and storing of post-event information, but it is also affected by the psychological need to eliminate uncertainties and inconsistences. Memories are therefore distorted "so that it all makes sense". Details are added to complete a fragmented picture.[80]

---

subjects witnessed an auto accident and post-event information supplied by a neutral party was incorporated by a significant number of subjects. However, if the same information was attributed to the defence lawyer, the effect was eliminated!

74 Wells, *supra*, note 31 at 32-38.
75 For a review of current research see, Cole & Loftus, *supra*, note 36 at 178.
76 S.J. Ceci, D.F. Ross & M.P. Toglia, "Age Differences in Suggestibility: Narrowing the Uncertainties", in Ceci, Toglia & Ross, *supra*, note 35 at 90.
77 King & Yuille, *supra*, note 35 at 28; G.S. Goodman & R.S. Reed, "Age Differences in Eyewitness Testimony" (1986), 10 Law and Human Behaviour 317.
78 See discussion this chapter, part 2(2)(d), Age.
79 Cole & Loftus, *supra*, note 36 at 195.
80 Woocher, *supra*, note 27 at 983.

Not only will a witness add detail through his or her own unconscious act, there also may be subtle pressure on a witness to guess. Witnesses generally want to be helpful and to provide as much information as possible.[81] If the police have gone to the trouble of composing a lineup, there may a tendency to guess despite an element of uncertainty. Guessing, however, is one way that memory gaps are filled in and guesses ultimately become certainties. Researchers have shown this through an experiment where subjects were asked questions and encouraged to guess about details of a staged crime they had witnessed.[82] After a short break their memory of the staged event was tested a second time, but this time they were warned not to guess if they did not know the answer. The results showed that the group that had guessed were much more likely than the control group to be wrong in detail. The "guesses" had been incorporated into memory and were now recalled as fact.

Another aspect to the same experiment was to show that answers originally reported with low confidence were later repeated with high confidence.[83] In other words, repetition establishes the answer in the mind and this is true whether or not the original answer was correct or incorrect.[84] This, in part, explains the witness who between preliminary inquiry and trial becomes more certain or adds more detail. The memory gaps have been filled in by guesses that have now become cemented in memory. The witness may report this as being due to extra thought or concentration, but since memory does not improve with time it is likely attributable to unconscious memory modification.

(3) Retrieval

(a) Questioning and Context Cues

Successful retrieval of information from memory is directly related to the quality of the acquisition and retention of the original material. There are two aspects to retrieval: recall and recognition. Recall requires positive action on the part of the individual; providing either a verbal or perhaps a pictorial representation of the

---

81   *Ibid.*
82   R. Hastie, R. Landsman & E.F. Loftus, "Eyewitness Testimony: The Dangers in Guessing" (1978), 19 Jurimetrics J. 1.
83   *Ibid.*
84   G.M. Whipple, "The Observer as Reporter" (1909), 6 Psychological Bull. 153.

memory.[85] Recognition is essentially a multiple choice test. The person must search his or her memory to determine if there is a match.[86] As a general statement recognition memory is superior to recall memory.[87] ("Your face looks familiar, but I can't remember your name.") Both forms of retrieval are, however, inherently poor when the object to be recalled or recognized is a face.[88]

Retrieval may be aided by proper questioning. The type of questioning used, however, may influence both the amount and accuracy of the information retrieved. Free recall, where the person provides a narrative without assistance, is the process most free of bias. It provides the most accurate information but is also the least complete.[89] Leading questions on the other hand may have a massive impact on the final report, one study showing that only 5% of subjects could avoid being misled somewhat by leading questions.[90] Retrieval may also be assisted by "controlled narrative". This involves the use of questions to help direct attention.

One of the most complete experiments conducted into the effect of various questioning techniques was a joint effort by a lawyer and two psychologists.[91] The experiment consisted of showing a movie to a total of 151 "witnesses" and then questioning them. All witnesses first provided a free recall and then were questioned in one of four ways: moderate guidance, where witnesses were asked such things as "what objects were visible?"; high guidance, where questions such as "how many houses did you see?" were asked; multiple choice questions; and extremely leading questions typical of a trial cross-examination. The experiment confirmed that the type of questioning had a profound effect on completeness and accuracy. During free recall, only about one quarter of all relevant information was reported, but with great accuracy. As the questions became more directed, more information was elicited, leading questions extracting approximately 85% of all relevant material. However, there was a concomitant decline

---

85   Wells, *supra*, note 31 at 8.
86   *Ibid.*
87   D.L. Postman, W.O. Jenkins & L. Postman, "An Experimental Comparison of Active Recall and Recognition" (1948), Amer. J. Psychology 511; Yarmey, *supra*, note 52 at 139.
88   *Infra*, this chapter, part 4, Pre-Trial Identification.
89   Loftus, *supra*, note 5 at 91, 92; Lipton, *supra*, note 62.
90   B.R. Clifford & J. Scott, "Individual and Situational Factors in Eyewitness Testimony" (1978), 63 J. Applied Psychology 352.
91   J. Marshall, K.H. Marquis & S. Oskamp, "Effects of Kind of Questions and Atmosphere of Interrogation on Accuracy and Completeness of Testimony" (1971), 84 Harv. L. Rev. 1620.

in accuracy. The study also established that alerting the subjects to be aware of the biasing effects of questions could decrease but not eliminate this negative effect.

The inverse relationship between accuracy and completeness creates a dilemma for law enforcement officers. University of Alberta psychologist Gary Wells, in a book written for law enforcement personnel, suggests that a free recall approach followed by unbiased specific questions will produce the best compromise between accuracy and completeness.[92] The development of an unbiased question, however, is not an easy task. Even the article used to preface a noun may have a subtle effect; a witness is more likely to report seeing a non-existent object when asked, "Did you see *the* . . .?", rather than, "Did you see *a* . . .?"[93] The false information may then become lodged in memory with the witness unable to discern the original from the reconstruction.[94]

Retrieval may also be aided by context cues. Context cues are nothing more than aids that assist in reconstructing the event in its original form. We do this, for example, if we misplace an article such as our car keys. We reconstruct our day trying to remember where we could have put the missing keys. The "crimestoppers" television reconstructions are also examples of this, trying to jog people's memory by placing the event in context.

Researchers have shown that context cues may be of assistance in helping to retrieve memories. For example, people show better memory for an event if the same emotional mood is recalled.[95] Law enforcement officers are therefore taught to encourage witnesses to relive the scene, including how they were feeling and what they were thinking.[96] Helping witnesses to reconstruct the actions and objects that constituted the original event can also help to improve face identification accuracy. Researchers Malpass and Devine were able to increase correct identification of a target suspect to 60% from 40% by using a guided memory interview which assisted the subjects in reliving the event.[97] However, research has also shown that dressing all lineup members in the same clothes to match a description given by a witness decreases

92   Wells, *supra*, note 31 at 32-38.
93   E.F. Loftus & G. Zanni, "Eyewitness Testimony: The Influence of the Wording of a Question" (1975), 5 Bull. Psychonomic Soc. 86.
94   See generally, this chapter, part 3(1), Post-Event Information.
95   G.H. Bower, "Mood and Memory" (1981), 36 Amer. Psychologist 129.
96   Wells, *supra*, note 31 at 61,62, and 75,76.
97   R.S. Malpass & P.G. Devine, "Guided Memory in Eyewitness Identification Lineups" (1981), 66 J. Applied Psychology 343.

identification accuracy. Rather than acting as a context cue, the repetitive clothing becomes disorienting and makes concentration on facial features more difficult.[98]

(b) Hypnosis

Hypnosis is another technique that has been used in an attempt to retrieve memories, however its use is highly controversial. It has been used successfully on occasion with dramatic results. For example, in 1976 a bus carrying 26 youngsters from Chowchilla, California was hijacked and the children and bus driver forced into an abandoned truck trailer buried six feet underground. After they were rescued, the bus driver was hypnotized and was able to recall all but one digit of the licence plate of the van used by the hijackers. This information, which had not been available through ordinary questioning techniques, assisted in the capture of the three suspects.[99] Results like this make hypnosis a useful tool, as long as its limitations are understood.

The hypnotic state is characterized by increased suggestibility, compliance and cooperation.[100] There is a desire to please the hypnotist and to comply with both the explicit and implicit demands of that person. The hypnotic technique involves the use of positive reinforcers such as "good" and "you are doing fine" and these words act to subtly encourage modifications in the memory that seem to please the hypnotist.[101] For example, under hypnosis, an individual may be asked to look at something that is clearly outside the range of visual acuity. The subject will report the details of this fantasized perception as real.[102] The term "confabulation" is used to describe the process in which the memory gaps are filled in and are accepted as real.[103] An individual can also lie while in an hypnotic state.[104] This is particularly true if the lie would serve that person's best interests. It is also possible to feign being under hypnosis and fool very experienced clinicians.[105]

---

98   G.S. Sanders, "Effects of Context Cues on Eyewitness Identification Responses" (1984), 14 J. Applied Social Psychology 386.
99   Loftus, *supra*, note 5 at 104, 105; Yarmey, *supra*, note 52 at 175, 176.
100 M.T. Orne, D.A. Soskis, D.F. Dinges & E.C. Orne, "Hypnotically Induced Testimony", in Wells & Loftus, *supra*, note 7 at 171.
101 *Ibid.*, at 175, 176.
102 *Ibid.*, at 177.
103 *Ibid.*
104 *Ibid.* The same is true for "truth sera" such as sodium Pentothal. See Yarmey, *supra*, note 52 at 175.
105 *Ibid.*

Hypnosis is also entirely ineffective in improving recognition memory. Subjects under the effects of hypnosis are significantly less accurate in recognizing faces in a lineup. The reason for this is the heightened suggestibility caused by the hypnosis. It leads to individuals identifying a person for reasons other than facial recognition.[106]

Without doubt hypnosis can assist in the recall of accurate and meaningful information. This positive gain is brought about by the increased relaxation and concentration. However, there is a corresponding increase in inaccurate information, the subject filling in the gaps with appropriate and plausible detail. Neither the subject nor the observer is able to distinguish what is fact from what is fiction. The memories and pseudomemories are melded into one.[107]

The use of hypnosis also brings about a misplaced confidence in the truthfulness and accuracy of the memories. The subject is much more certain of both the original and pseudomemories arrived at during the hypnosis. This misplaced confidence in inaccurate recall tends to make the witness more credible to third party viewers, who see not only a confident witness but one who is precise as to detail. The details, however, are as likely a product of confabulation as they are of reality.[108]

The admissibility of "hypnotically refreshed" testimony has generally been rejected in United States jurisdictions. The general argument against admissibility is that the probative value is outweighed by the prejudicial effect. In essence, the inability of the witness to be able to separate original memories from those produced by confabulation creates the prejudice.

This argument was first accepted by the Minnesota Supreme Court in *State v. Mack*.[109] Relying on expert testimony garnered from around the country, the Minnesota Supreme Court stated:[110]

> Expert testimony further indicated that a hypnotized subject is highly susceptible to suggestion, even that which is subtle and unintended ... The hypnotized subject is influenced by a need to "fill gaps". When asked a question under hypnosis, rarely will he or she respond, "I don't know". Another factor ... which can affect the

106   G.S. Sanders & W.L. Simmons, "Use of Hypnosis to Enhance Eyewitness Accuracy: Does It Work?" (1983), 68 J. Applied Psychology 70.
107   *Supra*, note 100 at 183-89. For an excellent judicial review of the limits of hypnosis see *State v. Peoples*, 319 S.E. 2d 177 (N.C., 1984).
108   *Supra*, note 100 at 192-94.
109   292 N.W. 2d 764 (Minn., 1980)
110   *Ibid.*, at 768, 769.

"memory" produced under hypnosis is the subject's desire to please either the hypnotist or others who have asked the person hypnotized to remember and who have urged that it is important that he or she remember certain events. Most significantly, there is no way to determine from the content of the "memory" itself which parts of it are historically accurate, which are entirely fanciful, and which are lies.

In addition to its historical unreliability, a "memory" produced under hypnosis becomes hardened in the subject's mind. A witness who was unclear about his "story" before the hypnotic session becomes convinced of the absolute truth of the account he made while under hypnosis. This conviction is so firm that the ordinary "indicia of reliability" are completely erased, and hypnotic subjects have been able to pass lie detector tests while attesting to the truth of statements made under hypnosis which researchers know to be utterly false.

Based on the scientific evidence the Minnesota Supreme Court determined that since the testimony cannot even be established as having first been perceived by the witness, as opposed to fantasized, its prejudice outweighed any probative value. As such the court ruled that evidence first revealed under hypnosis was inadmissible. The ruling has been followed in numerous other American jurisdictions.[111]

The general trend in the United States is to reject only the testimony which is a direct product of the hypnosis session. Guidelines have been suggested that recommend that all recollections before the session be recorded (preferably on videotape) so as to differentiate between pre- and post-session evidence.[112] However, the California[113] position is that once a witness is hypnotized, the witness' evidence on all topics covered in the session is inadmissible. The reasoning is that the increased confidence created by the hypnotic session is said to be unfair to the defendant. This extreme position is not generally accepted. For example, the

---

111 *Contreras v. State*, 718 P. 2d 129 (Alaska, 1986); *Collins v. Super. Ct.*, 644 P. 2d 1266 (Ariz., 1982); *People v. Shirley*, 641 P. 2d 775, cert. denied 459 U.S. 860 (Calif., 1982); *People v. Quintanar*, 659 P. 2d 710 (Colo. App., 1982); *State v. Davis*, 490 A. 2d 601 (Del., 1985); *Bundy v. State*, 471 So. 2d 9, cert. denied 479 U.S. 894 (Fla., 1985); *State v. Moreno*, 709 P. 2d 103 (Hawaii, 1985); *Peterson v. State*, 448 N.E. 2d 673 (Ind., 1983); *State v. Haislip*, 701 P. 2d 909, cert. denied 474 U.S. 1022 (Kan., 1985); *State v. Metscher*, 464 A. 2d 1052 (Md., 1983); *Commonwealth v. Kater*, 447 N.E. 2d 1190 (Mass., 1983); *People v. Gonzales*, 310 N.W. 2d 306 (Mich. App., 1981), affirmed 329 N.W. 2d 743 (Mich., 1982); *State v. Palmer*, 313 N.W. 2d 648 (Neb., 1981); *People v. Hughes*, 453 N.E. 2d 484 (N.Y. App., 1983); *State v. Peoples*, 319 S.E. 2d 177 (N.C., 1984); *Robison v. State*, 677 P. 2d 1080, cert. denied 467 U.S. 1246 (Okla. Cr., 1984); *Commonwealth v. Nazarovitch*, 436 A. 2d 170 (Pa., 1981); *State v. Martin*, 684 P. 2d 651 (Wash., 1984).
112 See, for example, *State v. Palmer*, ibid.
113 *People v. Shirley, supra*, note 111.

First Circuit held that the defendant's Sixth Amendment right to confrontation was not violated by allowing a witness to testify about pre-hypnotic memories. The fact that the witnesses' subjective belief in the truthfulness of the testimony had been enhanced did not negate the fact that the accused still had a full right of cross-examination and the right to call witnesses to explain the effects of hypnosis on confidence levels.[114]

The argument in favour of admitting hypnotically induced testimony is that the limitations can be explained to the trier of fact who can then assess the weight to be afforded the evidence. In *State v. Hurd*,[115] the New Jersey Supreme Court adopted this reasoning but required that a set of guidelines be followed, including a videotape of the session, before the evidence would be admitted. If this safeguard existed, the court felt that proper jury instructions could overcome any difficulties. This approach is also followed in Illinois,[116] New Mexico[117] and Wisconsin.[118]

Until recently, the general exclusionary rule has applied equally to hypnotically refreshed testimony by prosecution or defence witnesses. In 1987 however, the United States Supreme Court held, in *Rock v. Arkansas*,[119] that excluding the defendant's hypnotically refreshed testimony violated the accused's constitutional right to testify. The defendant Rock had no clear recollection of the events that led to her husband's death. Under hypnosis she described an accidental shooting. Independent evidence showed that the gun in question was defective and prone to fire if dropped. In a 5:4 decision, the Supreme Court ruled that the hypnotically refreshed testimony should be admitted as it was corroborated in a material way.

Two Canadian cases have allowed the accused to testify about events first "remembered" under hypnosis. In *R. v. Clark*,[120] the trial judge reviewed the expert evidence presented on the effects of hypnosis. He relied on the principle set out in *R. v. Wray*,[121] that evidence should be excluded only if it is of trifling probative value

---

114   *Clay v. Vose*, 599 F. Supp. 1505 (Mass., 1984), affirmed 771 F. 2d 1 (1st Circ., 1985).
115   432 A. 2d 86 (N.J., 1981).
116   *People v. Smrekar*, 385 N.E. 2d 848 (Ill. App., 1979).
117   *State v. Beachum*, 643 P. 2d 246 (N.M. App., 1981), cert. quashed 644 P. 2d 1040 (1982).
118   *State v. Armstrong*, 329 N.W. 2d 386 (Wisc., 1983), cert. denied 461 U.S. 946 (1983).
119   483 U.S. 44 (1987).
120   (1984), 13 C.C.C. (3d) 117 (Alta. Q.B.).
121   [1970] 4 C.C.C. 1 (S.C.C.).

and highly prejudicial, and ruled the evidence admissible. The same approach was followed in *R. v. Pitt*.[122]

The only reported Canadian case where the prosecution has attempted to call evidence first disclosed under hypnosis is *R. v. K*.[123] Provincial Court Judge Garfinkel also relied on *Wray*, ruling that the unreliability of the evidence made it highly prejudicial and of trifling probative value.

It does not appear logical that the admissibility of hypnotically induced evidence should be based on which party intends to proffer it. The inability of a witness to know truth from fiction, essentially an issue of competence,[124] is as relevant to the Crown as it is to the defence. If the trier of fact knows that the witness cannot separate fact from fiction, it seems impossible to give that evidence any weight. Evidence of no weight is clearly prejudicial and without any probative value and should be excluded. If a witness is to be hypnotized then care should be taken to preserve the pre-existing evidence to prevent contamination.[125] Hypnosis may then be properly used as an investigative tool but should not be used as a tool to create new evidence.

4. PRE-TRIAL IDENTIFICATION TECHNIQUES

(1) Identifying Faces

(a) The Cognitive Process

Our ability to discriminate between hundreds of faces in our daily lives, despite the many similarities between individuals, probably represents one of the brain's most remarkable perceptual skills. We exercise this skill constantly. We may not see a friend or relative for many years, but have no trouble recognizing that person the moment we see them again. On the other hand, it is also a common experience to have erred in face recognition; to mistake a stranger for a friend.

How the brain encodes a face is not well understood. There is no evidence of a special "face processing function" in the brain. Rather the face, like all objects, is encoded using the visual process-

---

122   [1968] 3 C.C.C. 342 (B.C.S.C.).
123   (1979), 47 C.C.C. (2d) 436 (Man. Prov. Ct.).
124   *R. v. Hawke* (1975), 29 C.R.N.S. 1 (Ont. C.A.).
125   Wells, *supra*, note 31 at 102.

ing functions of the brain's right hemisphere.[126] Because of the biological and social relevance of faces, human beings have developed processes particularly well suited for distinguishing faces.[127]

The ability to recognize a face is directly related to the frequency of exposure.[128] There is a difference in the processing of familiar and unfamiliar faces.[129] With familiar faces, the internal part of the face – the eyes, nose and mouth – are the most salient features. Thus a change of hairstyle or the growing of a beard does not affect recognition of familiar people. It may take several exposures before the brain is able to create a memory trace of the internal portion of the face so that the face becomes totally familiar and can be recognized if it is altered by a hairstyle, for example. One study showed that five exposures was insufficient to create a memory trace of the internal portion of the face when the only instruction was to remember the face.[130] However, three to five exposures was sufficient when subjects were asked to form impressions about the person such as likability and intelligence.[131] In a practical sense this means that humans can form a good memory trace after a few exposures to people with whom they have talked and interacted. Mere exposure, however, creates a poor memory trace even after several encounters.

The inability to form a good memory trace of an unfamiliar face means that when viewing an unfamiliar face, the elements that are stored are such things as hairstyle and hair colour, the presence or absence of glasses, and facial hair.[132] Not surprisingly, a change in hairstyle makes face recognition of an unfamiliar face particularly difficult.[133] Similar results have been shown by adding

---

126   A.W. Ellis & A.W. Young, "Are Faces Special?", in A.W. Young & A.W. Ellis (eds.), *Handbook of Research on Face Processing* (North-Holland, 1989), at 1.

127   Sergent, "Structural Processing of Faces", in Young & Ellis, *ibid.*, at 57.

128   V. Bruce, "Changing Faces: Visual and Non-visual Coding Processes in Face Recognition", (1982) 73 Br. J. Psychology 105; R.L. Klatzky & F.H. Forrest, "Recognizing Familiar and Unfamiliar Faces" (1984), 12 Memory and Cognition 60.

129   H.D. Ellis, J.W. Shepherd & G.M. Davies, "Identification of Familiar and Unfamiliar Faces from Internal and External Features: Some Implications for Theories of Face Recognition" (1979), 8 Perception 431; A.W. Young *et al.*, "Matching Familiar and Unfamiliar Faces on Internal and External Features" (1985), 14 Perception 737.

130   Endo, Takahashi & Maruyama, "Effects of Observer's Attitude on the Familiarity of Faces: Using the Difference in Cue Value Between Central and Peripheral Facial Elements as an Index of Familiarity" (1984), 43 Tohoku Psychologica Folia 23; A.W. Young & A.W. Ellis, "Semantic Processing", in Young & Ellis, *supra*, note 126 at 235.

131   *Ibid.*

132   A.W. Ellis, "Practical Aspects of Face Memory", in Wells & Loftus, *supra*, note 7 at 12.

133   *Ibid.*, at 15.

glasses.[134] Thus the memory reported by an eyewitness to a crime is likely to contain detail of external elements, the elements particularly amenable to disguise and alteration.

(b) Cross-Racial Identification

Considerable research has been done on cross-racial effects on identification; that is, the effect of a difference in race between the witness and the subject.

As a general rule, people can identify faces of their own race better than faces from other races.[135] The terms "own-race bias" or "cross-racial effect" have been coined to describe this phenomenon. The explanation for own-race bias is that through greater experience with people of one's own race, greater knowledge of subtle within-race variation is acquired. The subtle cues to help differentiate people from another race are not acquired. Thus the shape of the eyes of the Oriental may be well known but the ability of a non-Oriental to see slight variation is absent.

Own-race bias has application to the criminal justice system in two ways. First, it affects identification by a witness of a criminal. This may result in false identification because of an inability to distinguish between people of a different race. It may also lead to the witness declining to make an identification because "they all look the same to me".[136] Secondly, own-race bias affects the ability to prepare a fair lineup or photo array.[137] Researchers Brigham and Ready showed that much more careful selection goes into preparing a lineup of one's own race.[138] Presumably the selector is much

---

134 *Ibid.*
135 J.C. Brigham & P. Barkowitz, "Do They All Look Alike? The Effect of Race, Sex, Experience, and Attitudes On the Ability to Recognize Faces" (1978), 8 J. Applied Social Psychology 306; J. Chance, A.G. Goldstein & L. McBride, "Differential Experience and Recognition Memory for Faces" (1975), 97 J. Social Psychology 243; E.S. Eliott, E.J. Wells & A.G. Goldstein, "The Effects of Discrimination Training on the Recognition of White and Oriental Faces" (1973), 2 Bull. Psychonomic Soc. 71; R.S. Malpass, "Racial Bias in Eyewitness Identification" (1974), 1 Personality and Social Psychology Bull. 42; R.S. Malpass & Kravitz, "Recognition of Faces of Own and Other Races" (1978), 13 J. Personality and Social Psychology 330; J.W. Shepherd, J.B. Deregowski & H.D. Ellis, "A Cross-Cultural Study of Recognition Memory for Faces" (1974), 9 Int. J. Psychology 205.
136 R.C.L. Lindsay & G.L. Wells, "What Do We Really Know About Cross-Racial Eyewitness Identification?", in S.M.A. Lloyd-Bostock & B.R. Clifford, *Evaluating Witness Evidence* (New York: John Wiley and Sons, 1983), at 219.
137 Loftus & Doyle, *supra*, note 11 at 107.
138 J.C. Brigham & D.J. Ready, "Own Race Bias in Line-up Construction" (1985), 9 Law and Human Behaviour 415.

more attuned to the subtle facial details that cause similarities and differences in the members of one's own race.

(c) Delay

It is trite to say, but time is of the essence in face recognition.[139] The memory loss after viewing an unfamiliar face is originally rapid. Within five minutes a good portion of the memory trace is erased. There is then a more gradual loss over the next 48 hours. By this time most of the memory trace is gone.[140] In practice this means that identification tests done within 48 hours will produce the best results. There are not statistically significant differences between identifications done at one week, one month or three months.[141] Presumably after 48 hours only the most salient features remain.

(2) Identification Methods

(a) Composite Sketches

A composite sketch is not really an identification technique. It is an investigatory technique that is most often used when the police have no suspect in mind. The process involves the witness working with an artist or technician to prepare a pictorial likeness of the criminal. There is an issue whether the picture itself is admissible in evidence or whether it is a hearsay representation of the verbal description given by the witness.[142] If a suspect is arrested on the strength of the composite sketch, then the witness would likely be asked to attempt an identification using one of the methods outlined below.

The composite sketch techniques do not produce very good likenesses.[143] The process is limited by the fact that it requires a verbal description. This is a difficult process, since faces are ob-

---

139   K. Deffenbacher, "Forensic Facial Memory: Time is of the Essence," in Young & Ellis (eds.), *supra*, note 126 at 563.
140   *Ibid.*, at 565. In numerical terms, Deffenbacher estimates that 13.5% of the trace is erased in the first five minutes; a further 13.5% over the next 48 hours; and an additional 4% over the next five days.
141   J.W. Shepherd, "Identification After Long Delays", in Lloyd-Bostock & Clifford, *supra*, note 136 at 173.
142   See discussion, Chapter 3, part 6.
143   For a review of the tests done on the quality of two commercially produced kits, the Identi-kit and the Photo-fit, see G.M. Davies, "Forensic Face Recall: The Role of Visual and Verbal Information", in Lloyd-Bostock & Clifford, *supra*, note 136 at 103.

served holistically and not in individual pieces.[144] One study asked artists, who presumably have good visual skills, to describe faces while another artist prepared a sketch from their description.[145] The drawings were then given to a panel who were asked to identify the person in the drawing. The panel was able to do so only 50% of the time, even though they knew the people well. In contrast a control group was able to identify 93% of the people when the artist sketched the face directly. The study showed that even well-trained artists have difficulty translating a visual image into a verbal one.

Another problem with the preparation of a composite sketch is that the process carries with it the risk that the witness will become confused and the memory lost or distorted. To reduce this risk only one witness should be involved in the process. Also, if witnesses work together there is a tendency to bias one another's memory of the event.[146] If possible the other witnesses should not view the composite sketch, to prevent contamination of their independent memory.[147]

(b) "Mug-Shots"

If the police do not have a suspect in mind they may ask a witness to search through a collection of photographs, colloquially referred to as "mug-shots". The process is extremely biasing and inefficient. Any memory the witness had is quickly contaminated by repeated exposure to other faces.[148]

New systems are now being developed to use computers to assist in this process and at the same time reduce the contamination caused by viewing multiple pictures.[149] There are several prototypes being tested, but the general methodology is to use the computer to eliminate unlikely photographs. The "mug-shots" are entered into the computer memory. The witness then provides information which is used to prune the files and reduce the

---

144 *Ibid.*

145 L.D. Harmon, "The Recognition of Faces" (1973), 229, No.5, Scientific Amer. 71.

146 Wells, *supra*, note 31 at 42; see generally, Retention and Retrieval, this chapter, part 3, *supra*.

147 *Ibid.*

148 Laughery, Alexander & Lane, *supra*, note 12; G. Davies, J. Shepherd & H. Ellis, "Effects of Interpolated Mugshot Exposure on Accuracy of Eyewitness Identification" (1979), 64 J. Applied Psychology 232.

149 Bruce & Burton, "Computer Recognition of Faces", in Young & Ellis, *supra*, note 126 at 487; D.R. Lenorovitz & K.R. Laughery, "A Witness-Computer Interactive System for Searching Mug Files", in Wells & Loftus, *supra*, note 7 at 38.

number of targets. The witness works from a "typical" face and suggests changes to that face. For example, the witness may indicate that the lips of the suspect are thicker. The computer searches through the files eliminating all pictures that do not meet this criterion. The process continues until a manageable set of photographs is obtained. The witness then reviews these photographs in an attempt to make an identification.

The technology being developed has promise but it is not a panacea. The system is only as good as the information supplied and the information supplied is subject to all the limitations of memory. The difficulty in verbalizing facial features is not eliminated and the concern that the process will alter or influence the memory still exists.[150]

(c) Confrontations

A confrontation, sometimes referred to as a show-up, involves presenting a single suspect to a witness and asking the witness to attempt an identification. This is the most unsatisfactory method of pre-trial identification. It is highly suggestive. Any doubt in the witnesses' mind may be overcome by the powerful suggestion that the police have captured the guilty party. Any gaps in memory are filled in with the face of the suspect.[151] The witness is then entirely unable to separate the original memory from that supplanted by this suggestive procedure.

(d) Lineups and Photo Arrays

A lineup or a photo array is essentially a multiple choice test.[152] In theory "none of the above" is a possible choice, but most witnesses realize that if the police have gone to the trouble of assembling a lineup or photo array, they must have a suspect in mind. The witnesses will try hard to find a match between the memory and the person or photograph before them. Failing that, and using a process of elimination, the witnesses may choose the one that most closely resembles their recollection of the criminal.[153]

A great deal of psychological research has been devoted to investigating the proper way to compose and conduct a lineup or

---

150   See generally, Composite Sketches, *supra*, this chapter, part 4(2)(a).
151   See generally, *supra*, this chapter, parts 3(1), 3(2).
152   Loftus, *supra*, note 5 at 144.
153   *Ibid.*

photo array. Since these are generally considered the best methods to confirm eyewitness identification, the desire is to learn to do them fairly. If a lineup or photo array is fair then innocent suspects will not be chosen by people with a hazy memory for the event and people with a good memory will be able to identify the perpetrator. In other words, a well conducted lineup or photo array is a test. It separates those who are merely guessing from those with true knowledge.

If a lineup is to be a true test it must be composed fairly. Fairness in composition is measured by deciding if all of the foils (the known-to-be-innocent decoys) are plausible choice alternatives for the witness. At an extreme, placing an Oriental suspect in a lineup composed entirely of Caucasians would be unfair because the Caucasians would not be plausible choices.

Unfairness, however, need not be so blatant. If a foil does not match the witness' description in any important detail, then that person is eliminated as a plausible choice. For example, if the witness provides a description of a person who is 30 to 35 years of age, all persons who appear younger or older in the lineup are rejected as plausible choices.

If a lineup or photo array is fair, a witness who observed the offender should be able to make an identification, but a person who merely reads the description given by the witness should not be able to make an identification with a probability greater than chance. For example, if there are six people in a lineup, then a random sample of people should pick each person one sixth of the time.[154] If random people who never witnessed the crime eliminate foils because they are too tall or their hair is too dark, for example, then the functional size of the lineup is reduced.

Researchers at the University of Toronto put this premise to the test in the case of *R. v. Shatford*.[155] The eyewitness to a robbery could only describe the assailant as "rather good looking". She was, however, able to make an identification from a 12-person lineup. Professor Doob first showed the lineup pictures to a random group and determined that the accused was considered the best-looking person in the pictures. He then showed the lineup picture to 21 different subjects. They were told only that the criminal was "rather good looking" and were asked if they could make an identification. Eleven out of 21 subjects picked the ac-

---

154   *Ibid.*, at 145, 146.
155   A.N. Doob & H.N. Kirshenbaum, "Bias in Police Lineups — Partial Remembering" (1973), 1 J. Police Science and Admin. 287.

cused as the criminal. An additional four subjects indicated he was their second choice. If the lineup was fair, the accused should have been picked no more than one twelfth of the time (one or two people out of 21). The fact that 11 people chose him indicates he was chosen significantly more often than chance and the lineup was (unintentionally) unfair.

What this case shows is that it is not sufficient to know the actual size of a lineup or photo array to determine if it is fair. The important measurement is its effective or functional size. One proposed measure of functional size computes the total number of mock witnesses divided by the number identifying the subject.[156] A lineup or photo array is biased against the accused if the computed ratio is smaller than the actual size. The lineup or photo array is fair if the ratio is equal to or greater than actual size. To illustrate, if twenty mock witnesses view a six-person lineup, and based solely on the reading of the witnesses' description, ten choose the suspect, then the functional size is, twenty divided by ten, which equals two.[157] The lineup test is therefore not fair. Mere guessing eliminates most of the foils.

The fact that the police have taken the time to prepare a lineup or photo array will suggest to most people that the suspect is in there somewhere and their task is to find the closest match.[158] This was well illustrated by psychologists Malpass and Devine in a 1981 study.[159] Having staged a vandalism of university property, 100 students were asked to participate in viewing a lineup. Only half were told that the person may or may not be present (unbiased instructions). The other half were told that there was a suspect and were asked to view the lineup (biased instructions). When the offender was present in the lineup, 100% of the witnesses given the biased instructions chose someone (25% in error). Only 83% of the group given the unbiased instruction made a choice, all choices correct. When the suspect was absent from the lineup, 78% of the group receiving the biased instruction still chose someone, compared to 33% receiving the unbiased instruction. Of course all of these choices were wrong.

Because of this tendency to choose someone, it is extremely important that the witness be told directly that the suspect may not

---

156 G.L. Wells, M.R. Leippe & T.M. Ostrom, "Guidelines for Empirically Assessing the Fairness of a Line-up" (1979), 3 Law and Human Behaviour 285.
157 How to make use of functional size in the courtroom is illustrated, *infra*, Appendix C.
158 Wells, *supra*, note 31 at 74.
159 R.S. Malpass & T.G. Devine, "Eyewitness Identification: Line-up Instructions and the Absence of the Offender" (1981), 66 J. Applied Psychology 482.

be present in the lineup or photo array and that they should also be explicitly cautioned against guessing.[160] The witness should be asked whether he or she can make a positive identification. Under no circumstances should the witness be asked if "anyone looks familiar" or if "anyone is closest".[161] Prompts such as these invite a guess and encourage the witness to choose someone regardless of the strength and accuracy of the memory.

In order to fairly conduct a lineup or photo array it is also important that the authorities do not inadvertently bias the selection. It is obvious that a direction such as "take a good look at number five" is hopelessly inappropriate, but unconscious actions may also bias the selection. If police officers act as foils, their gait or posture may set them aside from the criminal.[162] They may unconsciously shift their eyes towards the suspect or may move slightly away, isolating the suspect actually or by attitude.[163] The officer conducting the lineup may also look towards the suspect or react slightly when that person is brought in, providing some clue to the witness.

The suspects may also unintentionally bias the selection by their own actions. For example, they may call attention to themselves by their posture, their eye movements, or any other nervous gestures, and thus alert the witness that this is the person the police suspect.[164]

A photo array may also be biased. The photo array used in *R. v. Sophonow*[165] contained one candid shot of the accused taken outdoors and seven photographs clearly discernable as police "mug-shots". The biasing effects of the photographs need not be so blatant. If the suspect's photograph shows the head at a distinctive angle or wearing a distinctive expression, this may be sufficient to bias the process.[166] The conduct of a photo array may be biased by the operator giving subtle non-verbal clues such as

160 Wells, *supra*, note 31 at 74, 75.
161 *Ibid.*
162 G.H. Williams & H.A. Hammelman, "Identification Parades", [1963] Crim. Law Rev. 479 at 487.
163 *Ibid.*, at 489.
164 *Ibid.*
165 *R. v. Sophonow (No.1)* (1984), 12 C.C.C. (3d) 272, affirmed 17 C.C.C. (3d) 128 (S.C.C.)[Man.]; *R. v. Sophonow (No.2)* (1986), 25 C.C.C. (3d) 415, leave to appeal to S.C.C. refused 67 N.R. 158 [Man.].
166 R. Buckhout, D. Figueroa & E. Hoff, "Eyewitness Identification: Effects of Suggestion and Bias in Identification From Photographs" (1975), 6 Bull. Psychonomic Soc. 71.

pausing at one photo or leaning over the witness as one photograph is examined.[167]

Some of these subtle biasing effects can be noticed after the fact. Others are only obvious if one is there to observe. This suggests that the presence of counsel at a lineup or photo array identification may be of importance.

The vast majority of psychological literature on lineup procedures deals with laboratory experiments. The experiments cannot capture the vast array of emotions that might affect a witness in a natural environment. More particularly, knowledge of the consequences of a false identification, the trial and possible conviction of an innocent person, is difficult to replicate in the laboratory. In an attempt to measure how witnesses react to the serious consequences of their actions, researchers Malpass and Devine carried out a very true to life experiment where police officers conducted the lineups and the witnesses were led to believe that the consequences to the accused would be severe.[168] Contrary to their hypothesis, knowing the true to life severe consequences did not inhibit the witness from making a choice. 83% made a choice as compared to only 26% who believed the consequences to the accused were trivial. When the witnesses believed the consequences would be severe, 73% chose incorrectly when the offender was absent from the lineup, and 25% did so when he was present.[169]

This experiment indicates that witnesses may not be attuned to the consequences of inaccuracy. Rather, a belief that the police have the right person, coupled with a belief in the utilitarianism of catching and punishing an offender, may override any reflection on the consequences of the action.[170] This re-emphasizes the need to ensure that identification techniques are carried out in a manner that is scrupulously fair to the accused.

---

167 J.E. Smith, R.J. Pleban & D.R. Shaffer, "Effects of Interrogator Bias and a Police Trait Questionnaire on the Accuracy of Eyewitness Identification" (1982), 116 J. Social Psychology 19.

168 R.S. Malpass & P.G. Devine, "Realism and Eyewitness Identification Research" (1981), 4 Law and Human Behaviour 347.

169 See also, D.M. Murray & G.L. Wells, "Does Knowledge that a Crime was Staged Affect Eyewitness Performance?" (1982), 12 J. Applied Social Psychology 42. The results of this study are much less dramatic, but do emphasize that knowing the consequences does not inhibit a witness from making an identification.

170 R.S. Malpass & P.G. Devine, "Research on Suggestion in Lineups and Photospreads", in Wells & Loftus, *supra*, note 7 at 64.

(e) Voice Identification

As with visual identification, voice identification of familiar voices is generally excellent. A few words is often sufficient to recognize a speaker one has not heard from in months or years. One cannot, however, extrapolate from this experience to the recognition of unfamiliar voices. The two situations are distinct.[171]

The study of voice identification is a fairly recent topic of interest. The studies are few and generally test recognition in ideal laboratory situations. The 1935 Lindbergh murder sparked early research in voice identification after Charles Lindbergh testified he recognized Hauptmann's voice several years after hearing a spoken ransom demand.[172] Research following that case showed that voice recognition of an unfamiliar speaker was good after two days (85% accuracy) but dropped off rapidly thereafter. More recent studies have shown somewhat poorer performance levels. Researchers Clifford, Rathborn, and Bull found identification accuracy to be 55% in choosing the target voice from ten distractors after a ten-minute delay.[173] This fell to 32% accuracy after 24 hours and 30% accuracy after seven days. The results suggest that for forensic application, where testing is likely to take place long after the event, voice identification would be highly suspect.

As with visual identification, there are several factors which will influence the ability to recognize an unfamiliar voice. Surprisingly, the length of speech sample does not appear to be one of them. One sentence appears to provide sufficient clues to allow recognition, at least in a laboratory where testing is done after a short interval.[174] Awareness of the importance of concentration on the speech appears to be significant. Bank and shop personnel did extremely poorly on voice recognition tests when they did not know they would be tested after an insignificant conversation.[175] Voice disguise significantly affects recognition ability. Whispering or changing tone from angry to normal causes a substantial decrease in recognition accuracy. It appears that disguising the voice

171   B.R. Clifford, "Memory For Voices: The Feasibility and Quality of Earwitness Evidence", in Lloyd-Bostock & Clifford, *supra*, note 136 at 189.

172   B.R. Clifford, "Voice Identification by Human Listeners: On Earwitness Reliability" (1980), 4 Law and Human Behaviour 373.

173   B.R. Clifford, H. Rathborn & R. Bull, "The Effects of Delay on Voice Recognition Accuracy" (1981), 5 Law and Human Behaviour 201.

174   *Supra*, note 171 at 195, 196.

175   R.B. Bull & B.R. Clifford, "Earwitness Voice Recognition Accuracy", in Wells & Loftus, *supra*, note 7 at 92.

hides the most salient vocal or speech features.[176] Voices heard over the telephone are also more difficult to recognize than those heard live, the telephone restricting in some way the unique qualities of the voice.[177]

Voice recognition research is in its infancy. Most studies are in non-stressful situations under optimum testing conditions. Under these ideal conditions recognition can be quite high. The effect of stress, delay, and disguise, however, may have a profound effect, making the forensic use of voice recognition doubtful.[178]

5. ASSESSING THE CREDIBILITY OF THE EYEWITNESS

(1) Confidence

The confidence exhibited by a witness is intuitively felt to reflect the accuracy of the information. The level of confidence displayed by a witness will influence the decision of the police on whether to lay charges, the prosecutor's decision on whether to proceed, and ultimately the judge's decision on whether to convict.

When the courts confront an eyewitness it is rarely the veracity of the witness that is in question. The issue is the correctness of the testimony. If a witness reports a high degree of confidence in the accuracy of his or her identification, does it follow that the identification is more likely to be correct? In other words, is there a positive correlation between witness confidence and witness accuracy?

The answer to this question is no.[179] Confidence is not an accurate predictor of accuracy. A confident witness is as likely to be wrong as an non-confident witness is to be right.[180]

There are probably several reasons why this is true. Certainly one reason is that accuracy and confidence are related to different factors.[181] Accuracy is a product of the quality of the perception,

---

176   *Supra*, note 171 at 196-99.
177   *Supra*, note 175.
178   *Ibid.*, at 123.
179   G.L. Wells & D.M. Murray, "Eyewitness Confidence", in Wells & Loftus, *supra*, note 7 at 155; Wells, *supra*, note 31 at 15, 16.
180   Wells, *ibid.*
181   *Ibid.*

retention and retrieval of the information. Confidence is a product of psychological and social variables that influence the witness.[182]

The effect of these psychological and social variables can be seen in the positive correlation some researchers have found between the decision to make a lineup choice and the confidence in that choice.[183] A witness who chooses someone from a lineup or photo array will often reflect a high degree of confidence in the accuracy of the choice. A witness who declines to make a choice, on the other hand, may have little confidence in that decision. This reflects the overwhelming belief that the suspect is in there somewhere and the witness has passed the identification test by choosing or alternatively has failed the test by non-choosing. The witness who has chosen is convinced of the correctness of the choice.

Another social variable that influences confidence is the criminal process itself. Studies have shown that witness confidence increases with knowledge that a cross-examination will take place.[184] Presumably this "test" encourages the witness to prove his or her accuracy. Confidence level is also increased by the positive feedback from police and prosecutors.[185] All of these factors influence confidence but are entirely unrelated to accuracy.

It is interesting to note that the one group most knowledgeable of the fact that confidence is unrelated to accuracy is the police.[186] Perhaps this is the result of having attended lineups where their police colleagues were confidently identified as heinous criminals. A limited survey of Canadian lawyers and judges showed that only 37% were aware that accuracy and confidence as to identification are not related.[187] Education is required to ensure that false intuition is replaced by correct scientific fact.

(2) Recall

Another factor that influences credibility is the extent of the recall of detail by the witness. Intuitively, a witness who can

---

182 *Ibid.*
183 Malpass & Devine, *supra*, note 159; Wells & Murray, *supra*, note 179 at 162.
184 G.L. Wells, T.J. Ferguson & R.C.L. Lindsay, "The Tractability of Eyewitness Confidence and its Implications for Triers of Fact" (1981), 66 J. Applied Psychology 688.
185 Wells & Murray, *supra*, note 179 at 168.
186 A.D. Yarmey & H. Jones, "Police Awareness of the Fallibility of Eyewitness Identification" (1982), 6 Can. Police College J. 113.
187 *Ibid.*

provide a wealth of detail must be a good observer. Does it follow that a good observer of detail is more likely to be an accurate identifier of faces?

The current research indicates that the answer to the question is no. There is no positive correlation between the accuracy of the description of the perpetrator and the ability to make a correct identification.[188] The reason is related to the different cognitive functions that control verbal recall and visual recognition.[189] The ability to be able to describe a face does not make you a good identifier. It is true, however, that there are distinctive faces and faces that are distinctive are easier to describe and easier to identify.[190] Conversely, faces that are difficult to describe are difficult to identify. Thus, witnesses who honestly say that they are unable to give any identifying characteristics because the "person looked typical", are in fact describing (or failing to describe) a difficult face. In such circumstances any recognition of the face must be considered suspect.

There is also no truth to the statement that memory for peripheral detail positively aids in face identification. In fact two studies have proved exactly the opposite; memory for peripheral detail is negatively correlated to face recognition accuracy.[191] Presumably, the person who is taking in all the external detail is spending little if any time on face processing. Memory for peripheral detail, however, is positively correlated to making a lineup choice.[192] This suggests the possibility that witnesses will be influenced to attempt an identification based in part on their ability to remember details of the crime.[193] The witnesses appear to be influenced by the false belief that if they have a good memory for the details of the crime, they must also have a good memory of the face.

Finally, it should be noted that there is no correlation between the ability to give accurate height and weight estimates and the

---

188   G.L. Wells, "Verbal Descriptions of Faces from Memory: Are They Diagnostic of Identification Accuracy?" (1985), 70 J. Applied Psychology 619; M. Pigott & J.C. Brigham, "Relationship Between Accuracy of Prior Description and Facial Recognition" (1985), 70 J. Applied Psychology 547.

189   Wells, *ibid.*

190   *Ibid.*

191   B.L. Cutler, S.D. Penrod & T.K. Martens, "The Reliability of Eyewitness Identification" (1987), 11 Law and Human Behaviour 233; G.L. Wells & M.R. Leippe, "How Do Triers of Fact Infer the Accuracy of Eyewitness Identifications? Using Memory for Peripheral Detail Can Be Misleading" (1981), 66 J. Applied Psychology 682.

192   *Ibid.*

193   Cutler, Penrod & Martens, *supra*, note 191 at 253, 254.

ability to recognize faces.[194] The explanation is likely related to the fact that some people are simply poor estimators of these variables and neither an accurate nor inaccurate estimate is any indication of their face recognition powers.

(3) Training

A third intuitive predictor of accuracy is training and experience. Sixty-five per cent of Canadian judges and lawyers believe that an eyewitness identification made by a police officer is superior to that of a store clerk.[195]

Training does have certain positive effects. It can be used to help provide strategies that are effective in remembering details, such as clothing or licence plate numbers.[196] It may be effective in reducing or eliminating cross-racial bias.[197] Training may also be used to increase the likelihood that a witness will pay attention to the face, thus increasing the length of exposure.[198] Training might also be helpful in reducing stress levels which may then improve the quality of the perception.[199]

Training, however, appears to be ineffective in the critical area of face recognition. Without doubt there are people with good visual memory.[200] It is possible to find a subset of the population that out-performs the general population in visual memory tests. Regrettably, people are very poor at assessing their own visual memory skills, which is a significant finding in assessing the credibility of a witness.[201] Science, unfortunately, has not been able to ascertain what causes a good visual memory and therefore all attempts to improve visual memory skills have met with no success.[202] One system designed to teach people to concentrate on facial components was entirely unsuccessful.[203] Human visual memory appears to require that the face be processed as a whole,

---

194 *Ibid.*
195 Yarmey & Jones, *supra*, note 186.
196 Loftus & Doyle, *supra*, note 11 at 62.
197 Lindsay & Wells, *supra*, note 136 at 219.
198 *Supra*, note 11 at 103.
199 See generally, the effects of stress on perception; *supra*, this chapter, part 2(2)(a).
200 A. Baddeley & M. Woodhead, "Improving Face Recognition Ability", in Lloyd-Bostock & Clifford, *supra*, note 136 at 125.
201 *Ibid.*, at 132.
202 *Ibid.*
203 *Ibid.*, at 126, 127.

not feature by feature.[204] Any attempt to teach a strategy contrary to this "natural" process is simply counter-productive.[205] Thus, given the state of the science, police officers and other law enforcement personnel cannot be trained so as to directly improve face recognition skills.

6. THE PSYCHOLOGIST AS A WITNESS

(1) The Purpose of the Evidence

This chapter has detailed several of the factors that influence eyewitness performance. Some, such as the effect of stress and the relationship between confidence and accuracy are counter-intuitive. Others, such as weapon fixation and the effect of post-event information may simply be outside the realm of general knowledge.

The usual tool to expose the weakness in evidence is cross-examination. Cross-examination is generally ineffective to test the quality of a visual identification however, because the witness is unaware of the effects of the intangible psychological factors on his or her memory. Even if it is possible to expose some of the factors that may have influenced memory, the value of such exposure will be greatly reduced without a full explanation of the effect.

Researchers in recent years have investigated the issue of whether lay jurors possess adequate knowledge about factors that influence eyewitness performance. In general the studies have shown that the jurors possess an inadequate knowledge base.[206] A very thorough study involving 321 subjects recently examined this issue.[207] The study used videotaped trials to independently assess the effects of a number of factors on jury decision-making. For example, in one of the trials the evidence established that the lineup members were similar in appearance; in the other trial the

---

204   *Ibid.*, at 128.
205   *Ibid.*
206   K.A. Deffenbacher & E.F. Loftus, "Do Jurors Share a Common Understanding Concerning Eyewitness Behaviour?" (1982), 6 Law and Human Behaviour 15; J.C. Brigham & R.K. Bothwell, "The Ability of Prospective Jurors to Estimate the Accuracy of Eyewitness Identifications (1983), 7 Law and Human Behaviour 19; Loftus, *supra*, note 5 at 171ff; G.L. Wells, "How Adequate is Human Intuition for Judging Eyewitness Testimony?", in Wells & Loftus, *supra*, note 7 at 256.
207   B.L. Cutler, S.D. Penrod & T.E. Stuve, "Juror Decision Making in Eyewitness Identification Cases" (1982), 12 Law and Human Behaviour 41.

witness testified that the lineup members were dissimilar. At issue was whether the jurors treated the lineup evidence differently during their deliberations. Other factors independently assessed in the same manner were the effect of disguise, weapon focus, stress, retention interval, prior photographic searches, lineup instructions and witness confidence. The lawyers conducting the trials spent extra time in closing argument emphasizing the factor that was being manipulated in the test. The results were disturbing, indicating that the jurors did not use the information to draw any inferences about the accuracy of the identification, the culpability of the defendant, or the strength of the prosecution case.[208]

It is important to note that this study was not concerned with whether the jurors were ultimately correct in convicting or acquitting the accused. The study was focused on process; that is, whether the jurors had sufficient knowledge to assess both the strengths and the weaknesses of the evidence. The legal system is as concerned about process as it is about outcome. Presumably the entire system benefits if the process by which evidence is assessed by the trier of fact is improved. It is this argument that generally gives rise to the motion to call expert evidence at trial; a desire to educate the jury members and give them a knowledge base with which to assess the quality of the evidence.

(2) The Admissibility of the Evidence

The admissibility of expert evidence is governed by the general principle that the information must be outside the experience of the judge or jury and be of assistance to them. The Supreme Court of Canada expressed this position in R. v. Abbey:[209]

> An expert's function is precisely this: to provide the judge and jury with a ready-made inference which the judge and jury, due to the technical nature of the facts, are unable to formulate. "An expert's opinion is admissible to furnish the Court with scientific information which is likely to be outside the experience of a judge or jury. If on the proven facts a judge or jury can form their own conclusions without help, then the opinion of the expert is unnecessary".

In R. v. Béland,[210] the Supreme Court cited with approval the following passage by Lord Cooper in Davie v. Edinburgh Magistrates:[211]

---

208 Ibid., at 54.
209 (1982), 68 C.C.C. (2d) 394 at 409 (S.C.C.), citing R. v. Turner (1974), 60 Cr. App. R. 80 at 83 (C.A.).
210 (1987), 36 C.C.C. (3d) 481 (S.C.C.).
211 [1953] S.C. 34 at 40.

> [The expert's] duty is to furnish the Judge or jury with the necessary scientific criteria for testing the accuracy of their conclusions, so as to enable the Judge or jury to form their own independent judgment by the application of these criteria to the facts proved in evidence.

Against this general background, Canadian courts have shown some reluctance to admit expert testimony on the frailties of identification evidence. The Ontario Court of Appeal considered the matter in *R. v. Audy (No. 2)*,[212] and declined to interfere with the trial judge's decision to refuse the evidence. The court did not close the door on admissibility in future cases but ruled:[213]

> There were no facts elicited on cross-examination or otherwise which made it necessary for the jury to be assisted, in arriving at its verdict, by the expert evidence tendered. We are not to be taken as saying that there cannot be a case in which evidence of this kind would be admissible. We simply hold that this was not such a case.

Relying on this caveat, Stortini D.C.J. recently admitted expert psychological evidence after defence counsel laid a proper evidentiary foundation.[214] The eyewitness testified that stress improved her powers of perception. Counsel also established that the witness had been unable to make an identification from photographs but later identified the accused during a confrontation.[215]

Three British Columbia cases have held that the evidence of psychologists on this issue is inadmissible. *R. v. Martel*,[216] *R. v. Low*,[217] and *R. v. Tsang*,[218] all relied on the principle that the evidence is inadmissible because the material to be canvassed was in the general knowledge of the jury. In *Tsang*, Huddart J. ruled that ordinary citizens would be aware of the effect of the prior viewing of photographs on the subsequent identification.

The most recent treatment of the issue is to be found in the *obiter dicta* of Mr. Justice O'Sullivan in *R. v. Sophonow (No. 2)*.[219] His Lordship stated that if the evidence is to be admitted it must not be of a general nature, such as the deterioration of memory with time,

---

212 (1977), 34 C.C.C. (2d) 231 (Ont. C.A.). For an Australian example adopting the same position see *R. v. Smith*, [1987] V.R. 907 (S.C.).

213 *Ibid.*, at 236.

214 *R. v. Marinelli*, Ont. Div. Ct., Stortini D.C.J., No. 1859/88, 20th June 1988 (not yet reported).

215 It is unclear from the case report whether or not the accused's picture had been shown to the witness.

216 [1980] 5 W.W.R. 577 (B.C.S.C.).

217 (1980), 23 B.C.L.R. 207 (Co. Ct.).

218 (1987), 1 W.C.B. (2d) 200 (B.C. Co. Ct.).

219 (1986), 25 C.C.C. (3d) 415, leave to appeal to S.C.C. refused 67 N.R. 158 [Man.].

but must be specific to an issue in the trial. For example, in *Sophonow*, one of the issues was the fact that four people had worked together on the creation of a composite sketch. O'Sullivan J.A. suggested that expert evidence could have been called to explain the biasing effects of such a process.

The *Sophonow* decision pre-dates the Supreme Court of Canada's most recent judgment on the issue of expert evidence, but would seem to be in accord with it. *R. v. Lavallee*[220] dealt with the admissibility of psychiatric testimony with respect to the "battered wife syndrome". The Crown had argued that the evidence was inadmissible on the basis that the psychiatrist was only discussing human nature. The court rejected this position stating:[221]

> The long-standing recognition that psychiatric or psychological testimony also falls within the realm of expert evidence is predicated on the realization that in some circumstances the average person may not have sufficient knowledge of or experience with human behaviour to draw an appropriate inference from the facts before him or her.

The Supreme Court accepted that the jury would benefit from expert evidence on such issues as why a woman would stay in an abusive relationship.

The *Lavallee* reasoning would appear to be applicable to psychological testimony concerning the frailties of eyewitness identification. The literature establishes that human nature is insufficient to appreciate the factors that influence the eyewitness. The trial judge should have a discretion to admit the evidence if it will assist the jury.

This is essentially the position in the United States. Most jurisdictions give the trial judge a discretion to determine if the evidence will in fact assist the trier of fact. One of the first cases to consider the issue was *U. S. v. Amaral*.[222] The Ninth Circuit Court of Appeals ruled that the trial judge had not abused his discretion in excluding the testimony. The basis of the decision was that the subject of the expert's testimony must be beyond the common sense understanding of the average lay person and not exposable through cross-examination. On the issue of stress, the court believed that this issue could be canvassed adequately in cross-examination and therefore declined to overrule the trial judge.[223]

---

220 (1990), 55 C.C.C. (3d) 97 (S.C.C.).
221 *Ibid.*, at 111.
222 488 F. 2d 1148 (9th Circ., 1973)
223 For similar decisions, see *U.S. v. Thevis*, 665 F. 2d 616 at 641 (5th Circ.), cert. denied 456 U.S. 1008 (1982); *U.S. v. Fosher*, 590 F. 2d 381 (1st Circ., 1979); *U.S. v. Brown*, 501 F. 2d 146 (9th Circ., 1974), reversed on other grounds 422 U.S. 225 (1975).

More recently, however, some appellate courts have recognized that though jurors may have some intuitive understanding of the issue, the body of experimental literature has proliferated beyond common knowledge and, in the appropriate case, expert testimony can assist the jury in reaching an informed decision. This position has been accepted by the Third and Sixth Circuits of the United States Court of Appeals in *U. S. v. Downing*[224] and *U.S. v. Smith*,[225] and by the Arizona and California Supreme Courts in *State v. Chapple*[226] and *State v. McDonald*.[227] For example, in *McDonald* the court referred specifically to the "counter-intuitive aspects" of cross-racial identification and the relationship between confidence and accuracy.[228] In *Chapple*, the court believed that the jury would benefit from information concerning "unconscious transfer" which might help to explain a subsequent lineup identification after a failure to recognize a photograph.[229]

These recent cases recognize that the adversarial system relies in large part on the use of effective cross-examination to expose weaknesses in the evidence. The eyewitness, however, is usually honest, and any mistake in identification is probably a result of unknown and unappreciated psychological factors. The expert witness may be the only method to provide the jurors with the information necessary to perform their function properly. As the California Supreme Court concluded in *State v. McDonald*:[230]

> The expert testimony in question does *not* seek to take over the jury's task of judging credibility: as explained above, it does not tell the jury that any particular witness is or is not truthful or accurate in his identification of the defendant. Rather, it informs the jury of certain factors that may affect such an identification in a typical case; and to the extent that it may refer to the particular circumstances of the identification before the jury, such testimony is limited to explaining the potential effects of those circumstances on the powers of observation and recollection of a typical eyewitness. The jurors retain both the power and the duty to judge the credibility and weight of all testimony in the case, as they are told by a standard instruction.

This argument is persuasive and would appear to be in accord with the reasoning of the judgments in *Audy*,[231] *Sophonow*,[232] and

224   753 F. 2d 1224 (3rd Circ., 1985).
225   736 F. 2d 1103 (6th Circ., 1984), cert. denied 105 S. Ct. 213 (1984).
226   660 P. 2d 1208 (Ariz., 1983).
227   690 P. 2d 709 (Calif., 1984).
228   *Ibid.*, at 721.
229   *Supra*, note 226 at 1221.
230   *Supra*, note 227 at 722.
231   (1977), 34 C.C.C. (2d) 231 (Ont. C.A.).
232   (1986), 25 C.C.C. (3d) 415, leave to appeal to S.C.C. refused 67 N.R. 158 [Man.].

Lavallee[233] discussed above. It also reflects the general purpose of expert testimony endorsed by the Supreme Court of Canada. To paraphrase Lord Cooper in *Davie v. Edinburgh Magistrates*,[234] the expert furnishes the scientific criteria so that the judge or jury may form their own independent judgment by the application of these criteria to the facts proved in evidence.

---

233 (1990), 55 C.C.C. (3d) 97 (S.C.C.).
234 [1953] S.C. 34 at 40.

Chapter Two

The Legal Framework

1. INTRODUCTION

The cases of wrongful conviction based on mistaken eyewitness identifications are too numerous to mention.[1] Given the inherent unreliability of this type of testimony, legal scholars, governmental commissions and the courts have attempted to develop a set of principles for use in the judicial process in order to prevent the occurrence of such miscarriages of justice. This chapter will present an outline of some of these proposals and the judicial response to them. As well, specific legal and evidentiary problems relating to eyewitness identification will be discussed.

2. GOVERNMENT REPORTS

There have been a number of reports written by various governmental bodies dealing with issues relating to eyewitness identification. In this part, recommendations made by three of those bodies will be discussed.[2]

(1) The Adolph Beck Case

In 1896 Adolph Beck was convicted of ten counts of fraud and sentenced to a total of seven years imprisonment. He spent ap-

---

1   For a list of publications setting out many of these cases, see Law Reform Commission of Canada, *Pretrial Eyewitness Identification Procedures: Police Guidelines*, (Ottawa: Law Reform Commission of Canada, 1983), endnote 24 at 182,183.

2   See, for example: U.K., *Identification Procedure under Scottish Criminal Law* (Cmnd. 7096) (Edinburgh: H.M.S.O., 1978); New Zealand Criminal Law Reform Committee, *Report on Identification* (Wellington: Government Printer, 1978). Other than the Law Reform Commission of Canada, *Pretrial Eyewitness Identification Procedures: Police Guidelines, supra,* note 1, there have been no Canadian reports on the issue.

proximately 5$\frac{1}{2}$ years in custody as a result of these charges. In 1904 he was again convicted of four counts of fraud. However, prior to sentence being passed, it was discovered that Beck was not the person involved in either the 1896 or 1904 crimes. As a result, Beck was eventually pardoned for both sets of offences.

In the 1896 trial Beck was positively identified as the perpetrator of the frauds by ten witnesses. These witnesses had spent anywhere from 45 minutes to two hours in the company of the person who actually committed the frauds. This pattern repeated itself in the trial of 1904.[3] The evidence of identity was of such a positive character that the trial judge in the 1896 trial characterized it as "overwhelming".[4]

As a result of this gross miscarriage of justice, a committee of inquiry was set up to examine the affair. In its report the committee effectively absolved the judicial process of any blame in the matter. However, it went on to state the following:[5] .

> ... since judges, however able and experienced, are fallible, and evidence as to identity based on personal impressions, however *bona fide*, is perhaps of all classes of evidence the least to be relied upon, and therefore, unless supported by other facts, an unsafe basis for the verdict of the jury.

The committee in effect stated that no conviction should be based on eyewitness identification unless there was corroboration. As will be seen, no court has followed this recommendation.

(2) The Criminal Law Revision Committee

This committee was constituted to review the law of evidence in criminal cases in England and to recommend relevant changes to the legal rules. As part of its 1972 report[6] it made certain recommendations in the area of eyewitness identification evidence.

The committee stated that it regarded "mistaken identification as by far the greatest cause of actual or possible wrong convictions".[7] Notwithstanding this statement, it refused to follow

---

3   For a comprehensive discussion of the *Beck* case see, E.R. Watson, *Trial of Adolph Beck* (London: Butterworth's, 1924).

4   *Ibid.*, at 155.

5   *Ibid.*, at 250.

6   Criminal Law Revision Committee, *Eleventh Report Evidence (General)* (Cmnd. 4991) (London: H.M.S.O., 1972).

7   *Ibid.*, at 116.

the Beck Committee's recommendation that corroboration be required in order to convict. However, it did recommend that the law be changed statutorily to provide the following:[8]

> 21. Without prejudice to the general duty of the court at a trial on indictment to direct the jury on any matter on which it appears to the court appropriate to do so, where at such a trial the case against the accused depends wholly or substantially on the correctness of one or more identifications of the accused which the defence alleges to be mistaken, the court shall warn the jury of the special need for caution before convicting the accused in reliance on the correctness of the identification or identifications, but in doing so shall not be required to use any particular form of words.

In making this recommendation, the committee took the middle ground between those who expressed the view that corroboration should be made a requirement and those who were of the view that no change was necessary. However, this advice was not acted upon and legislation has not been passed in England requiring a warning in cases of eyewitness identification.

(3) The *Devlin Report*

As set out in Chapter 1, a small committee under the chairmanship of Lord Devlin was formed to look into the wrongful conviction of two men which resulted from mistaken identification. The mandate of the committee was to review all aspects of the law of identification evidence and make appropriate recommendations.[9]

After a thorough study of the issue, the committee came to the following conclusion:[10]

> . . . the possibility of mistake in visual identification is sufficiently high to mean that as a rule of evidence visual identification standing by itself should not be allowed to raise the level of probability of guilt up to the standard of reasonable certainty that is required by the criminal law.

However, this committee also rejected the proposition that requiring corroboration was the method of resolving this problem to ensure "that in ordinary cases prosecutions are not brought on

---

8   *Ibid.*, at 185.
9   U.K., *Report to the Secretary of State for the Home Department of the Departmental Committee on Evidence of Identification in Criminal Cases (Devlin Report)*, (London: H.M.S.O., 1976).
10   *Ibid.*, para. 4.54.

eye-witness evidence only and that, if brought, they will fail."[11] It gave two reasons for this decision. The first was that in cases such as those where there was a frequent or prolonged observation the requirement would be an "excessive burden" on the prosecution. The second reason was that corroboration, as defined in the past, was a requirement that was "on the way out".[12]

Like the Criminal Law Revision Committee, the Devlin Committee recommended that a warning be given to juries of the dangers of convicting solely on the evidence of eyewitness identification. It also agreed that this warning requirement ought to be embodied in a statute. As it felt that the warning should be more elaborate than that set out by the previous committee, it recommended that:[13]

> (a) A judge shall direct the jury that experience has shown that as a general rule the chance of an eye-witness, even when he himself is quite certain, making a mistake about identification is high enough to induce a reasonable doubt, that a witness who is mistaken can give evidence as apparently convincing as one who is not and accordingly that it is not safe to convict upon such evidence unless the circumstances of the identification are exceptional or the identification is supported by substantial evidence of another sort.
>
> (b) A judge who gives such a direction shall indicate to the jury the circumstances, if any, which they might regard as exceptional and the evidence, if any, which they might regard as supporting the identification: if he is unable to indicate either such circumstances or such evidence, he shall direct the jury to return a verdict of not guilty.

Given the almost infinite number of possible fact situations, the committee chose not to set out in detail what it considered "exceptional circumstances". Nonetheless, it gave some examples of these circumstances, such as where the eyewitness is familiar with the accused,[14] or where the accused does not deny his or her presence but only denies participation in the event that gives rise to the charge.[15]

The committee also stated that the failure of the accused to counter credible identification evidence with his own story (pre-

---

11   *Ibid.*, para. 8.4.
12   *Ibid.*, para. 8.3. Corroboration is on the way out or has been abolished in most situations under Canadian law. See *Vetrovec v. R.; Gaja v. R.* (1982), 27 C.R. (3d) 304 (S.C.C.) (evidence of accomplices); s. 274 [re-en. R.S.C. 1985, c. 19 (3rd Supp.), s. 11] of the Criminal Code, R.S.C. 1985, c. C-46, (sexual offences); R.S.C. 1985, c. 19 (3rd Supp.), s. 15 (unsworn evidence of children), repealing s. 659 of the Criminal Code.
13   *Ibid.*, para. 4.83.
14   *Ibid.*, para. 4.62.
15   *Ibid.*, para. 4.63.

sumably an alibi) could also create an exceptional circumstance.[16]
It has been a longstanding right of an accused person not to give
evidence, nor to be faulted for not doing so. Unfortunately, the
committee did not discuss the larger ramifications of its conclusion.[17] Also, there was no discussion of why or in what circumstances the failure of the accused to testify would create an exceptional circumstance.

Again, no statute was passed embodying the committee's
recommendation.

3. THE JUDICIAL RESPONSE

Generally parliamentary bodies have not responded to the
call of various governmental commissions for statutory reform as a
means of alleviating the possibility of miscarriages of justice
caused by the inherent unreliability of eyewitness identification.[18]

---

16 *Ibid.*, para. 4.64.
17 In Canada, any mention of the failure of the accused to give his own story would
    probably be a violation of s. 4(6) of the Canada Evidence Act, R.S.C. 1985, c. C-5,
    which states:
      "(6) The failure of the person charged, or of the wife or husband of that
      person, to testify shall not be made the subject of comment by the judge or
      by the counsel for the prosecution."
    It also would be a violation of a right to silence inherent in the presumption of
    innocence. This is set out in s. 11(d) of the Canadian Charter of Rights and Freedoms,
    Part I of the Constitution Act, 1982 (Eng.), c. 11 (hereinafter called the Charter).
    In England, the prohibition on such comment is limited to the prosecutor (Criminal
    Evidence Act, 1898, c. 36, s. 1(b)). Although the judge can make such a comment, it
    has been held in *R. v. Bathurst*, [1968] 1 All E.R. 1175 at 1178, 1179 (C.A.), that it ought
    to be in the following form:
      ". . . the accused is not bound to give evidence, that he can sit back and
      see if the prosecution have proved their case, and that while the jury have
      been deprived of the opportunity of hearing his story tested in cross-
      examination, the one thing they must not do is to assume that he is guilty
      because he has not gone into the witness box".
18 A notable exception is New Zealand, where the Crimes Amendment Act, S.N.Z.
    1982, No. 46, provides:
      "344D. Jury to be warned where principal evidence relates to identification
      — (1) Where in any proceedings before a jury the case against the accused
      depends wholly or substantially on the correctness of one or more visual
      identifications of him, the Judge shall warn the jury of the special need for
      caution before finding the accused guilty in reliance on the correctness of
      any such identification.
        "(2) The warning need not be in any particular words but
            shall —
        "(a) Include the reason for the warning; and
        "(b) Alert the jury to the possibility that a mistaken witness may be

As a result, this difficult problem has been left in the hands of the judicial system.

(1) The First Comprehensive Responses: *Casey* and *Turnbull*

Prior to the decision of the Supreme Court of Ireland in *People v. Casey (No. 2)*,[19] there had been no reported appellate decisions setting out the nature of the directions to be given to a jury in cases involving eyewitness identification. *Casey* and the English Court of Appeal case of *R. v. Turnbull*[20] provide the basis for discussing the general principles that apply to eyewitness identification cases today.

Casey was charged with a number of offences relating to an indecent assault on a 5-year-old boy. He was identified by four witnesses and gave an unsupported alibi. The only issue before the court was whether a trial judge was required to direct a jury, in general terms, on the dangers inherent in eyewitness testimony. The court held that such a warning was required and that it ought to take the following form:[21]

> We consider juries in cases where the correctness of an identification is challenged should be directed on the following lines, namely that if their verdict as to the guilt of the prisoner is to depend wholly or substantially on the correctness of such identification, they should bear in mind that there have been a number of instances where responsible witnesses, whose honesty was not in question and whose opportunities for observation had been adequate, made positive identifications on a parade or otherwise, which proved to be erroneous; and accordingly that they should be specially cautious before accepting such evidence of identification as correct; but that if after careful examination of such evidence in the light of all the circumstances, and with due regard to all the other evidence in the case, they feel satisfied beyond reasonable doubt of the correctness of the identification they are at liberty to act upon it.

This warning is very general. It does not advert to the reasons for the danger, nor does it require the judge to point out any deficiencies in the evidence before the jury. Also, it does not

---

convincing; and
"(c) Where there is more than one identification witness, advert to the possibility that all of them may be mistaken."

19   [1963] I.R. 33 (S.C.).
20   [1976] 3 All E.R 549 (C.A.).
21   *Supra*, note 19 at 39, 40.

instruct the jury that mistaken witnesses can be convincing. Notwithstanding these omissions, the mere fact that a warning would be required was unique in the state of the common law as it stood at the time. In fact, it was this form of warning that was recommended by the Criminal Law Revision Committee nine years later.[22]

It was not until *Turnbull*[23] that a court set out the need for a comprehensive warning on the dangers of identification evidence. The English Court of Appeal chose three cases involving eyewitness identification to set out the parameters of this warning. In its view, a warning was required in order to reduce the number of miscarriages of justice occasioned by mistaken identifications.

The court held:[24]

> First, whenever the case against an accused depends wholly or substantially on the correctness of one or more identifications of the accused which the defence alleges to be mistaken, the judge should warn the jury of the special need for caution before convicting the accused in reliance on the correctness of the identification or identifications. In addition he should instruct them as to the reason for the need for such a warning and should make some reference to the possibility that a mistaken witness can be a convincing one and that a number of such witnesses can all be mistaken. Provided this is done in clear terms the judge need not use any particular form of words.
>
> Secondly, the judge should direct the jury to examine closely the circumstances in which the identification of each witness came to be made. How long did the witness have the accused under observation? At what distance? In what light? Was the observation impeded in any way, as for example by passing traffic or a press of people? Had the witness ever seen the accused before? How often? If only occasionally, had he any special reason for remembering the accused? How long elapsed between original observation and the subsequent identification to the police? Was there any material discrepancy between the description of the accused given to the police by the witness when first seen by them and his actual appearance?
> . . . Finally he should remind the jury of any specific weaknesses which had appeared in the identification evidence. Recognition may be more reliable than identification of a stranger; but, even when the witness is purporting to recognise someone whom he knows, the jury should be reminded that mistakes in recognition of close relatives and friends are sometimes made.

In addition to a simple caution, the court stated that the jury had to be told that an honest witness could nevertheless be mis-

---

22   *Supra*, note 6 at 118.
23   *Supra*, note 20.
24   *Ibid.*, at 551, 552.

taken, and required the trial judge to closely examine the identification evidence. The stated purpose of the warning was to ensure
that the jury examine the quality of the identification evidence
closely before coming to its determination.

The court further stated that when it formulated this warning
it tried to follow the recommendations of the *Devlin Report*.[25]
However, it chose not to adopt the requirement that a jury should
be told that it would be dangerous to convict in the absence of
exceptional circumstances or additional evidence.[26] By not referring to the fact that it would be dangerous to convict, the court
diminished the strength of the warning recommended by Devlin.
In practical terms it took an intermediate position between the
Devlin recommendation and the earlier recommendation of the
Criminal Law Revision Committee. It also specifically rejected any
corroboration requirement in eyewitness identification cases.[27]

The court also refused to adopt the Devlin Committee's recommendation that "exceptional circumstances" be taken into account in order to determine whether or not it would be dangerous
to convict. It gave the following reason for its decision:[28]

> In our judgment, the use of such a phrase is likely to result in the build-
> up of case law as to what circumstances can properly be described as
> exceptional and what cannot. Case law of this kind is likely to be a
> fetter on the administration of justice when so much depends on the
> quality of the evidence in each case. Quality is what matters in the end.
> In many cases the exceptional circumstances to which the report refers
> will provide evidence of good quality, but they may not; the converse
> is also true.

In the result, the *Turnbull* formulation focuses on the trial
judge's duty to deal with the quality of the evidence. The trial
judge has an obligation to deal with both those matters which
enhance the quality of the identification and those which detract
from it.

In this connection the court stated:[29]

> A jury, for example, might think that support for the identification
> evidence could be found in the fact that the accused had not given
> evidence before them. An accused's absence from the witness box
> cannot provide evidence of anything and the judge should tell the jury
> so. But he would be entitled to tell them that when assessing the

---

25   *Supra*, note 9.
26   *Ibid.*, para. 8.4.
27   *Supra*, note 20 at 552, 553.
28   *Ibid.*, at 554.
29   *Ibid.*, at 553.

quality of the identification evidence they could take into consideration the fact that it was uncontradicted by any evidence coming from
the accused himself.

It seems that the court agreed with the Devlin Committee's
assertion that the accused's failure to testify in some way bolsters
the identification evidence already before the jury. Unfortunately,
no reasons are given for this conclusion.[30]

Turnbull can legitimately be described as the "leading" case in
the law relating to eyewitness identification. Its formulation has
been discussed by most courts in the common law world. What
follows is a discussion of the law relating to the issue in some of
those jurisdictions.

(2) The Canadian Response

(a) The Supreme Court of Canada

The Supreme Court of Canada has never directly delineated
the character of the trial judge's charge to the jury in cases involving eyewitness identification.[31] In *Mezzo v. R.*,[32] the issue was
whether a trial judge could withdraw a case from the jury in the
face of direct eyewitness testimony, where that testimony was
weak or flawed. In the majority decision,[33] McIntyre J. discussed
Turnbull[34] and made the following observations:[35]

> It is impossible to disagree with Lord Widgery when he speaks of the
> danger of error in visual identification. Nobody could disagree with his
> assertion of the need for a careful and complete direction to the jury
> with regard to their treatment of such evidence.

---

30 In *R. v. Mutch*, [1973] 1 All E.R. 178 (C.A.), the court seemed to intimate that such a
direction was not advisable where the only issue was the identity of the accused.
31 Cases such as *R. v. Blackmore* (1971), 2 C.C.C. (2d) 514n, affirming 2 C.C.C. (2d) 397
(S.C.C.); *R. v. Bouvier* (1985), 22 C.C.C. (3d) 576 (S.C.C.); and *Canning v. R.* (1986), 27
C.C.C. (3d) 479 (S.C.C.), involved identification evidence. However, the points
raised in the court did not involve the adequacy of the general charge on eyewitness
identification.
   In *Chartier v. Que. (A.G.)* (1979), 9 C.R. (3d) 97 (S.C.C.), the court made the oft-
quoted statement, "Regardless of the number of similar characteristics, if there is one
dissimilar feature there is no identification." However, this was a civil case and no
further discussion of the legal issues took place.
32 [1986] 4 W.W.R. 577 (S.C.C.).
33 McIntyre J.'s judgment was concurred in by Beetz, Estey, Chouinard and Le Dain JJ.
Wilson J. (Dickson C.J.C. concurring) wrote a concurring judgment. Lamer J. (La
Forest J. concurring) dissented.
34 [1976] 3 All E.R. 549 (C.A.).
35 *Supra*, note 32 at 589.

> Turning to the case at bar ... It should have been left to the jury, with a proper caution in the terms suggested in *Turnbull*.

In view of these comments, it could be argued that the Supreme Court has implicitly adopted the *Turnbull* formulation as the appropriate warning for Canadian juries. However, given that the above remarks are clearly *obiter*, it cannot be said with confidence that any such requirement exists. Therefore, the approaches to the issue by the various provincial Appellate Courts are of importance.

These courts have made numerous comments on the manner in which juries ought to be instructed in cases of eyewitness identification. As these comments have not been uniform, it is necessary to examine them on a province by province basis.

(b) British Columbia

The law relating to eyewitness identification has led a roller-coaster existence in British Columbia. In the five-year period between 1946 and 1951, Mr. Justice O'Halloran wrote a series of judgments that emphasized the dangers of convicting an accused solely on the basis of eyewitness testimony. In *R. v. Yates*,[36] he maintained that:

> ... when the sole defence as here is an alibi, and the identification depends upon the evidence of a single witness, it is the duty of the trial Judge to deal carefully in his charge with the evidence relating to the identification, and to draw the attention of the jury to the weaknesses in that evidence and to warn them that such evidence must be weighed with the greatest care ... The necessity for that course arises out of the opportunity for honest mistake peculiar to cases of identity.

In *R. v. Harrison*,[37] he asserted:

> More important still, the jury were not informed of the opportunities of honest mistake peculiar to cases of identity.

In *R. v. Browne and Angus*,[38] he augmented these views by stating the following propositions:

> A positive statement "that is the man" when rationalized is found to be an opinion and not a statement of single fact. All a witness can say is, that because of this or that he remembers about a person, he is of the opinion that person is "the man".

---

36   (1946), 85 C.C.C. 334 at 337 (B.C.C.A.).
37   (1950), 99 C.C.C. 96 at 99 (B.C.C.A.).
38   (1951), 99 C.C.C. 141 at 147 (B.C.C.A.). These views were reasserted in *R. v. Harrison* (1951), 100 C.C.C. 143 (B.C.C.A.).

Unless the witness is able to testify with confidence what characteristics and what "something" has stirred and clarified his memory of
recognition, then an identification confined to "that is the man",
standing by itself, cannot be more than a vague general description
and is untrustworthy in any sphere of life where certitude is essential.

These cases envisage a relatively exacting standard of proof in
cases of eyewitness identification. A jury would have to be instructed that in effect, an identification without reasons was not to
be accepted by them. However, these propositions did not endure.

In a series of cases, the British Columbia Court of Appeal
effectively overruled these propositions. In *R. v. Still*,[39] the court
adopted the following analysis of the applicability of the principles
set out in *Browne and Angus*:[40]

"The court . . . has on a number of occasions indicated that it does not
require a witness testifying in respect of identification to be as minute
in his appraisal of the person being identified as one would gather the
judgments in those two cases require. I think those cases have been
either distinguished, or perhaps whittled down in their effect on a
number of occasions in this court and can no longer be considered as
setting the standard of proof required from a witness in order that
identification may be established."

It appears that the court has taken the view that ordinarily a
jury need only be told to view the evidence of identification with
the greatest care and little else. In *R. v. McCallum*,[41] the accused
argued that a jury ought to be charged in the manner set out in
People v. Casey (No.2).[42] This argument was rejected by a unanimous court. McFarlane J.A. held:[43]

. . . I am not prepared to hold that trial Judges must or ought to apply
any formula or set of words when charging juries in such cases. One
must have regard to the sophistication of modern juries in this
Province. I agree with the statement of MacKay, J.A., which I repeat "I
think in each case the extent and nature of the Judge's warning and
charge must, of necessity, depend on the circumstances of the particular case."

However, in *R. v. Virk*,[44] the court held that where the wit-

---

39   *R. v. Still*, [1987] B.C.W.L.D. 2161 (C.A.), Victoria No. CAV000242, 4th May 1987.
40   Taken from *R. v. Mongovius*, 5th October 1982, *per* Taggart J.A. (unreported). Earlier
      cases stated that the opinions expressed in such cases as *Browne and Angus* were only
      those of a single judge and not of the court. For example, see *R. v. McKay* (1966), 61
      W.W.R. 528 at 531 (B.C.C.A.), and *R. v. Nagy* (1967), 61 W.W.R. 634 at 636 (B.C.C.A.).
41   (1971), 4 C.C.C. (2d) 116 (B.C.C.A.).
42   [1963] I.R. 33 (S.C.). For a discussion of this case see, *supra*, this chapter, part 3(1).
43   *Supra*, note 41 at 121.
44   (1983), 33 C.R. (3d) 378 (B.C.C.A.). See also, *R. v. Hang* (1990), 55 C.C.C. (3d) 195
      (B.C.C.A.).

nesses have been shaken to some extent, a special direction as to identification ought to be given.[45] The suggested direction was taken from an Ontario Model Jury Charge[46] which effectively encompasses the constituent elements set out in *Turnbull*. It seems somewhat incongruous that the comprehensiveness of a jury charge is dependent upon defence counsel's ability as a cross-examiner. The requirement of a thorough jury charge is based on the inherent unreliability of eyewitness identification evidence, which unreliability is not affected by a witness's ability to stick to his or her story. The fact that eyewitnesses are often certain in their evidence is one of the primary reasons for a warning to be given. Certainty does not exclude the possibility of error.

Notwithstanding this statement, the court has never expressly adopted the guidelines in *Turnbull*. In fact, it could be said that these guidelines are not the basis upon which jury charges are tested. For example, the Court of Appeal has accepted the following charge as being adequate:[47]

> Now, there is only one issue in this case, and that is the question of identity. You have heard a good deal of evidence from witnesses who were there and gave some eyewitness evidence of identification. Now, this is not a case of identification of an acquaintance or someone of familiarity. None of the witnesses suggested they had seen the men who came into the bank before. So in cases such as this, you must of course use very, very, considerable care, the greatest care in scrutinizing that evidence. It is obvious to you of course, that misidentification can lead to the most grave form of injustice.
>
> Now, what I am about to say to you now pertains to your assessment of the eyewitnesses of identification. It is not to say that you should not look to the other evidence as a whole and whatever eyewitness identification is useful to you, but to the extent that you rely on eyewitness identification you must use substantial and grave caution.

Although the trial judge gave the jury a strong caution, he did not refer to the reasons behind the need for caution; the fact that a mistaken witness can be a convincing one or the fact that a number of witnesses can be mistaken. Notwithstanding these omissions, the charge was found to be complete.

In summary, it can fairly be said that as long as a jury in British Columbia is warned in general terms of the need for caution in relying on eyewitness identification, little more needs to be said by

---

45   *Ibid.*, at 385.
46   The complete charge is set out in Appendix B, *infra*.
47   *R. v. Van Beest*, [1988] B.C.W.L.D. 2147 (C.A.), Vancouver No. CA006060, 28th April 1988.

the trial judge. That is, the jury need not be informed of the additional factors set out in *Turnbull*. However, if the witnesses are shaken on cross-examination, a more comprehensive warning may be required.

(c) Alberta

The Alberta Court of Appeal has unreservedly subscribed to the guidelines articulated in *Turnbull*.[48]

This process was initiated in *R. v. Duhamel*.[49] In that case the accused was charged with a bank robbery. When a lineup was conducted, two witnesses to the robbery identified Duhamel. However, at trial one witness stated, "I wasn't certain", and the other testified that, "I wasn't quite sure".[50] Given the nature of the evidence, the trial judge withdrew the case from the jury and directed a verdict of acquittal. This decision was upheld by a unanimous Court of Appeal. In its decision the Court of Appeal cited *Turnbull* as authority for its conclusion. In the earlier case of *R. v. Lin*,[51] the court also employed *Turnbull* in its reasoning. In that case, the court held that the charge to the jury on the question of identity was incomplete in that it neither dealt adequately with the inherent frailties of identification evidence, nor were certain conflicts in the evidence drawn to the jury's attention.

The process was completed in *R. v. Atfield*.[52] In that case Belzil J.A., speaking for a unanimous court, specifically adopted *Turnbull*. He stated:[53]

> The authorities have long recognized that the danger of mistaken visual identification lies in the fact that the identification comes from witnesses who are honest and convinced, absolutely sure of their identification and getting surer with time, but nonetheless mistaken. Because they are honest and convinced, they are convincing, and have been responsible for many cases of miscarriages of justice through mistaken identity. The accuracy of this type of evidence cannot be determined by the usual tests of credibility of witnesses, but must be tested by a close scrutiny of other evidence. In cases where the criminal act is not contested and the identity of the accused as perpetrator the only issue, identification is determinative of guilt or innocence; its accuracy becomes the focal issue at trial and must itself be put on trial so to speak. As is said in *Turnbull*, supra, the jury (or the judge sitting

---

48   [1976] 3 All E.R. 549 (C.A.).
49   (1980), 56 C.C.C. (2d) 46 (Alta. C.A.).
50   *Ibid.*, at 48, 49.
51   (1979), 13 A.R. 597 (C.A.); see also, *R. v. Bryzgorni* (1982), 37 A.R. 156 (C.A.).
52   (1983), 25 Alta. L.R. (2d) 97 (C.A.).
53   *Ibid.*, at 98, 99.

alone) must be satisfied of both the honesty of the witness and the correctness of the identification. Honesty is determined by the jury (or judge sitting alone) by observing and hearing the witness, but correctness of identification must be found from evidence of circumstances in which it has been made or in other supporting evidence. If the accuracy of the identification is left in doubt because the circumstances surrounding the identification are unfavourable, or supporting evidence is lacking or weak, honesty of the witnesses will not suffice to raise the case to the requisite standard of proof, and a conviction so founded is unsatisfactory and unsafe and will be set aside. It should always be remembered that in the famous *Adolph Beck* case, 20 seemingly honest witnesses mistakenly identified Beck as the wrongdoer.

Some of the matters to be considered in determining the correctness of identification are found in the guidelines of Lord Widgery in *Turnbull*.

Nonetheless, it seems that a failure to adhere to the above guidelines will not necessarily result in a conviction being reversed. In the recent case of *R. v. Skani*,[54] the trial judge charged the jury in the following fashion:

"... the dangers of eyewitness identification, and that is dangerous, and all of you know that, that you see a person briefly, and you are called upon to identify that person, it is a very difficult thing to do. It is easy to make a mistake ...

"Still you may say it's dangerous, and you must be satisfied in your own mind, satisfied beyond a reasonable doubt that the person ... is, in fact, Mr. Skani.

"If there is a doubt in your mind, you must give that doubt to Mr. Skani, and acquit him.

"Only if you are satisfied beyond a reasonable doubt that the testimony of the witnesses discloses that the assailant . . . was Skani will you convict."

On appeal, it was argued that this charge did not sufficiently adhere to the *Turnbull* guidelines. McClung J.A., speaking for a majority of the court,[55] described the charge as one that was "praiseworthy in its simplicity."[56] He went on to say:[57]

The trial judge pointed out the ease of mistake in identification matters, perhaps not in the complete *Turnbull* format, but in simple and useful language for the jurors' guidance.

---

54   (1989), 95 A.R. 63 (Alta. C.A.).
55   Agrios J.A. concurred in the judgment. Côté J.A. dissented, citing *Turnbull* and *Duhamel*.
56   *Supra*, note 54 at 64, 65.
57   *Ibid.*, at 65.

This case illustrates the fact that even if *Turnbull* has been accepted as authority by a court, its guidelines need not be adhered to rigorously. It must be remembered the *Turnbull* guidelines are just that – "guidelines".

However, in light of the Alberta Court of Appeal's previous rulings, the decision in *Skani* ought to be looked at as an anomaly. It is safe to say that a jury charge not encompassing these guidelines will ordinarily find it difficult to survive appellate scrutiny in Alberta.

(d) Saskatchewan

In *R. v. Ross*,[58] the Saskatchewan Court of Appeal dealt with the issue although no complaint had been made about the charge to the jury. In that case, the trial judge's direction followed the *Turnbull* guidelines. The court took the opportunity to note the following statement from the English case of *R. v. Keane*:[59]

> It would be wrong to interpret or apply *Turnbull* . . . inflexibly. It imposes no rigid pattern, establishes no catechism, which a judge in his summing-up must answer if a verdict of guilty is to stand. But it does formulate a basic principle and sound practice. The principle is the special need for caution when the issue turns on evidence of visual identification: the practice has to be a careful summing-up, which not only contains a warning but also exposes to the jury the weaknesses and dangers of identification evidence both in general and in the circumstances of the particular case.

In the result, the court has indicated that some form of detailed warning must be given in cases involving eyewitness identification. However, there is flexibility in the form of that warning.

(e) Manitoba

In 1936 the Manitoba Court of Appeal reviewed a conviction based on the evidence of a 77-year-old woman.[60] This woman saw three men robbing her home. At the time, it was dark and she was not wearing her glasses. Evidence was tendered on appeal that with glasses, her vision was only 40% of normal. Despite these weaknesses, the conviction was upheld by a unanimous court. The judgment made no mention of the need for caution in assessing

---

58   Sask. C.A., No. 2280, 21st April 1986 (unreported); see also, *R. v. Lafond*, (1988) 69 Sask. R. 38 (C.A.).

59   (1977), 65 Cr. App. R. 247 at 248 (C.A.).

60   *R. v. Zarichney* (1936), 65 C.C.C. 214 (Man. C.A.).

such testimony. Fortunately, the state of the law in the province has changed in the intervening years.

Like Alberta, the Manitoba Court of Appeal has held that the guidelines set out in *Turnbull*[61] ought to form the basis of jury instructions when the case is based on eyewitness identification.

Within six months of *Turnbull* the Manitoba Court of Appeal released its decision in *R. v. Dunlop*.[62] In that case the trial judge gave the following direction on the issue of identification:[63]

> "Generally speaking, we, as ordinary members of society, do not identify people by remembering the colour of their eyes, or the shape of their noses, or by the colour of their hair, or ears, unless the person has some distinctive birthmarks, but in spite of that, we usually have no difficulty in remembering if we have met. I am satisfied that if somebody would ask me to describe the colour of his eyes, the shape of the nose or the ears or to estimate the weight, or how he combs his hair, I would have difficulty in describing my brother whom I have not seen for a year or two. Still I would have no difficulty in recognizing him as my brother."

This charge was held to be inadequate. O'Sullivan J.A., speaking for the majority,[64] referred to *Turnbull* when he held that it was necessary for a trial judge to warn the jury of the frailty of identification evidence. As there was no warning of any sort in this case, nothing was said about the other parts of the guidelines in *Turnbull*.

Ten years later, in *R. v. Sophonow (No. 2)*,[65] the court confirmed that a simple warning was not sufficient. Twaddle J.A., pronouncing the judgment of a unanimous court, held:[66]

> . . . where the case against an accused depends wholly or substantially on the correctness of one or more identifications of the accused which the defence alleges to be mistaken, there are guidelines . . . which should be observed by trial judges in charging juries.
>
> The guidelines may be stated thus:
> (i) the judge should warn the jury of the special need for caution before convicting in reliance on the correctness of the identification;

---

61   [1976] 3 All E.R. 549 (C.A.).
62   (1976), 33 C.C.C. (2d) 342 (Man. C.A.).
63   *Ibid.*, at 348.
64   Freedman C.J.M., Matas and Hall JJ.A. concurred in the judgment. Guy J.A. dissented.
65   (1986), 25 C.C.C. (3d) 415, leave to appeal to S.C.C. refused 67 N.R. 158 [Man.]. In the intervening years a number of trial decisions acknowledged the dangers of eyewitness testimony. See *R. v. Haag* (1980), 8 Man. R. (2d) 400 (Co. Ct.); *R. v. Tiginagas* (1981), 13 Man. R. (2d) 181 (Co. Ct.); *R. v. Bearbull* (1983), 24 Man. R. (2d) 121 (Co. Ct.).
66   *Ibid.*, at 438, 439.

    (ii) he should instruct them as to the reasons for the need for such a warning and make some reference to the possibility that a mistaken witness could be a convincing one and that a number of such witnesses could all be mistaken;

   (iii) he should point out that although identification by one witness can support that of another, even a number of honest witnesses can be mistaken;

   (iv) he should direct them to examine closely the circumstances in which the identification by each witness came to be made;

   (v) he should remind the jury of any specific weaknesses which had appeared in the identification evidence.

These guidelines are adapted from those expressed by the English Court of Appeal (Criminal Division) in *R. v. Turnbull et al* ... as adopted and amplified by Canadian courts in *R. v. Duhamel* ... and *R. v. Atfield*.

In addition to setting out the guidelines, he delineated both the reasons for these guidelines and the importance of giving those reasons. He stated:[67]

> ... the warning is given because of the experience of the legal system that in several cases a number of honest witnesses have identified someone only to be proved later to have been mistaken ...

> The need for giving the reasons for the warning as to the dangers of mistaken identification is a matter of elementary psychology. A warning of danger will often be disregarded unless the reason for it is explained. If a climber is told simply that a cliff is dangerous, it surely will allure his spirit of adventure and his will to climb it, regardless of the risk, but if he is told also that it is dangerous because the rock face is crumbling, he will exercise greater discretion before deciding to make the climb and even if he decides to do so, he will search for secure footholds at every stage of the ascent.

Twaddle J.A. also dealt with the need to remind the jury that they ought to focus on the initial identification rather than the subsequent identification(s) made in the courtroom. In this context he stated:[68]

> [The witnesses] were sure of their identification and getting surer not only with time, but also with each successive appearance to testify ... The jury should have been asked to consider whether the qualification given to their original identification was not more reliable than the assurance displayed in the witness-box. Subsequent affirmation of an earlier qualified identification can arise from a subconscious wish by a witness to defend the identification originally made. It should have been made clear to the jury that mistaken identification by several witnesses has occurred before.

---

67   *Ibid.*, at 440. The principles were reiterated in *R. v. Kies* (1987), 48 Man. R. (2d) 30 (C.A.).

68   *Ibid.*, at 446.

In the result, trial judges in Manitoba are required to give a comprehensive charge to the jury in cases where identification is an issue. Except in Alberta, the other provincial Appellate Courts that have considered the issue have not adopted the same stance.

(f) Ontario

The law in Ontario has taken several twists and turns. In 1946, the Ontario Court of Appeal recognized the necessity of a requirement that the trial judge point out any weaknesses in identification evidence to the jury.[69] Six years later, in *R. v. Smith*,[70] the court referred with approval to the statement of the Beck Committee of Inquiry that it is unsafe to convict on eyewitness identification alone.[71] In addition the court accepted the proposition that an identification which is not based on identifiable characteristics is not to be relied upon.[72] Mackay J.A. stated:[73]

> If the identification of an accused depends upon unreliable and shadowy mental operations, without reference to any characteristic which can be described by the witness, and he is totally unable to testify what impression moved his senses or stirred and clarified his memory, such identification, unsupported and alone, amounts to little more than speculative opinion or unsubstantial conjecture, and at its strongest is a most insecure basis upon which to found that abiding and moral assurance of guilt necessary to eliminate reasonable doubt.

The first statement by the court requiring a warning to be given to a jury came a year later. In *R. v. Cachia*,[74] Pickup C.J.O. held:

> . . . where the Crown's case depends entirely upon the evidence of one witness identifying the accused person, and that person is previously unknown to the witness, and the defence is alibi, the trial Judge should plainly point out to the jury the danger of convicting on such evidence alone.

As can be seen, the need for a warning was limited to cases where the identification evidence was that of a single witness and where an alibi defence was presented. The dangers of multiple

---

69 *R. v. Hederson* (1944), 81 C.C.C. 132 (Ont. C.A.).
70 (1952), 103 C.C.C. 58 (Ont. C.A.).
71 *Supra*, this chapter, part 2(1).
72 The court relied on the statements of O'Halloran J.A., in *R. v. Browne and Angus* (1951), 99 C.C.C. 141 (B.C.C.A), as authority for this proposition. See, *supra*, this chapter, part 3(2)(b).
73 *Supra*, note 70 at 61.
74 (1953), 107 C.C.C. 272 (Ont. C.A.).

witness error were not dealt with. Moreover, a bare warning without clarification was deemed to be sufficient.

The law in Ontario was effectively settled in a series of four cases decided between 1969 and 1971. In *R. v. Sutton*,[75] the trial judge directed the jury that it was dangerous to convict on the uncorroborated evidence of a single witness. The Court of Appeal held that this was insufficient. Jessup J.A., speaking for a unanimous court, expressed the following opinion:[76]

> In my opinion such a charge is insufficient with respect to an issue of identification by an eyewitness because it tends to caution the jury only on the credibility of the witness and not also on the inherent frailties of identification evidence arising from the psychological fact of the unreliability of human observations and recollection. As a model of direction for a charge on the issue of identification I would adopt what was said by Kingsmill Moore, J., delivering the judgment of the Supreme Court of Ireland in *The People v. Casey (No.2)*.

In the result, it seemed that the court had adopted *Casey*[77] as the required standard in Ontario. In *R. v. Spatola*,[78] Laskin J.A., speaking for the majority,[79] both modified and amplified *Sutton* to some degree. The modification came in the following form:[80]

> Without taking a position on whether in all cases where a conviction rests on identification evidence the trial Judge must direct the jury to view it with caution or warn them of its fallibility, I think it mandatory to give an instruction of this character where the identification evidence is offset either by evidence of a contrary nature or by evidence of a failure or inability of another witness equally in a position to see the alleged offender, to make an identification.

In the result, the question of whether a warning was mandatory in all cases of identification was left open. Laskin J.A.'s amplification of *Sutton* dealt with the form of the warning that had to be given. He stated:[81]

> The Court in the *Sutton* case adopted that statement as a desirable model in all such cases. The learned Irish Judge put his statement forward as a minimum warning, recognizing that particular circumstances attending a case may require amplification or variation, according to the probative value of the item of identification evidence.

---

75   [1970] 2 O.R. 358 (C.A.).
76   *Ibid.*, at 368.
77   [1963] I.R. 33 (S.C.).
78   [1970] 3 O.R. 74 (C.A.).
79   Jessup J.A. concurred, Aylesworth J.A. dissented.
80   *Supra*, note 78 at 81.
81   *Ibid.*, at 82.

The reasons for the kind of minimum warning to juries suggested in *The People v. Casey (No.2)* are not difficult to appreciate. Errors of recognition have a long documented history. Identification experiments have underlined the frailty of memory and the fallibility of powers of observation. Studies have shown the progressive assurance that builds upon an original identification that may be erroneous . . .

Bare recognition unsupported by reference to distinguishing marks and standing alone, is a risky foundation for conviction even when made by a witness who has seen or met the accused before. Of course, the extent of their previous acquaintanceship must have a very important bearing on the cogency of identification evidence, as will the circumstances in which the alleged recognition occurred. Where some distinguishing marks are noticed and later verified, there is a strengthening of credibility according to the nature of such marks. But the initial issue of the caution with which identification evidence must be received, particularly where it is the unsupported evidence of one witness, remains; all of this is, in a jury trial, for the jury to evaluate on proper direction. If that direction should embrace an admonition of caution where there is questioned identification evidence, and such direction is not given, an appellate Court cannot say that a conviction in such a situation must be sustained.

As a consequence, the Ontario position seemed to be that a warning might not be required in all cases, but if a warning was required, the minimum warning was a *Casey* type warning. As well, if a warning was required and not given, it seemed that any conviction would not be upheld by the Court of Appeal.

In *R. v. Howarth*,[82] the accused argued that the trial judge erred in not charging the jury in accordance with *Casey*. Gale C.J.O. held that this model charge "should again be recommended for all cases where identity of a person charged with an offence is a substantial issue". However, in this case, he dismissed the appeal on the grounds that, notwithstanding the error, no substantial wrong or miscarriage of justice occurred.[83] Jessup J.A. concurred in these reasons. MacKay J.A. agreed in the result, but went on to say:[84]

I think in each case the extent and nature of the Judge's warning and charge must, of necessity, depend on the circumstances of the particular case.

The issue was finally settled in *R. v. Olbey*,[85] where the court considered these three cases together with the decision of the

82   (1970), 1 C.C.C. (2d) 546 (Ont. C.A.).
83   In accordance with the provisions of the Criminal Code, S.C. 1953-54, c. 51, s. 592(1)(*b*)(iii) [am. S.C. 1968-69, c. 38, s. 60(1)] (now s. 686(1)(*b*)(iii)).
84   *Supra*, note 82 at 548.
85   (1971), 4 C.C.C (2d) 103 (Ont. C.A.).

House of Lords in *Arthurs v. Nor. Ireland (A.G.)*.[86] The conclusion the court[87] came to was as follows:[88]

> Without derogating in any way from the principle that in identification cases the trial Judge should carefully charge the jury on those matters which, *in the circumstances of the particular case*, should receive their anxious consideration in deciding whether they will accept the identification evidence, the weight of authority is against the necessity of a particular form of words, general or specific, failure to use which form must result in a new trial.

In the result, it seems that in Ontario there may be situations where no warning need be given. If a warning is given, it need not take any particular form.[89] However, the practice may be such that *Turnbull* type directions are given in most cases. As the Ontario Model Jury Charge[90] on identification is based on the guidelines set out in that case, this type of direction will be given by those trial judges who utilize this model when preparing a jury charge.

(g) Quebec

The Courts of Quebec seem to have taken cognizance of the need for a special direction or warning in cases based on identification evidence.

In *R. v. Peterkin*,[91] Blain J.S.P. accepted the proposition enunciated in *Browne and Angus*[92] that an identification without details is in effect no identification. He went on to state:[93]

> When the Crown bases its case solely on one witness who identifies the accused whom he had never seen before the crime, and when this accused had an alibi defence, the judge must warn the jury of the dangers of convicting on such identification, and he must enumerate to the jury the facts and the evidence that support the alibi defence:

---

86   (1970), 55 Cr. App. R. 161 (H.L.).
87   The panel was comprised of MacKay, McGillivray and Arnup JJ.A. The decision was given "by the court".
88   *Supra*, note 85 at 115.
89   This proposition was reiterated in the post-*Turnbull* decision of *R. v. Bouvier* (1984), 11 C.C.C. (3d) 257 at 271, affirmed, 22 C.C.C (3d) 576 (S.C.C.)[Ont.]. However, the question of the nature or content of any warning given was not a central issue in the case. The Supreme Court of Canada simply stated that they were not persuaded that the Ontario Court of Appeal had erred in its conclusion.
90   See, *infra*, Appendix B.
91   (1959), 30 C.R. 382 (Que. C.A.).
92   (1951), 99 C.C.C. 141 (B.C.C.A.). In *Sommer v. R.* (1958), 29 C.R. 357 (Que. C.A.), this case was distinguished on the facts. However, there was no disagreement with the principle set out.
93   *Supra*, note 91 at 390.

In *R. v. Deschamps*,[94] the Court of Appeal stated that the trier of fact must exercise "extreme caution" in identification cases. Also, particularly in cases where there was no other evidence, the court cited *Turnbull*[95] as a model for the instructions to be given to a jury. However, there was no indication that the warning must be given in that form.

It also seems that when there is other evidence, no such warning need be given. In *R. v. Auger*,[96] the trial judge failed to give such a warning. However, the Quebec Court of Appeal stated:[97]

> The identification did not, therefore, stand alone as the sole evidence against the appellant, and the special warning suggested by the Court of Appeal in *R. v. Turnbull* . . . was not required.

If any conclusion can be reached from the above cases it is that a warning is recommended in Quebec in all cases involving identification evidence. It is not required in those cases where there is other evidence implicating the accused, and if a warning is given it is suggested that it be in the form set out in *Turnbull*.

(h) New Brunswick

The New Brunswick Courts have not dealt directly with the question of whether or not a warning is required, and in particular, they have not discussed the form of such warning. If one were to use the case of *R. v. Lanigan*[98] as a model, it could be said that not much of a warning is required. In that case the trial judge gave the following direction on the question of identity:[99]

> ". . . therefore the question arises as to identity and when a case – mistakes can be made with respect to juries and judges and when mistakes are made many times they can be made with respect to identity. So you've got to keep your eyes and ears open when you're making decisions as to identity, who was there, who was not there . . . but when it comes to identity and when you people are going to be making decisions as to the identity of the accused being there, having been stated by Crown witnesses, and you keep your eyes and your ears very, very much open with respect to identity. And if you have a reasonable doubt about these points it goes to the benefit of the accused and not to the Crown."

---

94 (1980), 60 C.C.C. (2d) 364 (Que. C.A.).
95 [1976] 3 All E.R. 549 (C.A.).
96 (1982), 4 C.C.C. (3d) 282, leave to appeal to S.C.C. refused 4 C.C.C. (3d) 282n [Que.].
97 *Ibid.*, at 288.
98 (1984), 53 N.B.R. (2d) 388 (C.A.).
99 *Ibid.*, at 392, 393.

This relatively cursory charge was criticized by the court not for its content, but because the trial judge did not adequately deal with the strengths and weaknesses of the eyewitness evidence presented.

In the same case, the court accepted the concepts set out by O'Halloran J.A. in *Browne and Angus*.[100] Angers J.A. outlined the duty of a trial judge in the following terms:[101]

> Accordingly, it is the duty of the trial judge in such cases to tell the jury of the weaknesses of direct evidence of identification and review for them the matters which give weight to such evidence such as prior knowledge, opportunity to observe, duration of observation, presence of distinguishing features and finally he should review the circumstances of the subsequent identification if it be by photograph, line-up or otherwise.

Therefore, until the point is argued directly, the nature of the jury charge in New Brunswick is open to question. From the few cases that have been decided on the issue, it seems that as long as the evidence is thoroughly reviewed by the trial judge, no special warning need be given.

(i) Nova Scotia

Nova Scotia is another province that seems to accept the notion that care must be taken when identification is the key issue in a given case, but the form of any warning to be given to a jury has not been delineated. The Appellate Division of the province acknowledged the need for care in the case of *R. v. Smith*.[102] In that case, the court accepted earlier statements of the Ontario Court of Appeal in *R. v. Sutton*[103] and *R. v. Spatola*[104] to this effect. However, the statements in these two cases setting out the type of warning to be given are not dealt with.[105]

In *R. v. Bowser*,[106] the trial judge repeated the warning in *Casey*[107] which was said to be a proper caution by the court.

---

100   (1951), 99 C.C.C. 141 (B.C.C.A.). See, *supra*, this chapter, part 3(2)(b), for a full discussion of this case. The court had accepted the statements almost 30 years earlier in *Ayles v. R.* (1956), 119 C.C.C. 38 (N.B.C.A.). See also, *R. v. Boyle* (1987), 81 N.B.R. (2d) 43 (Q.B.).
101   *Supra*, note 98 at 392.
102   (1975), 12 N.S.R. (2d) 289 (C.A.). See also, *R. v. Bailey* (1987), 81 N.S.R. (2d) 288 (C.A.).
103   [1970] 2 O.R. 358 (C.A.).
104   [1970] 3 O.R. 74 (C.A.).
105   See, *supra*, this chapter, part 3(2)(f).
106   (1974), 8 N.S.R. (2d) 601 (C.A.).
107   [1963] I.R. 33 (S.C.).

However, *Turnbull*[108] has not been discussed in this context. Nevertheless some trial judges have obviously accepted *Turnbull* as the model for an appropriate charge to the jury. For example, in *Langille v. R.*,[109] the trial judge gave the following charge to the jury:

> "Now the next issue which I'm going to deal with is the question of identification. The case against the accused depends, in my view, wholly on the correctness of his identification by Marlene Kaizer. I must warn you, therefore, that there is a very special need for caution before convicting in reliance on the correctness of that identification. The reason for that need for caution is that all identification evidence suffers from an inherent frailty. Human observation and recollections are notoriously unreliable in this area. Most miscarriages of justice have been due to mistaken identity. I'm sure that you have no doubt that Marlene Kaizer is convinced in her own mind that she has identified the right man. But a witness, though perfectly honest, may also be mistaken. You must therefore examine closely the circumstances in which the identification was made in this case and I now propose to review that evidence with you."

This instruction was accepted as a proper one by the Appellate Division. However that court has yet to comment on whether this form of warning is required or even suggested in the province. The only statements to come from the court are very general and in all probability are not of much assistance to either the lower courts or counsel. For example, in *R. v. Robertson*,[110] the court stated:

> Identification evidence must be dealt with very carefully in order to avoid a miscarriage of justice based on misidentification.

As well, it seems that the court has reduced the proposition that there can be no conviction if there is a reasonable doubt from a rule of law to a rule of practice. This curious statement has been repeated in a number of cases. For example, in *R. v. MacDonald*,[111] the following statement was made:

> Where the issue of identification is the sole issue to be determined by the trial judge the rule of practice is that the evidence to justify conviction must be such that it leaves no room for reasonable doubt of guilt.

In the result, the status of the warning requirement is unsettled in the province. The Appellate Division has not set out any

---

108   [1976] 3 All E.R. 549 (C.A.).
109   (1981), 24 C.R. (3d) 88 at 92 (N.S.C.A.).
110   (1978), 29 N.S.R. (2d) 529 at 533 (C.A.).
111   (1984), 65 N.S.R. (2d) 229 at 231 (C.A.). See also, *R. v. Shaver* (1970), 2 N.S.R. (2d) 225 (C.A.), and *R. v. Jarrett* (1975), 12 N.S.R. (2d) 270 (C.A.).

need for a warning, nor has it stated what such a warning should contain.

(j) Prince Edward Island

There are no reported cases dealing with the issue.

(k) Newfoundland

The Newfoundland Court of Appeal has not dealt with the question of appropriate jury directions in cases of eyewitness identification. However, in a trial decision, *R. v. Power*,[112] Barrett J. charged himself in the following manner:[113]

> Under these circumstances there is a very special need for caution before convicting on the correctness of that identification.
>
> This need for caution arises out of the inherent frailty from which all such identification evidence suffers – human observation and recollections are notoriously unreliable in this area.
>
> The case [sic] of miscarriage of justice due to mistaken identity are legion.

He then went on to outline the factors that must be looked at in order to determine the trustworthiness of such evidence.[114] Many of these factors were taken directly from the judgment in *Turnbull*. Therefore, it would appear that, notwithstanding the absence of direction from the Court of Appeal, trial judges are utilizing the leading cases in their instructions.

(3) Post-*Turnbull* Developments in England

The English Court of Appeal has considered *Turnbull*[115] on numerous occasions.[116] Although some qualifications have been enunciated, it is safe to say that in most cases involving eyewitness identification, a direction along the lines suggested by Lord Widgery is required.

---

112 (1987), 67 Nfld. & P.E.I.R. 272 (Nfld. T.D.).
113 *Ibid.*, at 274.
114 *Ibid.*, at 274, 275.
115 [1976] 3 All E.R. 549 (C.A.).
116 The House of Lords has not dealt with the case directly. However, in two other cases, it has implicitly acknowledged its reasoning as appropriate in cases involving eyewitness identification. See *Holgate-Mohammed v. Duke* (1984), 79 Cr. App. R. 120; *R. v. Spencer; R. v. Smails* (1986), 83 Cr. App. R. 277.

The first of these qualifications came in *R. v. Keane*.[117] In that case the court held that there was flexibility in the *Turnbull* guidelines.[118] This proposition was later repeated by the Privy Council in *Nembhard v. R.*[119] In that case the board stated:[120]

> *Turnbull* does not purport to change the law. It provides a most valuable analysis of the various circumstances which common sense suggests or experience has shown may affect the reliability of a witness's evidence of identification and make it too dangerous in some of the circumstances postulated to base a conviction on such evidence unless it is supported by other evidence that points to the defendant's guilt. *Turnbull* sets out what the judgment itself described as "guidelines for trial judges" who are obliged to direct juries in such cases. But those guidelines are not intended as an elaborate specification to be adopted religiously on every occasion. A summing-up, if it is to be helpful to the jury should be tailored to fit the facts of the particular case and not merely taken ready-made "off the peg".

The Court of Appeal has also indicated that the *Turnbull* warning need not be given in every case where identity is an issue. For example, in *R. v. Oakwell*,[121] the accused was involved in an altercation with a police officer. The primary issue was whether or not the police officer was to be believed when he related the nature of the accused's involvement in that altercation. However, counsel argued that the officer might have been mistaken when he stated that the other person in the altercation was the accused. As a result, it was argued that the trial judge ought to have given the jury a *Turnbull* type of direction. The court held that this was not the type of case where such a direction was required. It also went on to state that the *Turnbull* guidelines were primarily meant to deal with cases of "fleeting encounters". Other cases also seem to indicate that warnings are not required where the accused admits to being at the scene and the issue is the extent to which he or she is involved in the events before the court.[122]

However, where the primary issue is the identity of the accused, the courts have emphasized the need to "strictly follow"[123]

---

117   (1977), 65 Cr. App. R. 247 (C.A.).
118   *Ibid.*, at 248.
119   (1981), 74 Cr. App. R. 144 (P.C.).
120   *Ibid.*, at 148.
121   (1978), 66 Cr. App. R. 174 (C.A.).
122   See, *R. v. Curry; R. v. Keeble*, [1983] Crim. L.R. 737 (C.A.), and *R. v. Hewett*, [1977] Crim. L.R. 554 (C.A.).
123   *McShane v. Northumbria Chief Constable* (1980), 72 Cr. App. R. 208 (Div. Ct.). See also, *R. v. Hunjan* (1978), 68 Cr. App. R. 99 (C.A.); *R. v. Weeder* (1980), 71 Cr. App. R. 228 (C.A.); *R. v. Breslin* (1984), 80 Cr. App. R. 226 (C.A.); *R. v. Tyson*, [1985] Crim. L.R. 48 (C.A.); *R. v. Clifton*, [1986] Crim. L.R. 399 (C.A.).

the principles set out in *Turnbull*. In addition, the Court of Appeal has held that where identification is the issue in a sexual case, the directions in *Turnbull* are the only directions that are required.[124] In effect the court has abrogated the need for corroboration on the issue of identity in sexual cases[125] and replaced it with the *Turnbull* directions.

In the result, it seems that *Turnbull* is alive and well in England. The courts have required that the directions set out in that case are to be given in any case where identity is a major issue. The only exception seems to be those cases where the accused's presence at the event in question is not at issue and his or her role in the events is.

(4) The Australian Response

The Australian courts have held that in a proper case, a warning about the inherent problems in identification evidence is required.[126] In *Kelleher v. R.*,[127] the High Court of Australia held:

> ... it is in practice generally desirable that where the case for the prosecution includes evidence of visual identification by a person previously unfamiliar with the accused, an appropriate warning should be given to the jury, since jurors may not appreciate as fully as a judge may do, or even at all, the serious risk that always exists that evidence of that kind may be mistaken. The failure to give an adequate warning where one is required may have the result that the conviction must be quashed. . . . If a warning is necessary, the duty to give it will not be satisfactorily discharged by the perfunctory or half-hearted repetition of a formula, and a warning in general terms will not alone be sufficient; the jury should be given careful guidance as to the circumstances of the particular case and their attention should be drawn to any weaknesses in the identification evidence.

The courts have also stated that no particular form or content is required in such a warning.[128]

---

124   *R. v. Chance* (1988), 87 Cr. App. R. 398 (C.A.).
125   The requirement of corroboration in sexual cases was abolished legislatively in Canada: Criminal Code, s. 274.
126   The need for a warning was first set out in the dissenting judgment of Evatt and McTiernan JJ., in *Craig v. R.* (1933), 49 C.L.R. 429 (Aust. H.C.).
127   (1974), 131 C.L.R. 534 at 551 (Aust. H.C.). See also, *R. v. Bromley* (1986), 161 C.L.R. 315 (Aust. H.C.); *R. v. Boardman*, [1969] V.R. 151 (S.C.); *R. v. Hentschel*, [1988] V.R. 362 (S.C.); *R. v. Goode*, [1970] S.A.S.R. 69 (S.C.); *R. v. Harris* (1971), 1 S.A.S.R. 447 (S.C.); *R. v. Easom* (1981), 28 S.A.S.R. 134 (S.C.); *R. v. Evans* (1985), 38 S.A.S.R. 344 (S.C.).
128   See, *R. v. Aziz*, [1982] 2 N.S.W.L.R. 322 (C.C.A.), and *R. v. De-Cressac* (1985), 1 N.S.W.L.R. 381 (C.C.A.).

However, some courts, particularly those in Victoria, have indicated that at least two basic propositions must be included in a warning. These are that judicial experience has shown that there can be cases of mistaken identification and that an honest witness can be mistaken. For example, in *R. v. Dickson*,[129] the Supreme Court of Victoria stated:

> It is difficult to convey to the jury the reality of particular dangers which exist in the evidence without drawing to the attention of the jury two things they are unlikely to know. The first is that experience in the courts over the years has shown that in a not insignificant number of cases erroneous identification evidence by apparently honest witnesses has led to wrong convictions. For this knowledge the judge draws largely on accumulated judicial experience. One sees instances of erroneous identification from time to time . . .
>
> The second thing which the jury are unlikely to know is the substantial degree of risk that honest witnesses may be wrong in their evidence of identification. Jurors, who unlike trial lawyers, have not given thought to the way in which evidence of visual identification depends on the witness receiving, recording and recalling accurately a fairly subjective impression on the mind are unlikely to be aware of the extent of the risk that honest and convincing witnesses may be mistaken, especially where their opportunities for observing a previously unknown offender were limited. The best way of explaining and bringing home to the jury the extent of this risk is by explaining the reasons for there being the risk and that it is essential to distinguish between honesty and accuracy and not assume the latter because of belief in the former.

In Western Australia[130] and Tasmania[131] the courts have referred to *Turnbull*[132] with approval. In *Oates v. R.*,[133] the Tasmanian Court of Criminal Appeal described these guidelines as "helpful and useful." Notwithstanding these statements, the courts have been careful to state that detailed rules will not be set out.[134] The courts in Australia obviously acknowledge the need for a warning, but wish to retain maximum flexibility as to the contents of such a warning.

---

129   [1983] 1 V.R. 227 at 231 (S.C.). See also, *R. v. Burchielli*, [1981] V.R. 611 (S.C.), and *R. v. Clune*, [1982] V.R. 1 (S.C.). In these cases the court emphasized that whether a warning is adequate or not depends on the facts of the particular case.
130   *Sutton v. R.*, [1978] W.A.R. 94 (S.C.).
131   *McCusker v. R.*, [1977] Tas. S.R. 140 (C.C.A.); *Oates v. R.*, [1979] Tas. R. 140 (C.C.A.).
132   [1976] 3 All E.R. 549 (C.A.).
133   *Supra*, note 131.
134   For example, in *Oates, supra*, note 131 at 141, the court stated: "Detailed rules binding on this Court as to the circumstances in which such a warning should be given and as to the terms of such a warning have not been and, in my view should not be laid down."

4. PRE-TRIAL DISCOVERY

In a case involving eyewitness identification there are a number of pieces of information that could be helpful to the accused in the preparation of his or her defence. This information would include the names and addresses of all the witnesses to the event in question, the descriptions of the perpetrator given by those witnesses, copies of any statements made by the witnesses, whether or not all of these witnesses participated in pre-trial identification procedures, and, if they did, the results of these proceedings.

This information is almost always in the hands of, or available to, the prosecutor. In England, a unitary state, the prosecutor on request will supply the name and address of any witness who has seen or was likely to have seen the criminal. In addition, a copy of the description given by that witness is provided.[135] In Canada, a federal state, such policies would have to be set by the various Attorneys General.[136] The result is that there is no uniform policy of pre-trial disclosure in Canada.

A prosecutor ought to disclose all evidence that would be of assistance to the accused. However, this duty is not an absolute one.[137] The determination of whether or not a given piece of evidence is of assistance is, in many instances, a matter of judgment. What may seem irrelevant to the prosecutor may be viewed as crucial by defence counsel. As a result, unless all of the information in the prosecutor's hands is disclosed, vital information may be withheld from the trier of fact. In recent years courts have begun to take the position that disclosure ought to be the rule rather than the exception. Although none of the cases discussed below deal with identification evidence, the principles enunciated in them are obviously applicable to these fact situations.

---

135 This policy was set out in a written answer tabled in the House of Commons on 27th May 1976 (Hansard, Vol. 912, No. 115). This followed the publication of the *Devlin Report.*

136 By virtue of s. 92(14) of the Constitution Act, 1867, jurisdiction over the administration of justice in the provinces is in the hands of the province. As a result, the vast majority of offences are prosecuted by the provincial Attorneys-General. The federal government conducts prosecutions under certain federal statutes, but these are of almost no significance for the purposes of this book.

137 See, *Re Cunliffe and Law Soc. of B.C.; Re Bledsoe and Law Soc. of B.C.* (1984), 13 C.C.C. (3d) 560 (B.C.C.A.). In *R. v. C. (M.H.)* (1988), 46 C.C.C. (3d) 142 (B.C.C.A.), the court seemed to indicate that failure to disclose will only affect the verdict if an oblique motive on the part of the prosecutor can be demonstrated.

In *R. v. Savion*,[138] the defendants asked for production of their own statements at their trial. One of the accused asked for production of an original tape recording of a conversation between him and an undercover police officer. The trial judge refused both requests. The Ontario Court of Appeal held that the trial judge was in error in refusing these requests. In so holding, the court enunciated the following principle:[139]

> However, I cannot conceive that the power to compel the Crown to produce the statement of a witness is a narrow and isolated power; I conceive it to be but one facet of a wider power to order production that flows from the ability of the Court to control its own process so as to manifestly ensure fundamental fairness and see that the adversarial process is consistent with the interests of justice. Such a power must include the power to order production of the statement of an accused.

In *R. v. Davies*,[140] this broad principle was used by the same court to state that a trial judge ought to have ordered that the name and the last known whereabouts of an individual who had served as an agent of the police in setting up a drug transaction be provided to the accused. The principle was extended to statements made by Crown witnesses in *R. v. Doiron*.[141] In expressly adopting what was said in *Savion*, the Appellate Division of the Nova Scotia Supreme Court stated that in the absence of a cogent reason to the contrary, production should be ordered.[142] Although all of the above cases involved proceedings at the trial, the same principles would apply to any request for information prior to the trial. The Saskatchewan Court of Appeal gave this principle constitutional standing in *R. v. Bourget*.[143] In that case, counsel for the accused had made a pre-trial request for the production of a certain type of ampoule used in a breathalyzer. The purpose of this request was to have these ampoules tested independently. This request was refused by the Crown. The court held that the ampoules ought to have been produced. In so doing, the court made the following general remarks:[144]

> In my opinion s. 7 of the Charter gives the court broad power to promote the proper administration of justice by ordering disclosure and discovery of material and objects for the purpose of independent

---

138   (1980), 52 C.C.C. (2d) 276 (Ont. C.A.).
139   *Ibid.*, at 284.
140   (1982), 1 C.C.C. (3d) 299 (Ont. C.A.).
141   (1985), 19 C.C.C. (3d) 350 (N.S.C.A.).
142   *Ibid.*, at 363.
143   (1987), 35 C.C.C. (3d) 371 (Sask. C.A.).
144   *Ibid.*, at 380. These principles were accepted by the Appellate Division of the Nova Scotia Supreme Court in *R. v. Eagles* (1988), 88 N.S.R. (2d) 337 (C.A.).

testing. Section 7 is no longer limited to the notion of procedural fairness in court and encompasses the whole process including discovery and disclosure. If our system of criminal justice is to be marked by a search for truth, then disclosure and discovery of relevant materials, rather than suppression, should be the starting point . . .

If disclosure and discovery do not work effectively by the mutual efforts of counsel under the adversary system, then the court, in cases where the application is made and the need is demonstrated, must supervise disclosure and discovery so that the ends of criminal justice are properly served. Where life, liberty and security of the person is at stake, gamesmanship is out of place.

Furthermore, pre-trial disclosure and discovery have societal benefits which should not be overlooked. If such procedures work effectively they should promote an expeditious as well as a fair disposition of charges, whether by plea or trial; they should provide the defendant with sufficient information to make an informed plea; they should permit thorough preparation for trial and minimize the potential for surprise or delay; they should eliminate as much as possible the procedural and substantive inequities among similarly situated defendants. In this way, not only are the immediate concerns of the judiciary, the state, the community and the litigants served, so are the longer-range concerns about the over-all operation of the criminal justice system.

On the basis of the above cases, it can be easily argued by counsel that there is a right to receive all necessary information from the Crown on request. These arguments can be based on common law principles or by utilizing the Charter. As a result, counsel in identification cases ought to be making such requests as a matter of routine.

5. THE PRELIMINARY INQUIRY

(1) The Purpose of the Preliminary Inquiry

The stated purpose of the preliminary inquiry is to determine whether or not the Crown has sufficient evidence to warrant putting the accused on trial. In practice, the hearing also provides a useful forum for discovery. There is growing recognition by the Courts of this aspect of the inquiry. For example, in *Re Skogman and R.*,[145] Estey J., speaking for the majority[146] of the Supreme Court of

---

145   (1984), 13 C.C.C. (3d) 161 (S.C.C.).
146   Dickson, Lamer and Wilson JJ. concurring. McIntyre J. dissented on other grounds. Beetz and Chouinard JJ. concurred in the dissent.

Canada, stated:[147]

> The purpose of a preliminary hearing is to protect the accused from a needless, and indeed, improper, exposure to public trial where the enforcement agency is not in possession of evidence to warrant the continuation of the process. In addition, in the course of development in this country, the preliminary hearing has become a forum where the accused is afforded an opportunity to discover and to appreciate the case to be made against him at trial where the requisite evidence is found to be present.

Given that discovery is a legitimate goal, the preliminary inquiry can be very useful for determining such things as the details surrounding the initial event; specifics of any identification procedures used by the police; initial descriptions given by the identification witnesses; and the names of other witnesses to the event, including those who could not identify the accused. This information is vital to trial preparation.

(2) Jurisdictional Error

There is no mechanism that permits an appeal from a decision made by a judge at a preliminary inquiry. As a result, any decision must be challenged by means of the prerogative writs. It is beyond the scope of this book to discuss the intricacies of this manner of judicial review. It is sufficient to say that the superior courts will not interfere with a decision made at a preliminary inquiry unless the error made at the inquiry can be classified as jurisdictional error.[148]

Jurisdictional errors are those that ensue where there is a failure to observe a mandatory provision of the Criminal Code or where the error results in a denial of natural justice.[149] In addition, it is jurisdictional error to commit an accused for trial where there is a complete absence of evidence relating to one of the essential

---

147 *Supra*, note 145 at 171. In the earlier case of *Caccamo v. R.* (1975), 21 C.C.C. (2d) 257 at 275 (S.C.C.), the majority of the court stated: "It is, of course, now settled law that the sole purpose of the preliminary inquiry is to satisfy the Magistrate that there is sufficient evidence to put the accused on trial". This statement can be reconciled with the statement in *Skogman*. The purpose of the preliminary inquiry is to determine if there is sufficient evidence to put the accused on trial. However, in the process of achieving that purpose, the accused is permitted to discover aspects of the Crown's case.

148 *Patterson v. R.* (1970), 2 C.C.C. (2d) 227 (S.C.C.); *A.G.(Que) v. Cohen* (1979), 46 C.C.C. (2d) 473 (S.C.C.); *Forsythe v. R.* (1980), 53 C.C.C. (2d) 225 (S.C.C.); *Re Skogman and R.*, *supra*, note 145.

149 *Ibid.*

elements of the charge.[150] As a result, even if an error is made at the preliminary inquiry, the practical effect may be that there is no method available to rectify the error. To put it another way, the judge at the preliminary inquiry has the right to be wrong.

(3) The Accused's Position in the Courtroom

In some cases, the preliminary inquiry is the first occasion on which an identifying witness would have the opportunity of seeing the accused. These cases would arise where no out-of-court identification procedures have taken place or where such identification was by means of photographs. In these cases the accused might wish to test the witnesses' ability to make an identification by placing himself or herself in the general audience in the courtroom, rather than sitting in the prisoner's box or at the counsel table. In the latter cases, the accused would be conspicuous and subject to identification as the perpetrator by his or her position in the courtroom rather than by bodily and facial features.

An example of the lengths to which the accused might go in testing a witness' ability to make an identification is set out in *Re R. and Grant*.[151] The accused, a black man, appeared at the preliminary inquiry accompanied by five other black men dressed in identical or substantially similar clothing to that of the accused. On a review of an order preventing the accused from testing identification in this way, Fraser J. of the Ontario High Court stated:[152]

> I know of no authority or principle giving an accused the right at a preliminary hearing to have persons present assist in identification . . . Such a practice would be very inconvenient, and it would be quite contrary to the normal practice that has prevailed for many years and it would not be in the interests of justice to make such a practice a mandatory one.

This proposition was expressly disagreed with in the case of *Re Vaudrin and R.*[153] In dealing with *Grant*, Spencer J. of the British Columbia Supreme Court held:[154]

150 *Re Skogman and R., supra*, note 145; *Re Martin and R.; Re Nichols and R.* (1978), 41 C.C.C. (2d) 342 (S.C.C.).

151 (1973), 13 C.C.C. (2d) 495 (Ont. H.C.).

152 *Ibid.*, at 498, 499. In *R. v. Dunlop* (1976), 33 C.C.C. (2d) 342 (Man. C.A.), the 45 chairs in the courtroom were occupied by men with black jackets, long hair and beards. Although not an issue, no adverse comment was made on this procedure. This case illustrates the danger of placing the accused in the audience, as the complainant identified all of the accused. Obviously, given the circumstances, this identification would be given more weight than one made of an accused in the prisoner's dock.

153 (1982), 2 C.C.C. (3d) 214 (B.C.S.C.).

154 *Ibid.*, at 218, 219.

... I think that case to be wrongly decided. It proceeds on the basis that an accused at a preliminary hearing has no right to have friends in the body of the court for the purpose of assisting in testing the Crown's evidence of identification . . . Spectators being in the court as of right, I think defence counsel may make whatever use of them is reasonable to assist in his cross-examination of a witness upon the issue of identification. That . . . is the recognized practice of the courts in this province . . .

Although there are disagreements concerning this practice, there is no disagreement on the effect of not conforming to the practice. The courts have uniformly held that even if it is an error to prevent the accused from sitting in the body of the courtroom in order to test identity, this error is not a jurisdictional error and, if made, will not affect the validity of the proceedings at the preliminary inquiry.[155] As a result, once such an order is made, it is a final order and cannot be challenged.

(4) The Right of Cross-Examination

The Criminal Code gives the accused the right to cross-examine Crown witnesses at a preliminary inquiry.[156] This right is the most effective discovery tool available to the accused. However, the failure to permit certain questions to be put to a witness or the disallowance of a certain line of questioning, even if erroneous, will not necessarily result in jurisdictional error. In *Forsythe v. R.*,[157] the Supreme Court of Canada held:

... jurisdiction will be lost by a Magistrate who fails to observe a mandatory provision of the *Criminal Code* ... Canadian law recognizes that a denial of natural justice goes to jurisdiction ... In the case of a preliminary inquiry, I cannot conceive that this could arise otherwise than by a complete denial to the accused of a right to call witnesses or of a right to cross-examine prosecution witnesses. Mere disallowance of a question or questions on cross-examination or other rulings on proffered evidence would not, in my view, amount to jurisdictional error.

Courts have held that it is jurisdictional error to put an arbitrary time limit on cross-examination[158] or to force a preliminary inquiry to proceed in the absence of counsel. This latter ruling would put the accused in the position of having to cross-examine

---

155   *Re R. and v. Grant, supra,* note 151; *Re Vaudrin and R., ibid.; Dubois v. R.* (1975), 29 C.R.N.S. 220 (B.C.S.C.); *R. v. MacDougall* (1987), 12 M.V.R. (2d) 126 (P.E.I.S.C.).
156   Criminal Code, s. 540(1)(a).
157   *Supra,* note 148 at 229.
158   *Re R. and Roulette* (1972), 7 C.C.C. (2d) 244 (Man. Q.B.).

the chief Crown witness without having heard the evidence in chief.[159] Also, in the case of *R. v. Cover*,[160] the court held that it was jurisdictional error to prohibit the cross-examination of a police officer which was designed to set up a foundation for an argument at trial that certain evidence was obtained in violation of the Charter of Rights and, as a result, ought to be excluded at trial.[161] Nevertheless, the weight of authority is that simply disallowing certain questions or a line of questioning does not constitute jurisdictional error.[162]

The difficulty of determining where mere irregularity ends and jurisdictional error begins is illustrated by the cases involving identification evidence. In *R. v. Churchman and Durham*,[163] the magistrate at the preliminary inquiry refused to permit counsel for the accused to ask for the names of all the persons who witnessed a lineup of which the accused was a member. In holding that this refusal amounted to jurisdictional error, LeBel J. stated:[164]

> At a preliminary hearing an accused person is always entitled to cross-examine for the purpose of demolishing the Crown's case then and there if he can, or, as more frequently happens, for the purpose of demolishing it later at the trial, and where the defence is misidentification he is entitled to the widest latitude in delving into the circumstances of the alleged identification. In this connection what is more important for him to know — and to know without delay — than the names and addresses of the persons who claim to have identified him as well as the same particulars concerning those who have either failed to identify him or, as sometimes happens, have picked out a stranger to the crime? If he does not secure this information at the preliminary hearing he may never be able to obtain it. It has been said before, but I think it should be said again, that the Crown has no monopoly on such witnesses.

159 *Re Durette and R.* (1979), 47 C.C.C. (2d) 170 (Ont. H.C.).
160 (1988), 44 C.C.C. (3d) 34 (Ont.H.C.).
161 A judge at a preliminary inquiry does not have the jurisdiction to exclude evidence or to give any other relief based on the Charter; *Mills v. R.* (1985), 26 C.C.C. (3d) 481 (S.C.C.).
162 *Re Légaré and R.* (1975), 24 C.C.C. (2d) 123 (Que. C.A.) (cross-examination of an expert witness on his role in proceedings in another forum involving the case before the court); *A.G. (Que.) v. Cohen* (1979), 46 C.C.C. (2d) 473 (S.C.C.) (preventing cross-examination on previous statements made by the witness); *Forsythe v. R.* (1980), 53 C.C.C. (2d) 225 (S.C.C.) (refusing the right to cross-examine a police officer on notes made by that officer); *Re Ferrero and R.* (1981), 59 C.C.C. (2d) 93 (Alta. C.A.) (refusal to allow cross-examination on the role or the identity of an individual involved in a drug transaction. The issue was whether this individual was an informer or an *agent provocateur*); *Re Dumont and R.* (1984), 15 C.C.C. (3d) 273 (Que. S.C.) (refusal to allow questions relating to the identity of persons questioned by the police or the number of witnesses who gave statements to the police during their investigation).
163 (1954), 110 C.C.C. 382 (Ont. H.C.).
164 *Ibid.*, at 385, 386.

In *Re DePagie and R.*,[165] the judge at the preliminary inquiry refused to permit the accused to ascertain the description of her assailant given by the complainant. The court held that even if this decision was erroneous, it was not a jurisdictional error. Given the state of the authorities, it is probable that questions asked for the purpose of discovery in identification cases are proper. However, if the judge at the preliminary inquiry does not allow such questions to be asked, that decision is in all probability immune from any challenge.

Different considerations apply when defence counsel attempt to have statements previously made by the witness produced at the preliminary inquiry. In the leading case of *Patterson v. R.*,[166] the majority of the Supreme Court of Canada[167] held that the judge sitting at a preliminary hearing does not have the power to order the production of previous statements made by a witness. It was further held that even if such a power exists, failure to order production is not jurisdictional error. Subsequent cases have relied on the notion of no jurisdictional error as the reason for declining to interfere in decisions not ordering the production of other types of documents.[168]

Patterson was circumvented in *R. v. Boucher*.[169] In that case, the judge ordered the production of the witness' statement where the witness had used that statement to refresh his memory prior to testifying at the preliminary inquiry. Also, in *R. v. Williams; Ex parte Barnett*,[170] the court held that it was jurisdictional error to refuse to permit cross-examination on the circumstances surrounding the taking of a statement from the accused. These cases could be used to argue that production of a statement used to refresh memory can be ordered. Of particular importance in identification cases is the fact that police officers and the identifying witness can be asked to describe the process by which the initial description of the perpetrator was obtained. In particular, this would permit discovery of whether or not any suggestions were made to the witness by the interviewer.

---

165   (1976), 32 C.C.C. (2d) 89 (Alta. C.A.).

166   (1970), 2 C.C.C. (2d) 227 (S.C.C.).

167   Judson J., Abbott, Martland, Ritchie and Pigeon JJ. concurring. Hall J., concurring in the result, held that there was no error on the facts of the case. Spence J. dissented.

168   *Re Hislop and R.* (1983), 7 C.C.C. (3d) 240, leave to appeal to S.C.C. refused 1 D.L.R. (4th) 424n [Ont.] (an accounting summary used by the witness); *Re Nichols and R.* (1977), 41 C.C.C. (2d) 308 (Ont. C.A.) (a police officer's notes).

169   (1978), 44 C.C.C. (2d) 177 (Ont. Prov. Ct.)

170   (1970), 2 C.C.C. (2d) 298 (Ont. H.C.).

In the result, although there is a statutory right to cross-examination at a preliminary inquiry, the requirement of jurisdictional error often leaves an accused without a remedy when there is a partial denial of this right.

(5) The Right to Call Witnesses

After the Crown has presented its case, the accused is given the opportunity to make an unsworn statement.[171] In a case where the issue is identity, this right would often permit an accused to proffer an alibi. The alibi could then be investigated by the police sufficiently in advance of the trial to prevent any inference of recent fabrication.[172]

In addition, the Criminal Code provides that the accused has the right to call witnesses at a preliminary inquiry.[173] This right can be used as a productive discovery device. If the Crown chooses not to call all of the witnesses present at the event or at any subsequent identification procedures, this right permits the accused to call these witnesses and determine what, if anything, they have to add to the case. This also prevents the accused from being surprised should such witnesses testify at the trial.

Failure to comply with this right on the part of the judge at the preliminary inquiry results in jurisdictional error. This is the case even when that judge is satisfied that the Crown has presented sufficient evidence to put the accused on trial.[174]

However, in some circumstances, the accused will discover the existence of a witness or witnesses as a result of the evidence given at the preliminary inquiry. In order to call these persons as witnesses, an adjournment would be required. The question of whether the refusal to grant such an adjournment constitutes jurisdictional error is unclear. Ordinarily, the granting of an adjournment is a matter of discretion and failure to grant one does not constitute jurisdictional error.[175] However, if refusal to grant an adjournment results in a denial of natural justice, including the

---

171 Criminal Code, s. 541(1),(2).
172 See generally, Chapter 7, part 4.
173 Criminal Code, s. 541(3),(4).
174 *R. v. Mishko* (1945), 85 C.C.C. 410 (Ont. H.C.); *R. v. Brooks*, [1965] 1 C.C.C. 290 (Alta. T.D.); *Re Ward and R.* (1976), 31 C.C.C. (2d) 466, affirmed 31 C.C.C. (2d) 466n (Ont. C.A.).
175 *R. v. Solloway; R. v. Mills* (1930), 53 C.C.C. 180 (Alta. C.A.); *R. v. Botting*, [1966] 3 C.C.C. 373 (Ont. C.A.).

right to make full answer and defence, it does constitute jurisdictional error.[176] Obviously, whether or not a superior court will interfere with this discretion is very much dependent on the facts of the case. If, for example, the accused was aware of the existence of the witnesses, and was in a position to issue a subpoena to them prior to the preliminary inquiry, a refusal of an adjournment might not constitute a denial of natural justice. However, if the existence of these witnesses was only discovered during the preliminary inquiry itself, then such a refusal would in all probability constitute jurisdictional error. The care with which reviewing courts attempt to limit their intervention to the facts of the case before them is illustrated by the case of *Re Fernandes and R.*[177] In that case, counsel for the accused mistakenly believed that the Crown would call certain witnesses. The Crown chose not to call these witnesses and an adjournment for the purpose of subpoenaing these officers was refused. In holding that the accused was denied the right to make full answer and defence, Cory J. (as he then was) held that his conclusion was based on the particular facts of the case, and in particular the misunderstanding of counsel for the accused.[178]

Given this diversity of opinion in the courts, it is difficult to predict with any certainty the circumstances in which a denial of an adjournment would constitute jurisdictional error.

(6) The Test for Committal

The determination of whether the evidence is sufficient to commit an accused for trial is the same test as used by a trial judge in deciding whether to withdraw a case from the jury. In the case of *U.S.A. v. Sheppard*,[179] the majority of the Supreme Court of Canada[180] dealt with this issue in the following manner:[181]

> ... the duty imposed upon a "justice" under s. 475(1) [now s. 548(1)] is the same as that which governs a trial Judge sitting with a jury in deciding whether the evidence is "sufficient" to justify him in withdrawing the case from the jury and this is to be determined according to whether or not there is any evidence upon which a reasonable jury

---

176   *R. v. Dick*, [1969] 1 C.C.C. 147 (Ont. H.C.); *Re R. and Carter* (1972), 7 C.C.C. (2d) 49 (Ont. H.C.).
177   (1975), 26 C.C.C. (2d) 309 (Ont. H.C.).
178   *Ibid.*, at 312.
179   (1976), 30 C.C.C. (2d) 424 (S.C.C.).
180   *Per* Ritchie J. (Martland, Judson, Pigeon and de Grandpré JJ. concurring). Spence J. (Laskin C.J.C., Dickson and Beetz JJ. concurring) dissented.
181   *Supra*, note 179 at 427.

properly instructed could return a verdict of guilty. The "justice", in accordance with this principle, is, in my opinion, required to commit an accused person for trial in any case in which there is admissible evidence which could, if it were believed, result in a conviction.

The courts have required that an accused be committed for trial unless there is an absence of evidence on an essential ingredient in a charge.[182] The Supreme Court of Canada reconfirmed the principle in *Sheppard* in *Mezzo v. R.*.[183] In that case it stated that where there is direct evidence of identification a case ought to be left to the jury, regardless of the quality of the evidence. Unless it can be argued that the evidence of identification is so uncertain as to amount to no evidence at all,[184] there must be a committal for trial where a witness identifies the accused as the perpetrator of the crime. The quality of the identification must be left to the trier of fact.

Committing an accused for trial where there is "no evidence" on an essential ingredient of a charge constitutes jurisdictional error.[185] However, if the same judge discharges an accused where there was in fact "some evidence" this does not constitute jurisdictional error.[186]

---

182   *Re Martin and R.; Re Nichols and R.* (1978), 41 C.C.C. (2d) 342 (S.C.C.); *Re Skogman and R.* (1984), 13 C.C.C. (3d) 161 (S.C.C.).

183   [1986] 4 W.W.R. 577 (S.C.C.).

184   *Re Joly and R.* (1978), 41 C.C.C. (2d) 538 (Ont. H.C.); *Re MacDonnell and R.* (1984), 14 C.C.C. (3d) 383 (Ont. H.C.).

185   *Re Skogman and R., supra*, note 182.

186   *Dubois v. R.* (1986), 25 C.C.C. (3d) 221 (S.C.C.). In this case, the court quashed a discharge in an identity case where the judge presiding at the preliminary inquiry stated that he was not satisfied beyond a reasonable doubt on the question of identity. The court held that it was not jurisdictional error merely to apply the wrong test for the sufficiency of evidence. However, in this case, applying the test reserved for another forum constituted jurisdictional error. In *Sask. (A.G.) v. Fenwick* (1988), 70 Sask. R. 185 (Q.B.), the court held that discharging an accused where there was direct evidence of identification did not constitute jurisdictional error. See also, *R. v. Tremblay* (1989), 47 C.C.C. (3d) 88 (S.C.C.).

It is important to note that, upon a discharge, the Crown has the option, pursuant to s. 577 of the Criminal Code, of obtaining the consent of the Attorney General and either laying a new information or preferring an indictment. The only remedy available to the accused is to apply to have the committal for trial quashed by a superior court.

6. THE TRIAL

(1) The Position of the Accused in the Courtroom

When an accused is charged with a summary conviction offence,[187] an absolute jurisdiction offence,[188] or elects to be tried by a Provincial Court Judge[189] when charged with an indictable offence, the first opportunity for a corporeal identification will often take place in the courtroom itself. In some cases, defence counsel may wish to place the accused in the body of the courtroom in order to test the ability of the witness to identify the accused. Whether or not this practice is permitted is at the discretion of the trial judge.[190] However, given the fact that most courts do not approve of "dock" identifications,[191] it is difficult to conceive of a situation where a judge would deny such a request. As O'Hearn C.C.J. stated in *R. v. Gillis*:[192]

> Ordinarily, the court is quite justified in insisting that the defendant . . . take his assigned place in the courtroom. Where there is a genuine question of identity, however, this arrangement can be prejudicial in foreclosing that question, or, at least, giving the witnesses to identity a strong clue, especially if they are police officers familiar with the arrangement of the courtroom.

(2) Withdrawing the Case from the Jury

In *R. v. Turnbull*,[193] the English Court of Appeal stated that:

> When, in the judgment of the trial judge, the quality of the identifying evidence is poor, as for example when it depends solely on a fleeting glance or on a longer observation made in difficult conditions, the situation is very different. The judge should then withdraw the case from the jury and direct an acquittal unless there is other evidence which goes to support the correctness of the identification.

This statement gives the trial judge a role in assessing the quality of identification evidence, even where a witness directly identifies the accused as the perpetrator of the offence. If that quality is wanting, the judge can withdraw the case from the jury and direct a verdict of acquittal.

---

187 Criminal Code, s. 798.
188 Criminal Code, s. 553.
189 Criminal Code, s. 536(2).
190 *Re Conrad and R.* (1973), 12 C.C.C. (2d) 405 (N.S.T.D.).
191 See, *infra*, Chapter 3, part 1.
192 (1980), 42 N.S.R. (2d) 259 at 263 (N.S. Co. Ct.).
193 [1976] 3 All E.R. 549 at 553 (C.A.).

The Supreme Court of Canada considered this proposition in *Mezzo v. R.*,[194] and rejected it. In that case, the trial judge withdrew the case from the jury where the observation was made in difficult circumstances and the accused was subject to an improper identification procedure. McIntyre J., for the majority[195] of the court, stated:[196]

> It is impossible to disagree with Lord Widgery when he speaks of the danger of error in visual identification. Nobody could disagree with his assertion of the need for a careful and complete direction to the jury with regard to their treatment of such evidence. When, however, he introduces the suggestion that the trial judge should consider the quality of the evidence and where he finds it wanting, take the case from the jury, he enters more controversial ground and authorizes the trial judge to encroach upon the jury's territory. Such a step blurs or even obliterates the clear line separating the functions of judge and jury. Questions of credibility and the weight that should be given to evidence are peculiarly the province of the jury. The term "quality", as applied by Lord Widgery, is really nothing but a synonym for "weight". To consider it, the trial judge exceeds his function. I am fully aware that untruthfulness on the part of a witness is not the only factor which may render his evidence weak or even useless. The most honest witness may be mistaken or, by external interference or distraction or by lack of opportunity to observe, the value of his evidence may be diminished or even eliminated so that it should receive little if any weight. All these considerations affect the weight of the evidence and the jury, 12 indifferent persons who must be unanimous to convict the accused, may after a careful direction from the trial judge take account of all these relevant factors and reach a conclusion with at least as much reliability as a single judge.

In the result, absent a complete lack of identification, these cases will be decided by the jury without the possibility of intervention by the trial judge.

(3) Evidentiary Issues

(a) Excluding Identification Evidence

In Canada, the only common law basis upon which it could be argued that identification evidence ought to be excluded would be dependent upon the ruling of the majority of the Supreme Court of

---

194 [1986] 4 W.W.R. 577 (S.C.C.).
195 Beetz, Estey, Chouinard and Le Dain JJ. concurring. Wilson J. (Dickson C.J.C. concurring) wrote a separate opinion concurring in the result. Lamer J. (La Forest J. concurring) dissented.
196 *Ibid.*, at 589. This endorsement of the ability of the jury to decide was reiterated by Dickson C.J.C. in *R. v. Corbett* (1988), 64 C.R. (3d) 1 at 19 (S.C.C.).

Canada in *R. v. Wray*.[197] In that case, Martland J.[198] set forth the following proposition:[199]

> . . . the idea of a general discretion to exclude admissible evidence is not warranted . . . the exercise of a discretion by the trial Judge arises only if the admission of the evidence would operate unfairly. The allowance of admissible evidence relevant to the issue before the Court and of substantial probative value may operate unfortunately for the accused, but not unfairly. It is only the allowance of evidence gravely prejudicial to the accused, the admissibility of which is tenuous, and whose probative force in relation to the main issue before the Court is trifling, which can be said to operate unfairly.

This discretion is extremely limited. Eyewitness identification in most cases would be of sufficient probative value to pass this test of admissibility. However, it could be argued that some evidence is of such dubious quality that its value could be said to be trifling. For example, in *R. v. Faryna*,[200] the identification of the accused was based upon an incident that took from six to nine seconds. It could be argued that the probative force of such an identification was trifling and as a result, the evidence ought to be excluded. However, it is unlikely that a court would hold that a positive identification of an accused person by a witness would meet this test.

It could also be argued that if a pre-trial identification procedure such as a lineup is conducted in an improper manner, such evidence ought to be excluded on the basis of this principle. In *R. v. Engel*,[201] the accused, dressed differently than the others, was placed in a room with 10 police officers and there identified by the complainant. The court held that this form of lineup was a "farce" and no weight should be given to it.[202] Surely an argument can be made that this evidence was of trifling probative value and highly prejudicial and as a result ought to have been excluded. The possibility of evidence obtained as a result of improper police identification procedures being excluded was specifically recognized by Wilson J. in *Mezzo v. R.*.[203] It remains to be seen whether or not these arguments will be adopted by the courts.

---

197   [1970] 4 C.C.C. 1 (S.C.C.).
198   Fauteux, Abbott, Judson, Ritchie and Pigeon JJ. concurring. Cartwright C.J.C., Hall J. and Spence J. wrote dissenting judgments.
199   *Ibid.*, at 17.
200   (1982), 3 C.C.C. (3d) 58 (Man. C.A.).
201   (1981), 9 Man. R. (2d) 279 (C.A.).
202   *Ibid.*, at 284.
203   [1986] 4 W.W.R. 577 (S.C.C.). Dickson C.J.C. concurred in the judgment.

At least four judges of the Supreme Court of Canada have questioned the principle in *Wray*.[204] In *Morris v. R.*,[205] Lamer J. (as he then was), in a dissenting judgment, stated that the admissibility of evidence of an accused's disposition is to be determined by weighing its probative value against its prejudicial effect. He went on to state:[206]

> The degree of probative value required to overcome the exclusionary rule is presently the object of some disagreement and the law is as a result somewhat unclear.

This was the first indication that the *Wray* test was open to reconsideration.

The second indication came in *Clarkson v. R.*,[207] where Wilson J. offered this opinion:

> ... the common law acknowledges a discretionary power on the part of trial judges to exclude evidence obtained in a way that violates a principle of adjudicative fairness or fair treatment of the accused at the hands of the police, notwithstanding the otherwise reliable nature of such evidence. Whether this discretion is applied so as to narrow the ambit in which an exclusionary rule can operate, as preferred by Martland J. in *R. v. Wray* ... or is perceived as a discretion to exclude evidence in recognition that "[c]onvictions obtained by the aid of unlawful or unfair acts may be obtained at too high a price" (*per* Barwick C.J. in *R. v. Ireland* (1970), 126 C.L.R. 321 at p. 335 (Aust. H.C.)), the process is one of weighing two competing and frequently conflicting concerns.

Then in *R. v. Corbett*,[208] La Forest J. expressed the view that it was an open question whether:[209]

> ... a judge has a discretion to weigh considerations of probative value and prejudice ... not only if its probative weight is "trifling" but whenever its "prejudicial effect would be 'out of proportion to its true evidential value' ".

Lastly, La Forest J., with Dickson C.J.C. concurring, again considered the issue in *R. v. Potvin*.[210] On that occasion, La Forest J.

---

204 *Supra*, note 197.
205 (1983), 7 C.C.C. (3d) 97 (S.C.C.).
206 *Ibid.*, at 107.
207 (1986), 25 C.C.C. (3d) 207 at 216 (S.C.C).
208 (1988), 64 C.R. (3d) 1 (S.C.C.). However, his decision was given in dissent. The dissent was not based on this point.
209 *Ibid.*, at 52. In *R. v. Morin* (1988), 66 C.R. (3d) 1 at 24 (S.C.C.), Sopinka J. (Dickson C.J.C., McIntyre and La Forest JJ. concurring) approved the general principles set out in both *Morris* and *Corbett*.
210 (1989), 47 C.C.C. (3d) 289 (S.C.C.). This case involved the interpretation of s.

specifically stated that he did not accept the restrictive approach of Martland J. in *Wray*, and enunciated the proposition that "the trial judge may exclude admissible evidence if its prejudicial effect substantially outweighs its probative value."[211] Thus there are strong indications that at least four members of the court are of the opinion that *Wray* may no longer be good law.

The position in England is much clearer than in Canada: a common law discretion permits a trial judge to exclude otherwise admissible evidence. The discretion applies whenever the probative value of the evidence is outweighed by its prejudicial effect.[212] It is obviously a wider discretion than the one recognized by the Supreme Court of Canada in *Wray*. This discretion has been held to apply to evidence of identification. For example, in *R. v. Horsham Justices: Ex parte Bukhari*,[213] the Divisional Court specifically recognized the right of the trial judge to exclude dock identifications since they were extremely unreliable. As well, in *R. v. Leckie and Ensley*,[214] the Crown Court excluded the evidence of a confrontation.

In addition to this common law discretion, there is a statutory discretion available to English Courts. This discretion is set out in s. 78 of the Police and Criminal Evidence Act, 1984, c. 60. This legislation provides that:

> 78. (1) In any proceedings the court may refuse to allow evidence on which the prosecution proposes to rely to be given if it appears to the court that, having regard to all the circumstances, including the circumstances in which the evidence was obtained, the admission of the evidence would have such an adverse effect on the fairness of the proceedings that the court ought not to admit it.
> (2) Nothing in this section shall prejudice any rule of law requiring a court to exclude evidence.

As can be seen, this legislation does not involve a balancing of probative value against prejudicial effect. It focuses on one issue,

---

643(1)[now s. 715(1)] of the Criminal Code. See, *infra*, this chapter, part 6(3)(c). Wilson J. (Lamer and Sopinka JJ. concurring) held that there was a statutory discretion which would permit the exclusion of evidence proffered under that section. As a result, she did not consider the common law discretion set out in *Wray*. However, she did acknowledge, at 309, that "reservations" had been expressed about the "restrictive formulation" in that case. La Forest J. stated that the discretion was the same as that at common law.

211   *Ibid.*, at 314.
212   *R. v. Sang* (1979), 69 Cr. App. R. 282 (H.L.).
213   (1982), 74 Cr. App. R. 291 (Div. Ct.). See also, *R. v. Flemming* (1987), 86 Cr. App. R. 32 (C.A.).
214   [1983] Crim. L.R. 543 (Crown Ct.).

the effect of the evidence on the fairness of the trial. This provision has been held to be applicable to identification evidence.[215] As well, it is a supplement to, and not a replacement for, the common law discretion.[216]

In the result, there is a broad discretion in the trial judge to exclude identification evidence. However, as Appellate Courts rarely interfere with the exercise of this discretion,[217] it may take some time to develop the principles upon which either the statutory or the common law discretion will be exercised.

The Australian courts also have the discretion to exclude evidence if its probative value is outweighed by its prejudicial effect.[218] This is the same general discretion that exists in England. Similarly, this discretion is applicable in cases involving eyewitness identification.[219]

There is an additional discretion to exclude evidence in Australia where that evidence is obtained by improper, unfair or illegal means. This discretion was outlined in the following manner by Barwick C.J. of the High Court of Australia in *R. v. Ireland*:[220]

> Evidence of relevant facts or things ascertained or procured by means of unlawful or unfair acts is not, for that reason alone, inadmissible. This is so, in my opinion, whether the unlawfulness derives from the common law or from statute ... Whenever such unlawfulness or unfairness appears, the judge has a discretion to reject the evidence. He must consider its exercise. In the exercise of it the competing public requirements must be considered and weighed against each other. On the one hand there is the public need to bring to conviction those who commit criminal offences. On the other hand there is the public interest in the protection of the individual from unlawful and unfair treatment. Convictions obtained by unlawful or unfair acts may be obtained at too high a price. Hence the judicial discretion.

It is important to note that this discretion is not based on any concept of fairness to the accused or of a fair trial. As was stated by Stephen and Aickin JJ. of the same court in *Bunning v. Cross*:[221]

215 *R. v. Beveridge* (1987), 85 Cr. App. R. 255 (C.A.); *R. v. O'Leary* (1988), 87 Cr. App. R. 387 (C.A.).

216 *R. v. O'Leary, ibid.; Matto v. D.P.P.*, [1987] Crim. L.R. 641 (Div. Ct.).

217 *R. v. O'Leary, ibid.*

218 *Alexander v. R.* (1981), 145 C.L.R. 395 (Aust. H.C.); *Stephens v. R.* (1985), 58 A.L.R. 753 (Aust. H.C.).

219 *Alexander v. R., ibid.; R. v. Easom* (1981), 28 S.A.S.R. 134 (S.C.); *R. v. Aziz*, [1982] 2 N.S.W.L.R. 322 (C.C.A.); *R. v. Haidley and Alford*, [1984] V.R. 229 (S.C.).

220 (1970), 44 A.L.J.R. 263 at 268 (Aust. H.C.). The court held that a photograph of the accused's hand taken by the police and the results of a medical examination carried out in contravention of statute ought to be excluded.

221 (1978), 19 A.L.R. 641 at 659 (Aust. H.C.).

What *Ireland* involves is no simple question of ensuring fairness to an accused but instead the weighing against each other of two competing requirements of public policy, thereby seeking to resolve the apparent conflict between the desirable goal of bringing to conviction the wrongdoer and the undesirable effect of curial approval, or even encouragement, being given to the unlawful conduct of those whose task it is to enforce the law. This being the aim of the discretionary process called for in *Ireland* it follows that it by no means takes as its central point the question of unfairness to the accused. It is, on the contrary, concerned with the broader questions of high public policy, unfairness to the accused being only one factor which, if present, will play its part in the whole process of consideration.

These principles were applied to some of the identification issues that came up in the case of *R. v. Clune*.[222] In that case the accused, on the advice of his solicitor, refused to go into a lineup. The police then gathered up 18 men and put them in a room with the accused. When a witness was brought to the room the accused covered his face and launched a protest about the fairness of the lineup. The court held that the evidence relating to this latter lineup was obtained improperly or unfairly since it was designed to subvert the accused's right not to participate in such a procedure. The court also held that this evidence could be excluded on the proper exercise of the court's discretion.

Given the existence of these broad discretionary powers of exclusion in both Australia and England, there is authority for an argument that the Canadian position ought to be reconsidered. In addition, given the comments of four judges of the Supreme Court of Canada set out above, the time may be ripe for such an argument to be made. In identification cases, these arguments might put into question the admissibility of weak eyewitness identifications and improper pre-trial identification techniques.[223]

(b) The Admissibility of Out-of-Court Identifications

In most cases involving identification issues, witnesses will have identified the accused as the perpetrator in some manner prior to trial. In addition to the identification at trial, evidence of these previous acts of identification are admissible as part of the

---

222   [1982] V.R. 1 (S.C.).
223   It may also be argued that improper pre-trial identification procedures infringe on or deny an accused's rights pursuant to the Charter of Rights and Freedoms, and that the evidence be excluded pursuant to s. 24(2) of the Charter. See, *infra*, Chapter 4, for a discussion of these issues.

case for the prosecution. Wigmore puts the reasons for this admissibility in the following manner:[224]

> Ordinarily, when a witness is asked to *identify* the assailant, or thief, or other person who is the subject of his testimony, the witness act of pointing out the accused (or other person), then and there in the courtroom, is of little testimonial force. After all that has intervened, it would seldom happen that the witness would not have come to believe in the person's identity. The failure to recognize would tell for the accused; but the affirmative recognition might mean little against him . . .
>
> To corroborate the witness therefore it is entirely proper . . . to prove that *at a former time*, when the suggestions of others could not have intervened to create a fancied recognition in the witness' mind, he recognized and declared the present accused to be the person . . .
>
> This is a simple dictate of common sense, and was never doubted in orthodox practice.

This principle has long been accepted by the courts. For example, in 1914 in *R. v. Christie*,[225] a 5-year-old boy identified the accused in court as the one who indecently assaulted him. No questions were asked of him about any previous identifications. His mother and a police constable were then called as witnesses to describe a previous act of identification that took place within hours of the assault. The admissibility of this previous act of identification was not questioned[226] except as to what words would be admissible. In fact, one Canadian court has indicated that an accused could validly object on appeal if such evidence was not presented by the Crown.[227]

In general, the only evidence that is admissible is what was said or what was done by the witness as part of the act of identification. So, for example, in *R. v. Christie*,[228] the court held that evidence, in which the boy described the acts done to him, taken at the time that he identified the accused, ought not to have been admitted. The test seems to be whether "what was said or done by the identifier can fairly be said to be part of the identification or as

---

224 *Wigmore on Evidence*, Chadbourn revision, vol. 4 (Toronto: Little, Brown & Co.(Canada) Ltd., 1972), at 277.
225 [1914] A.C. 545 (H.L.).
226 *Ibid.*, at 563.
227 *R. v. Knittel*, [1983] 3 W.W.R. 42 (Sask. C.A.). In *R. v. Harrison*, [1928] 1 W.W.R. 973 (B.C.C.A.), the court held that it was proper to introduce this evidence in order to permit the accused to show by means of cross-examination that the identification procedure was unfair.
228 *Supra*, note 224.

indicative of its reliability or its unreliability."[229] In this regard, the reaction of the witness on seeing the accused is admissible.[230]

It is trite law that an accused can cross-examine witnesses as to both the initial description given by the identifying witness[231] and statements made by the witness at any out-of-court identification procedures. In fact, if the prosecution chooses not to call the persons to whom the description is given, the accused has the right to call that evidence.[232] This ability to cross-examine removes any unfairness occasioned by the repetitive nature of the evidence. Cross-examination gives an accused the opportunity to point out deficiencies both in the circumstances surrounding the event itself and the subsequent identification procedures. As well, it gives the accused the ability to highlight the differences between the descriptions initially given and the accused's appearance at the time of the crime.[233]

Thus far, the cases have dealt with the situation where the accused has been identified in court and then evidence of previous identifications is given to bolster that identification. However, since trials may take place long after these identification procedures and even longer after the event itself, a witness may be unable to identify the accused at trial. This may be a result of the fact that the accused has changed in appearance in the interim or simple forgetfulness on the part of the witness. The courts have long held that evidence of previous out-of-court identifications is admissible even if the witness fails to identify the accused at the trial. For example, in *R. v. Burke and Kelly*,[234] the judges admitted this testimony where the witness stated that he had identified a man who had robbed him, at the police station two days after the event, but could not say that it was the accused since the accused was very differently dressed. The court held that the Crown could

---

229   *R. v. Collings*, [1976] 2 N.Z.L.R. 104 at 114 (C.A.). In this case, involving a gang rape, evidence that the victim described the part played by each of the men she identified was held to be properly admitted. However, evidence of the conversation she had with one of the accused ought not to have been admitted.

230   *R. v. Simpson (No.2)* (1981), 58 C.C.C. (2d) 122 at 130 (Ont. C.A.). In this case the evidence was that the complainant's left hand started to shake and she went white when she saw the accused in court at a docket type of identification. For comment on the propriety of this procedure see, *R. v. Faryna* (1982), 3 C.C.C. (3d) 58 (Man. C.A.). See also, *Mezzo v. R.*, [1986] 4 W.W.R. 577 (S.C.C.), *per* Wilson J.

231   *R. v. Sophonow (No.2)* (1986), 25 C.C.C. (3d) 415 at 447 (Man. C.A.), *per* Twaddle J.A.; *R. v. Travers* (1966), 49 C.R. 339 at 343 (B.C.C.A.).

232   *R. v. Geneau* (1980), 4 W.C.B. 442 (Ont. C.A.).

233   *R. v. Clarke* (1930), 22 Cr. App. R. 58 (C.C.A.).

234   (1847), 2 Cox C.C. 295.

call witnesses to prove that one of the accused was the man who had been identified on that earlier occasion.[235]

The British Columbia Court of Appeal came to the same conclusion in *R. v. Swanston*.[236] In that case, the victim of a robbery had identified the accused at a lineup and at the preliminary hearing. At the trial, which took place 1¹/₂ years after the robbery, he was unable to identify the accused. This inability to make an identification probably stemmed from the fact that the accused had shaved off his beard and moustache in the interim. The witness testified that he had identified the perpetrator of the robbery on these earlier occasions. The court stated that police witnesses could testify that the accused had been identified on two previous occasions. It came to the conclusion that "evidence of extrajudicial identification is admissible not only to corroborate an identification made at trial but as independent evidence going to identity".[237]

Even in the above situation, that is, where the witness states that an identification was made on a previous occasion but cannot at trial identify the accused as that person, third party evidence linking the previous identification with the accused does not unfairly inhibit the accused's ability to cross-examine the witnesses on the quality of the earlier identification(s).[238]

This principle was extended by the English Court of Appeal in *R. v. Osbourne; R. v. Virtue*.[239] In that case, one of the witnesses stated that she could not identify the accused, nor could she remember if she picked anyone out at lineup held some 7¹/₂ months earlier. The court stated that it could see no "reason ... in principle" why the evidence of police officers present at the lineup

---

235 Notwithstanding this evidence, both accused were acquitted.
236 (1982), 65 C.C.C. (2d) 453 (B.C.C.A.). See also, *Alexander v. R.* (1981), 145 C.L.R. 395 (Aust. H.C.); *R. v. Smith*, [1984] 1 N.S.W.L.R. 462 (C.D.), reversed on other grounds (1987), 7 N.S.W.L.R. 444 (C.C.A.).
237 *Ibid.*, at 455.
238 *R. v. Skipper* (1988), 69 Sask. R. 7 (Q.B.). In the United States, the Federal Rules of Evidence, Rule 801(d)(1)(C) 28 U.S.C.A., is to the same effect. It states:
  "A statement is not hearsay if -
    (1) ... The declarant testifies at the trial or hearing and is subject to cross-examination concerning the statement, and the statement is ... (C) one of identification of a person made after perceiving the person ..."
  See also, *U.S. v. Lewis*, 565 F. 2d 1248 (2nd Circ.,1977). The evidence has also been held to be admissible on the basis of the common law. *People v. Gould*, 354 P. 2d 865 (Calif., 1960).
239 [1973] 1 All. E.R. 649 (C.A.).

should not be admitted.[240] In this situation, the right to cross-examine is clearly inhibited. Since the witness cannot be questioned on the factors which made her identify the accused at the lineup, the only answer that the witness could give would be, "I don't remember". As well, she could not be cross-examined on what caused her to identify the accused at trial as she was unable to make such an identification. In the result, the only evidence of identity at the trial would be the bald assertion of the police officer that the witness had identified the accused at the lineup, which assertion could not be effectively challenged. It is of interest to note that the court in *Swanston*[241] stated that it was not necessary for them to reach the same conclusion on the facts before them.

In addition, the court in *Swanston* was careful not to criticize the result in its earlier decision in *R. v. McGuire*.[242] In that case, two witnesses testified that the accused was not the man they saw. The court held that the Crown could not lead evidence that these two witnesses had previously identified the accused. In reaching this conclusion the court held that, "if at the trial the person does not identify the accused, evidence that he did identify him at an earlier occasion cannot be admitted."[243] In *Swanston*, the court held that this statement ought no longer to be followed. They went on to state that the applicable principle was:[244]

> None of the exclusionary principles of evidence is infringed by permitting the identifying witness, who cannot identify the accused in Court, to state that whoever he identified on an earlier occasion was the culprit. The Crown may, then, prove by another witness that the man identified by the identifying witness was the accused in the dock.

In the result, it seems that the court was very careful not to extend the principle beyond the situation where the witness is able to testify that an identification was made at an earlier date. In light of this it is doubtful that the extension in *R. v. Osbourne; R. v. Virtue*,[245] will be followed by the Canadian courts.

Finally, there have been no cases in Canada, England, Australia or New Zealand where the prosecution has attempted to put in the evidence of identity without calling the identifying witness at the trial. In a number of American cases, courts have also held

240   *Ibid.*, at 657.
241   *Supra*, note 236 at 457.
242   (1975), 23 C.C.C. (2d) 385 (B.C.C.A.).
243   *Ibid.*, at 391.
244   *Supra*, note 236 at 458.
245   *Supra*, note 239.

that evidence of identity cannot be admitted when the identifying witness is not called to testify.[246]

This evidence would clearly be hearsay and inadmissible. However, in some situations this evidence might be of assistance to the accused. For example, in *Sparks v. R.*,[247] the 3-year-old victim of an indecent assault was not called as a witness at the trial. As a result, the accused was not permitted to bring out the fact that the girl had stated that the perpetrator was a "coloured boy", whereas the accused was caucasian.

In summary, if a witness testifies and identifies the accused in court or states that he or she made an identification at a previous time but cannot now identify the person, then evidence of the circumstances of that previous identification may be given by both the witness and persons present at that identification. It is still an open question in Canada if the evidence of the pre-trial identification will be admissible where the witness does not recall whether or not an identification was made previously. Nonetheless, if the identifying witness does not testify, the evidence of any previous identification procedure will not be admissible.

(c) Evidence Given at Previous Judicial Proceedings

In certain situations, evidence may be given at a trial by reading in evidence given at either a previous trial on the same charge or the preliminary hearing. In cases where identity is an issue, the finder of fact would be unable to assess the witness' demeanour; a factor that may be crucial in determining whether the identification made by the witness was accurate either in identifying the accused in court or at a previous identification procedure. The admissibility of this evidence is governed by the provisions of s. 715(1) of the Criminal Code, R.S.C. 1985, c. C-46, which states:

> 715.(1) Where, at the trial of an accused, a person whose evidence was given at a previous trial on the same charge . . . or on the preliminary inquiry into the charge, refuses to be sworn or to give evidence, or if the facts are proved upon oath from which it can be inferred reasonably that the person
> (a) is dead,
> (b) has since become and is insane,

---

246   *U.S. v. Ariza-Ibarra*, 605 F. 2d 1216 (1st Circ., 1979); *People v. Howard*, 599 P. 2d 899 (Colo., 1979); *People v. Cuadra*, 367 N.Y.S. 2d 21 (App. Div., 1975); *People v. Owens*, 337 N.E. 2d 60 (Ill. C.A., 1975); *Knight v. State*, 373 So. 2d 52 (Fla. App., 1979).
247   [1964] A.C. 964 (P.C.).

(c) is so ill that he is unable to travel or testify, or
(d) is absent from Canada,
and where it is proved that his evidence was taken in the presence of the accused, it may be read as evidence in the proceedings without further proof . . . unless the accused proves . . . that he did not have full opportunity to cross-examine the witness.

As can be seen, one of the key determinations of admissibility is the fact that the accused has had the full opportunity to cross-examine the witness at the former hearing. In *R. v. Potvin*,[248] the Supreme Court of Canada held that because of this opportunity, the section did not violate the provisions of the Charter of Rights and Freedoms. The court went on to say that the opportunity has a constitutional dimension and as a result must be construed in a "broad and generous manner".[249] However, the mere fact that counsel may choose to cross-examine differently at a preliminary inquiry than at a trial does not deny the accused the full opportunity to cross-examine.[250]

In an identification case, it might be argued that this right would be denied if, for example, the accused, at the initial hearing, was unaware of material discrepancies in the initial description given by an identifying witness or of certain statements made by that witness putting into doubt the identification that was made. As well, if, due to the nature of the evidence presented at the initial hearing, deficiencies in pre-trial identification procedures were not made known to the accused, this might be said to be a denial of the full opportunity to cross-examine. Of course, a ruling by the judge at a preliminary hearing which curtails cross-examination on an important issue such as credibility would also affect the admissibility of the evidence on the subsequent hearing.

In *Potvin*, the court also held that a judge has a discretion whether or not to admit this evidence.[251] Although the court was unanimous on the existence of such a discretion, it was divided on the nature of that discretion. Wilson J.[252] held that the discretion was a statutory one. As a result, in her view, it was broader than the common law discretion to exclude evidence if its prejudicial effect outweighed its probative value.[253] This statutory discretion would

---

248 (1989), 47 C.C.C. (3d) 289 (S.C.C.).
249 *Ibid*, at 302.
250 *Ibid.*, at 303.
251 This overruled a number of previous decisions which had held that there was at best a limited discretion. The leading case asserting this proposition was *R. v. Tretter* (1974), 18 C.C.C. (2d) 82 (Ont. C.A.).
252 Lamer and Sopinka JJ. concurring.
253 *Supra*, note 248 at 308.

apply where the admission of the evidence would operate unfairly to the accused.[254] This unfairness could result from the manner in which the evidence was obtained or where its admission would be unfair.[255] In the result, the focus would be on protecting the accused from unfairness rather than the admission of probative evidence.[256]

Although Wilson J. stated that "such circumstances would be relatively rare",[257] it may well be of some importance in cases where the evidence proffered is that of an eyewitness. An argument could be made that it would be unfair to admit such evidence where the quality of an identification is poor. Whether the lack of quality comes about as a result of the environmental factors at the time of the initial incident, or as a result of defects in the pre-trial identification procedures, is immaterial. In these cases, it would be argued that a witness' non-verbal reactions on being confronted with these weaknesses would be utilized by the trier of fact as a key factor in determining what weight, if any, to give to the evidence of identity. As a result, it would be unfair to the accused to admit this evidence without that key factor being present.

Also, if any of the above factors inhibiting cross-examination were present but were not sufficiently serious to amount to a constitutional infringement or denial of the accused's right to a full opportunity to cross-examination at the original proceeding, it might well be argued that, absent the constitutional violation, it would be unfair to admit the evidence, and a judge ought to exercise the appropriate discretion and exclude the evidence.

La Forest J.[258] took the view that the discretion to exclude evidence was a common law discretion rather than a statutory one.[259] In his view a judge had a discretion to exclude where "its prejudicial effect substantially outweighs its probative value".[260] This formulation of the discretion is more restrictive than that of Wilson J. The requirement that the prejudicial effect "substantially" outweigh the prejudicial value would result in evidence being admitted that would not have been admitted if the test articulated by Wilson J. were utilized. For although such evidence may have a prejudicial effect which might be unfair to the accused,

---

254 *Ibid.*, at 304.
255 *Ibid.*, at 308.
256 *Ibid.*, at 309.
257 *Ibid.*, at 304.
258 *Ibid.*, Dickson C.J.C. concurring.
259 *Ibid.*, at 314. See, *supra*, this chapter, part 6(3)(a).
260 *Ibid.*, at 314.

this effect might not "substantially" outweigh the probative value of the evidence. Given that there were only five judges involved in this decision and that they split 3:2 on reasoning, it remains to be seen which reasoning will predominate.

Finally, the court held that in cases where evidence is admitted pursuant to s. 715(1), it is desirable that the trial judge point out to the jury that they assess this evidence in light of the fact that they have not had an opportunity of observing the witness give evidence.[261] The court cannot inform the jury that this evidence is no different from any other evidence.[262]

(d) Photographs and Videotapes

Modern technology has developed security systems that will produce photographs or videotapes of a crime as it is being committed. These devices will often provide evidence that is determinative of the identity of the perpetrator of the offence. Two evidentiary issues arise as a result of these developments; the admissibility of the photographs and videotapes themselves, and whether or not witnesses can be called to identify the persons shown in the images portrayed.

Admissibility of both photographs and videotapes is governed by the principles set out by the Nova Scotia Supreme Court Appeal Division in *R. v. Creemer*.[263]

In that case, McKinnon J.A. stated:[264]

> All the cases dealing with the admissibility of photographs go to show that such admissibility depends on (1) their accuracy in truly representing the facts; (2) their fairness and absence of any intention to mislead; (3) their verification on oath by a person capable to do so.

These principles have been applied to videotapes as well as to photographs.[265] Ordinarily security systems are passive in the sense that no human is present when the photographic images are being taken. As a result, verification that the images accurately represent what they portray must be done indirectly. This is usually accomplished by having someone familiar with the system

---

261   *Ibid.*, at 300.
262   *Ibid.*, at 311.
263   [1968] 1 C.C.C. 14 (N.S.C.A.).
264   *Ibid.*, at 22.
265   *R. v. Schaffner* (1988), 44 C.C.C. (2d) 507 (N.S.C.A.); *R. v. Leaney* (1987), 38 C.C.C. (3d) 263 at 275 (Alta. C.A.), reversed in part 50 C.C.C. (3d) 289 (S.C.C.); *R. v. Maloney (No.2)* (1976), 29 C.C.C. (2d) 431 (Ont. Co. Ct.).

testify as to its operation. This has been held to be acceptable by the courts.[266] In the result, unless accuracy can be challenged, the images are usually admitted.

Once admitted, the finder of fact is in a position to compare the images with the accused and determine whether the person portrayed and the accused are one and the same. As a result, identity can be proved simply by having the photograph or videotape admitted into evidence. As well, earlier photographs of the accused may be admitted to assist in the identification process. This process was approved by the English Court of Appeal in the following terms:[267]

> Moreover, we reject the attempt made here to persuade this court to prevent a jury from looking at photographs taken by means of this technique, looking at a defendant in the dock and then to conclude if it be safe to do so that the man in the dock is the man shown in the photographs. Photographs of the same man taken at other times we regard as permissible aids in this process, bearing in mind that some offenders after the commission of crime by one device or another change their appearances.
>
> In performing this task juries cannot possibly in our judgment be regarded as acting as experts, as for instance they might be if they were invited to be judges of handwriting and fingerprints, in which specialties special training and expertise are demanded. They are called upon to do no more than the average person in domestic, social and other situations does from time to time, namely to say whether he is sure that a person shown in a photograph is the person he is then looking at or who he has seen recently.

A more difficult question arises if the Crown wishes to call witnesses to testify that the image entered into evidence is that of the accused. A case in point is that of *R. v. Leaney.*[268] The trial judge admitted the evidence of five police officers who stated that the person on the videotape was one of the accused. Four of these officers had no contact or minimal contact with the accused prior to his arrest. The fifth had known the accused for approximately 15 years and knew him well. The Alberta Court of Appeal and the Supreme Court of Canada held that the evidence of the four officers who were not familiar with the accused ought not to have been admitted as they were in no better position than the trier of fact to give an opinion.[269] The evidence of the fifth officer was held

---

266   See cases, *ibid.* See also, *Kajala v. Noble* (1982), 75 Cr. App. R. 149 (Div. Ct.).
267   *R. v. Dodson; R. v. Williams* (1984), 79 Cr. App. R. 220 at 228 (C.A.). An example of how this process was implemented by a trial judge sitting alone is *R. v. Walker*, [1989] B.C.W.L.D. 646 (Co. Ct.), 13th January 1989.
268   (1989), 50 C.C.C. (3d) 289 (S.C.C.), reversing in part 38 C.C.C. (3d) 263 (Alta. C.A.).
269   *Ibid.*, at 301, 303 (S.C.C.).

to be admissible. Harradence J.A. of the Alberta Court of Appeal explained the distinction:[270]

> Notwithstanding this general principle of exclusion, there may be occasions when non-expert opinion evidence will be relevant and admissible. Where a witness is so familiar with the accused that he can identify idiosyncracies of physical appearance or movement, not apparent to the trier of fact in the court-room, that witness should be able to give his opinion. Two criteria must be satisfied. First the witness must be sufficiently familiar with the accused so as to be aware of the unique features which form the basis of the opinion. Secondly, the witness must be able to state with particularity what the idiosyncracies are and show where and how they are revealed on the video tape. In this way the witness is contributing knowledge not otherwise available to the trier of fact.

In the result, it seems that once an independent image exists, extraneous evidence of identity will usually not be admitted into evidence.

The boundaries of the use of this technology as a means of proof were extended in *Taylor v. Chief Constable of Cheshire*.[271] In that case the videotape was accidentally erased. Notwithstanding this fact, the court held that a store manager and a number of police officers, who had seen the tape, could testify as to its contents, because there was no difference between the evidence of a person who has viewed a videotape and an eyewitness. If this case is followed, the technology permits the testimony of eyewitnesses who have not seen the event.[272]

The English courts have also stated that a jury must be warned as to the perils of this type of evidence. As was stated by the English Court of Appeal:[273]

> Evidence of this kind is relatively novel. What is of utmost importance with regard to it, is that the quality of the photographs, the extent of the exposure of the facial features of the person photographed, evidence, or the absence of it, of a change in the defendant's appearance and the opportunity a jury has to look at a defendant in the dock and over what period of time are factors, among other matters of relevance in this context in a particular case, which the jury must receive

---

270 *Ibid.*, at 277, 278 (Alta. C.A.). Harradence J.A. stated that the admissibility of this evidence ought to have been the subject of a *voir dire*. His dissent was based on other grounds. See also, *R. v. Fowden and White*, [1982] Crim. L.R. 588 (C.A.); *R. v. Grimer*, [1982] Crim. L.R. 674 (C.A.).

271 (1987), 84 Cr. App. R. 191 (Div. Ct.).

272 It should be noted that this is a different situation from that of *Leaney*. In this case, the court was not in as good a position as the witnesses to make the identification since there was no videotape before it.

273 *R. v. Dodson; R. v. Williams, supra,* note 267 at 229.

guidance upon from the judge when he directs them as to how they should approach the task of resolving this crucial issue.

In summary, evidence of photographs and videotapes of the event constituting the offence are admissible and can in certain circumstances be supported by *viva voce* evidence of identity. Provided that a jury is properly instructed as to their deficiencies, they can provide sufficient evidence of identity to result in a conviction.

(e) Evidence of Children

At common law, evidence not given under oath was inadmissible. As a result, children who were incapable of taking an oath were incompetent to testify.[274] This rule has been modified by statute in Canada to permit the reception of the unsworn evidence of a child under the age of 14 to be received if that child is able to communicate the evidence and promises to tell the truth.[275] This provision, which came into force in 1988, removed the requirement in the earlier legislation that such evidence be corroborated.[276] The question that has to be dealt with is whether the removal of this requirement will affect the way in which the evidence of children will be treated. That is, will it be treated in the same way as evidence given by an adult, or will it be dealt with by the courts in some special manner?

The common law treated the evidence of children differently from that of adults. Even if children were sworn, juries had to be warned as a matter of practice that it was dangerous to act on such evidence unless it was corroborated.[277] The reasons behind this rule are generally based on the immaturity of such children. In an early case, one English Court stated:[278]

> ... small children are possibly more under the influence of third persons – sometimes their parents – than are adults, and they are apt to allow their imaginations to run away with them and to invent untrue stories.

A more charitable view was recently taken by a judge in charging a jury when he stated:[279]

---

274   *Cross on Evidence*, 6th ed. (London: Butterworth's, 1985), at 192.
275   The Canada Evidence Act, R.S.C. 1985, c. C-5, s. 16(3), as enacted by R.S.C. 1985, c. 19 (3rd Supp.), s. 18.
276   R.S.C. 1970, c. E-10, s. 16(2).
277   *R. v. Dossi* (1918), 13 Cr. App. R. 158 (C.A.); *R. v. Sawyer* (1959), 43 Cr. App. R. 187 (C.A.).
278   *R. v. Dossi, ibid.,* at 161.
279   *R. v. Willoughby* (1988), 88 Cr. App. R. 91 at 93 (C.A.).

"Furthermore, in regard to children of tender years, because of their inexperience of life, it may be in an anxiety to find the culprit, or to please parents and persons in authority, that they may also give evidence which is either not true or mistaken. So, once again, caution is to be exercised in relying on their evidence."

The Supreme Court of Canada has focused on the child himself or herself rather than the effect of the influence of others upon that child. In *R. v. Kendall*,[280] Judson J. put this reasoning in the following terms:

> The basis for the rule of practice which requires the Judge to warn the jury of the danger of convicting on the evidence of a child, even when sworn as a witness, is the mental immaturity of the child. The difficulty is fourfold: 1. His capacity of observation. 2. His capacity of recollection. 3. His capacity to understand questions and frame intelligent answers. 4. His moral responsibility.

If the change in the statute is interpreted so as to remove any requirement for a warning in cases of the unsworn evidence of children, the illogical result would be that there would be a required warning in the case of the sworn evidence and no warning requirement for unsworn evidence. This is obviously an unacceptable situation.

Although it could be argued that the above problems relate to the evidence of all children and as a result the requirement of a warning should be extended to unsworn testimony, this would fly in the face of Parliament's intention to remove any need for corroboration of children's testimony. A more likely and logical result is that the requirement of a warning in the case of the sworn testimony of children will be modified by the courts.

An appropriate analogy is the case of *Vetrovec v. R.; Gaja v. R.*[281] In that case, the Supreme Court of Canada held that in Canada it was no longer a rule of law that a jury had to be warned about the dangers of accepting the evidence of an accomplice without corroboration. One of the reasons for rejecting this rule was that the dangers inherent in such testimony do not exist in every case. As the court stated, "credibility will vary with the facts of the particular case".[282]

The court resolved the question in the following manner:[283]

280   (1962), 132 C.C.C. 216 at 220 (S.C.C.). See also, *Horsburgh v. R.*, [1968] 2 C.C.C. 288 (S.C.C.); *R. v. Tennant* (1975), 23 C.C.C. (2d) 80 (Ont. C.A.); *R. v. Burdick* (1975), 27 C.C.C. (2d) 497 at 509 (Ont. C.A.).
281   (1982), 27 C.R. (3d) 304 (S.C.C.).
282   *Ibid.*, at 314.
283   *Ibid.*, at 315.

Rather than attempting to pigeonhole a witness into a category and then recite a ritualistic incantation, the trial judge might better direct his mind to the facts of the case and thoroughly examine all the factors which might impair the worth of a particular witness. If, in his judgment, the credit of the witness is such that the jury should be cautioned, then he may instruct accordingly. If on the other hand, he believes the witness to be trustworthy, then regardless of whether the witness is technically an "accomplice", no warning is necessary.

This reasoning is equally applicable to children's testimony. Some children are more mature than others, some are more prone to suggestion than others, and some are more subject to the influence of others. A trial judge ought to be able to assess these factors in a child witness, sworn or unsworn, and warn the juries of the need for caution if such need exists. If, based on that assessment, no need exists, no warning need be given. Given the trend away from strict categorization in the law of evidence, this seems the most likely resolution to the present anomaly in the law.

7. APPEALS

(1) Unreasonable Verdicts

Where identity is the key issue, most cases will be decided on their facts. As a result, in Canada, most acquittals based on the evidence of eyewitnesses are not the subject of an appeal.[284] Most conviction appeals are based on the ground that the verdict was unreasonable or could not be supported by the evidence.

This ground of appeal is based on the powers granted to the Court of Appeal in s. 686(1)(*a*)(i) of the Criminal Code, which states:

> 686. (1) On the hearing of an appeal against a conviction . . . the court of appeal
> (*a*) may allow the appeal where it is of the opinion that
> (i) the verdict should be set aside on the ground that it is unreasonable and cannot be supported by the evidence . . .

Although earlier cases interpreting this section had stated that the Court of Appeal could come to its own "original and independent conclusions on fact",[285] this is no longer the case. The

---

284 Section 676(1) of the Criminal Code only permits appeals by the Crown on questions of law alone. The sufficiency of identification evidence is not a question of law.
285 *R. v. Smith* (1952), 103 C.C.C. 58 (Ont. C.A.).

principles to be applied by a Court of Appeal in applying the provision were clarified by the Supreme Court of Canada in *Yebes v. R.*[286] In addition to holding that the application of this section raised a question of law which permitted an appeal to the Supreme Court of Canada, McIntyre J. enunciated the following proposition:[287]

> The function of the Court of Appeal . . . goes beyond merely finding that there is evidence to support a conviction. The court must determine on the whole of the evidence whether the verdict is one that a properly instructed jury, acting judicially, could reasonably have rendered. While the Court of Appeal must not merely substitute its view for that of the jury, in order to apply the test the court must re-examine and to some extent reweigh and consider the effect of the evidence. This process will be the same whether the case is based on circumstantial or direct evidence.

That is, the conviction will only be overturned where no jury could have reasonably found the accused guilty beyond a reasonable doubt.[288] In cases involving identity, one court has stated that "the inherent danger in faulty identification is so great that the evidence to justify a conviction must be such that it leaves no reasonable doubt of guilt".[289]

As can be seen, these principles give a Court of Appeal wide scope for overturning verdicts of guilty. In identification cases such verdicts have been reversed where the identifying witnesses have expressed uncertainty in court;[290] where the identifying witness

---

286   (1987), 36 C.C.C. (3d) 417 (S.C.C.). This case clarified the following statement of Pigeon J. in *Corbett v. R.* (1973), 14 C.C.C. (2d) 385 at 386, 387 (S.C.C.):

"Of course, if the Judges of the majority had held that their function was only to decide whether there was evidence, this would be reversible error. The *Criminal Code* expressly provides that the appeal may be allowed, not only when the verdict cannot be supported by the evidence but also when it is unreasonable. In other words, the Court of Appeal must satisfy itself not only that there was evidence requiring the case to be submitted to the jury, but also that the weight of such evidence is not so weak that a verdict of guilty is unreasonable. This cannot be taken to mean that the Court of Appeal is to substitute its opinion for that of the jury. The word of the enactment is 'unreasonable', not 'unjustified'. The jurors are the triers of the facts and their finding is not to be set aside because the Judges in appeal do not think they would have made the same finding if sitting as jurors. This is only to be done if they come to the conclusion that the verdict is such that no 12 reasonable men could possibly have reached it acting judicially."

287   *Ibid.*, at 430.

288   *R. v. Gale* (1984), 15 C.C.C. (3d) 143 (B.C.C.A.).

289   *R. v. Ghaney* (1988), 83 N.S.R. (2d) 236 (C.A.).

290   *R. v. Rehberg* (1973), 5 N.S.R. (2d) 14 (C.A.); *R. v. Albert* (1984), 4 O.A.C. 50 (C.A.); *R. v. Lambert*, [1989] B.C.W.L.D. 469 (C.A.), 7th December 1988.

has been seen to be unreliable;[291] where there is insufficient detail given in the initial description;[292] where the pre-trial identification procedures used by the police have been unreliable or unfair;[293] and where a witness identified the accused in court after failing to identify him in a photo array.[294]

On the other hand, verdicts of guilty have been upheld where the witness has stated that he was not certain that the accused was the perpetrator;[295] where the witnesses stated that the accused resembled the robber;[296] where the identifying witness made two mistaken identifications from photographs but identified an accused at a lineup;[297] where the witnesses testified that the robber ran from the scene of the crime and the accused led medical evidence that at the relevant time he would only have been able to walk with a pronounced limp;[298] and where the identification was made at an improperly conducted lineup when the witness had only a brief glance at the perpetrator at the crime scene.[299]

In addition, in *Corbett v. R.*,[300] the Supreme Court of Canada held that a Court of Appeal could take into account the accused's failure to testify in determining whether the verdict was unreasonable. This proposition is somewhat incongruous since the reasonableness of a verdict would ordinarily be dependent solely on the strength of the case for the Crown. Nonetheless, the reasoning behind this proposition was stated by Pigeon J. in the following terms:[301]

---

291 *R. v. Deschamps* (1980), 60 C.C.C. (2d) 364 (Que. C.A.); *Abel v. R.*, [1986] N.W.T.R. 345 (S.C.).

292 *R. v. Browne and Angus* (1951), 99 C.C.C. 141 (B.C.C.A.); *R. v. Harrison* (1950), 99 C.C.C. 96 (B.C.C.A.); *R. v. Yates* (1946), 85 C.C.C. 334 (B.C.C.A.); *R. v. McDonald* (1951), 101 C.C.C. 78 (B.C.C.A.); *R. v. Shaver* (1970), 2 N.S.R. (2d) 225 (C.A.).

293 *R. v. Smierciak* (1946), 87 C.C.C. 175 (Ont. C.A.); *Nepton v. R.* (1971), 15 C.R.N.S. 145 (Que. C.A.); *R. v. Whonnock* (1980), 4 W.C.B. 209 (B.C.C.A.); *R. v. Faryna* (1982), 3 C.C.C. (3d) 58 (Man. C.A.); *R. v. Lecaine* (1983), 22 Sask. R. 50 (C.A.); *R. v. Atfield* (1983), 25 Alta. L.R. (2d) 97 (C.A.); *R. v. Babb* (1971), 17 C.R.N.S. 366 (B.C.C.A.).

294 *R. v. Still*, [1987] B.C.W.L.D. 2161 (C.A.).

295 *R. v. Harvey* (1918), 42 O.L.R. 187 (C.A.).

296 *R. v. Jarrett* (1975), 25 C.C.C. (2d) 241 (N.S.C.A.).

297 *R. v. Dixon* (1953), 105 C.C.C. 16 (B.C.C.A.).

298 *R. v. Reakes*, [1987] B.C.W.L.D. 2215 (C.A.), affirmed [1988] 1 S.C.R. 395.

299 *R. v. Hutton* (1980), 43 N.S.R. (2d) 541 (C.A.).

300 (1973), 14 C.C.C. (2d) 385 (S.C.C.).

301 *Ibid.*, at 388. It is interesting to note that this statement approved a similar statement made by Branca J.A. of the British Columbia Court of Appeal in the same case, (1973), 11 C.C.C. (2d) 137 at 150, 151 (B.C.C.A.). In an earlier case, *R. v. McGeachy*, [1969] 2 C.C.C. 98 at 113 (B.C.C.A.), the same judge stated:

... the Canada Evidence Act ... provides that the failure of a person charged "shall not be made the subject of comment by the judge, or by counsel for the prosecution", it does not prevent the jury from taking the fact into account without being told. No one can reasonably think that a jury will fail, in reaching a verdict, to take into account the failure of the accused to testify, specially in a case like this. This being so, it is a fact properly to be considered by the Court of Appeal when dealing with the question: "Is this a reasonable verdict?"

This factor is likely to be re-examined in light of the provisions of s. 11(*c*) of the Canadian Charter of Rights and Freedoms, which gives constitutional force to the proposition that an accused cannot be compelled to testify at his or her trial. This matter was raised by the Ontario Court of Appeal in *R. v. Mammolita.*[302] In that case the court viewed the issue as an open one. The only reported case dealing with the issue is the Manitoba Court of Appeal decision in *R. v. B.(J.N.).*[303] Although the matter was not addressed by counsel, Twaddle J.A., speaking for the majority,[304] used the following reasoning to hold that this concept was not unconstitutional:[305]

> One of the most difficult decisions which defence counsel has to make is whether to call an accused to testify. In making the decision, counsel will be conscious of the fact that, if the accused does not testify, there is more likelihood of the trier of fact believing the Crown's witnesses and making adverse inferences. This fact may put pressure on the accused to testify, as is his right, but it does not compel him to do so. He is entitled, without giving evidence, to invite the trier of fact to doubt the truth of what the witnesses have said or, where the evidence is indirect, to reject the inferences suggested by the Crown as the only reasonable ones. I do not construe the Charter as abrogating the rule of common sense that, in deciding whether to believe a witness or draw

---

"The appellant did not testify. The defence called no witnesses. The appellant was entitled to the protection of the presumption of innocence. It was no part of his task to prove his innocence or whereabouts on the evening in question. He was under no duty to explain and was perfectly entitled to refrain from giving evidence and to rely upon the onus lying upon the Crown to prove his guilt in this case, as in all criminal cases, beyond a reasonable doubt, in the sense that he was the only man implicated and that the crime charged has been committed by him."
Other identity cases where this factor was taken into account by the Court of Appeal include: *R. v. Jarrett* (1975), 25 C.C.C. (2d) 241 (N.S.C.A.); *R. v. Martell* (1977), 23 N.S.R. (2d) 578 (C.A.); *R. v. Hahn* (1983), 23 Sask. R. 105 (C.A.); *R. v. Gill*, 50 Man. R. (2d) 33, affirmed [1989] 1 S.C.R. 295.

302 (1983), 9 C.C.C. (3d) 85 (Ont. C.A.).
303 (1989), 48 C.C.C. (3d) 71 (Man. C.A.).
304 Huband J.A. concurring. O'Sullivan J.A. dissented.
305 *Ibid.*, at 79, 80. On the other hand, O'Sullivan J.A. stated: "The adoption of a principle that an adverse inference can be drawn against an accused by an appellate tribunal would create a subtle but very real pressure on an accused to testify at trial, and this is contrary to the express guarantees in the Charter of Rights".

an inference, a trier of fact may consider as one factor the lack of contradictory evidence.

When it is alleged that a verdict is unreasonable, this court must have regard to all the factors which the trier of fact was entitled to consider. One of these factors is, where applicable, the absence of a denial or an explanation by the accused. There is an immense difference between a trial judge accepting the uncontradicted evidence of a complainant as establishing guilt beyond reasonable doubt and his preferring the unsupported evidence of the complainant over that of the accused. In the former circumstance, it is more difficult for this court to say the verdict was unreasonable. The fact that this court takes the absence of denial or explanation into account in that circumstance does not, in my opinion, infringe the accused's right to remain silent.

In summary, given the wide variety of circumstances that can occur, and the generality of the principle enunciated by the Supreme Court of Canada, it is almost impossible to predict with any certainty whether or not a conviction will be regarded as unreasonable by an Appellate Court.

(2) Fresh Evidence on Appeal

The Criminal Code has given the Courts of Appeal a broad discretion to consider and admit evidence not heard at trial.[306] The Supreme Court of Canada has stated that the following principles apply to the admission of such evidence:[307]

(1) the evidence should not be admitted if by due diligence it could have been adduced at trial, provided that this general principle will not be applied as strictly in a criminal case as in civil cases . . .

(2) the evidence must be relevant, in the sense that it bears upon a decisive or potentially decisive issue in the trial;

(3) the evidence must be credible, in the sense that it is reasonably capable of belief; and

(4) it must be such that, if believed, it could reasonably, when taken with the other evidence adduced at trial, be expected to have affected the trial.

Given the above principles, fresh evidence is admitted infrequently. However, in light of the fourth principle, if the evidence is admitted, the appeal must be allowed.[308]

In cases involving identification evidence, there are few cases where fresh evidence has been permitted. In an early case, the

---

306 Section 683(1).
307 *Palmer v. R.* (1979), 14 C.R. (3d) 22 at 38 (S.C.C.).
308 *Stolar v. R.* (1988), 62 C.R. (3d) 313 (S.C.C.).

court admitted evidence that the accused had a moustache at the time of the offence, where the true offender was clean shaven.[309] Evidence also has been admitted that an identifying witness questioned the veracity of his identification shortly after it was made.[310]

In certain instances evidence has been admitted that another person committed the crime in question. For example, in *R. v. Lakatos*,[311] the court admitted the evidence of a co-accused that the accused was not one of the men with him at the time the offence was committed. Similarly, in *R. v. Walker and Malyon*,[312] evidence of a third party stating that he, and not the accused, was one of the perpetrators was admitted. However, in *R. v. Byrne*,[313] the English Court of Appeal refused to admit such evidence of a person purporting to be the actual culprit on the grounds that the other evidence was of such strength that this person's evidence was not credible.

Finally, fresh evidence cannot be used as a device to correct counsel's incomplete investigation. In *R. v. Grigoreshenko and Stupka*,[314] the court refused to admit the evidence of witnesses called at the trial as to the lighting conditions at the place where the offence took place. The court held that this evidence could have been discovered if counsel had fully cross-examined these witnesses at the preliminary hearing. As a result, after-acquired knowledge is no substitute for thorough initial preparation.

309   *R. v. Gilling* (1916), 12 Cr. App. R. 131 (C.A.).
310   *R. v. Williams* (1912), 8 Cr. App. R. 84 (C.A.).
311   (1961), 129 C.C.C. 387 (B.C.C.A.).
312   (1910), 5 Cr. App. R. 296 (C.A.).
313   (1988), 88 Cr. App. R. 33 (C.A.)
314   (1945), 85 C.C.C. 129 (Sask. C.A.).

Chapter Three

Pre-trial Identification

There is no legislation in Canada governing the means by which the police obtain pre-trial eyewitness identifications. In contrast to the position in Canada, England has adopted a legislative scheme that details the manner in which pre-trial identifications are to be done. In 1986 (revised 1991), the *Code of Practice for the Identification of Persons by Police Officers* (Code D),[1] was passed pursuant to the Police and Criminal Evidence Act, 1984.[2] As a legislative instrument, Code D has the force of law. It is, however, drafted in a flexible manner that does recognize the need for some administrative options to meet exceptional circumstances.

Code D is subject to the provisions of s. 78(1) of the Police and Criminal Evidence Act, 1984.[3] This section gives the court a wide discretion to exclude evidence tendered by the prosecution if it appears to the court that, "having regard to all the circumstances, including the circumstances in which the evidence was obtained, the admission of the evidence would have ... an adverse effect on the fairness" of the trial. This section, combined with Code D, gives the court the discretion to exclude identification evidence if Code D is not adhered to. The evidence of identification is to be excluded if its admission would result in an unfair trial. The test is not whether the police acted reasonably, but whether the trial is fair. The concept of fairness cannot be defined with any precision, but the Court of Appeal has made it clear that Code D is a legislative scheme designed to create fair identification pro-

---

1   Police and Criminal Evidence Act, 1984 (Codes of Practice) (No. 1), Order 1985, SI 1985/1937 (London: H.M.S.O.). Code D was revised in 1991, and the revised code is reproduced in its entirety, with the permission of the Controller of Her Majesty's Stationery Office, *infra*, Appendix A.
2   1984 (Eng.), c. 60, s. 67(4).
3   The section is reproduced, *supra*, Chapter 2, part 6(3)(a).

cedures. It is therefore to be followed unless there are exceptional circumstances.[4]

In 1983, the Law Reform Commission of Canada released an extensive study paper on pre-trial eyewitness procedures that recommended legislation similar to that in England.[5] Legislation was felt to be necessary in order to establish uniform procedures, increase the reliability of identifications, reduce the risk of mistaken identifications, and protect the rights of suspects.[6] To date there is no legislation in Canada incorporating the study paper recommendations. The court's ability to control this aspect of criminal procedure therefore rests on a variety of common law principles that are reviewed in this chapter.

1. THE NEED FOR PRE-TRIAL IDENTIFICATION

The courts have long recognized that witnesses should be asked to identify a suspect or an accused at the earliest opportunity and under the fairest of circumstances.[7] As a general rule, little if any weight can be given to the evidence of a witness whose first opportunity to identify the accused takes place in court; the so-called "dock identification".[8] Though a dock identification may be necessary to establish the legal averments of the indictment, it is quite obvious in most cases which person in the courtroom is the accused. Therefore, the dock identification is a formality and not a test of memory. There is, however, no rule of evidence that excludes dock identification.[9] Rather, the weight is to be assessed by the trier of fact. The jury however, must be warned about the

---

4   *R. v. Lamb* (1980), 71 Cr. App. R. 198 (C.A.); *R. v. Gall* (1990), 90 Cr. App. R. 64 (C.A.); *R. v. Conway* (1990), 91 Cr. App. R. 143 (C.A.). See also, *R. v. Grannell* (1990), 90 Cr. App. R. 149 (C.A.), where evidence from a group identification was admitted because the suspect's unusual appearance made a lineup impractical.

5   N. Brooks, *Pre-Trial Eyewitness Identification Procedures: Police Guidelines*, (Ottawa: Law Reform Commission of Canada, 1983).

6   *Ibid.*, at 17.

7   *R. v. Cartwright* (1914), 10 Cr. App. R. 219 (C.A.); *R. v. Gardner and Hancox* (1915), 80 J.P. 135 (C.A.); *Davies v. R.; Cody v. R.* (1937), 57 C.L.R. 170 (Aust. H.C.); *R. v. Browne and Angus* (1951), 99 C.C.C. 141 (B.C.C.A.).

8   *R. v. Atfield* (1983), 25 Alta. L.R. (2d) 97 (C.A.); *R. v. Horsham Justices; Ex parte Bukhari* (1982), 74 Cr. App. R. 291 (Div. Ct.); *R. v. Izzard* (1990), 54 C.C.C. (3d) 252 (Ont. C.A.).

9   *R. v. Glass*, [1945] N.Z.L.R. 496 at 506 (C.A.); *R. v. Donnini*, [1973] V.R. 67 (S.C.). See, however, Law Reform Commission study paper, *supra*, note 5 at 45-50. The study paper recommends that, except in special circumstances, a dock identification be prohibited unless a pre-trial identification has taken place.

weakness inherent in a dock identification.[10] If that is the only evidence of identification it may be so "valueless" as to render a conviction unsafe.[11]

2. INTERVIEWING WITNESSES

When interviewing witnesses it is important to ensure that the memories of each are kept independent. As such, it is important to separate witnesses during identification procedures.[12] In *R. v. Armstrong*,[13] Des Brisay C.J.B.C. recognized the danger of failing to do this:[14]

> I would add that it is most objectionable to provide books of photographs for inspection by more than one person at a time. This gives opportunity for discussion between the persons examining photographs, and it may well happen that the one who is uncertain in his identification, or who is unable to identify, may be influenced or persuaded by what appears to be the confidence or certainty of another person. Each witness should be required to make his own inspection and selection, if any, and to reach his own conclusion without the opportunity for consultation or discussion with any other person . . .

Mr. Justice Twaddle, of the Manitoba Court of Appeal described the dangers of collaboration in these metaphoric terms:[15]

> The image resulting from the collaboration of several witnesses is in danger of resembling, to adopt a well-known expression, the zebra materializing from the committee's attempt to construct a horse.

It is also important that investigating officers should obtain from each identification witness, as soon as possible, the fullest description of the person observed.[16] This preserves the original memory in as accurate a form as possible. The original description

---

10   *R. v. Gaunt*, [1964] N.S.W.R. 864 (C.A.).
11   *R. v. Browne and Angus, supra,* note 7, *per* O'Halloran J.A., at 150:
     "In my judgment, with deference, identification of the kind presented in this case, is valueless in the sense that it is dangerous for a Court to act upon it in any respect. Its inherent tendencies toward honest mistake and self-deception are so pervasive that they destroy any value that could otherwise attach to it even in a lesser role of 'some evidence' ".
12   See Law Reform Commission study paper, *supra,* note 5 at 52-54.
13   (1959), 31 C.R. 127 (B.C.C.A.).
14   *Ibid.,* at 130.
15   *R. v. Sophonow (No.2)*(1986), 25 C.C.C. (3d) 415 at 447, leave to appeal to S.C.C. refused 67 N.R. 158 [Man.].
16   *R. v. Atfield, supra,* note 8 at 114; *R. v. Power* (1987), 67 Nfld. & P.E.I.R. 272 at 281 (Nfld. T.D.). See also Law Reform Commission study paper, *supra,* note 5 at 88-95.

can then be cross-checked with the description given by other witnesses, with the actual appearance of the accused, and with the description given at trial. Variations between the original description and that given at trial may be as a result of the numerous psychological factors that tend to distort memory over time.

3. LINEUPS

The Commonwealth law is consistent in recommending lineups as the most appropriate method of pre-trial identification.[17] Long before psychologists turned their attention to the issues of identification, the common law had developed principles, the validity of which have been proved by subsequent experimentation. As early as 1911, the Court of Criminal Appeal quashed a conviction that depended on identification evidence from children, who had identified the accused after being asked, "Is that the man?"[18] Lord Alverstone, C.J. stated:[19]

> That is not a satisfactory way of identification whether the [witnesses] were young or old. It is not right to point out and ask questions in this way. The usual and proper way in such cases is to place the suspected man with a sufficient number of others, and have the identifying person pick out a man without assistance.

If a lineup is used the weight to be afforded the evidence of the identification is increased. This point was made by the Ontario Court of Appeal in *R. v. Todish*:[20]

> Evidence of identification may be strengthened where the identifying witness has picked out the person whom he claims to have seen on a

---

17   *Marcoux and Solomon v. R.* (1975), 24 C.C.C. (2d) 1 at 9 (S.C.C.), quoting Glanville Williams, "Identification Parades - I", [1963] Crim. L.R. 479 at 481: " 'The courts have come to expect that evidence of identification should be subjected to the test of a parade ... ' "; *R. v. Browne and Angus* (1951), 99 C.C.C. 141 at 148 (B.C.C.A.): "In cases of identification a line-up is almost a routine step in the preparation of the prosecution case"; *R. v. Baxter* (1984), 6 O.A.C. 225 at 226 (C.A.): " ... it would have been preferable if the police had conducted a proper lineup."; *R. v. Smith* (1975), 12 N.S.R. (2d) 289 at 299 (C.A.): "I think it is desirable for the police to hold an identification parade before the arrest, trial, or preliminary inquiry, as the case may be."
     See also, *R. v. Chapman* (1911), 7 Cr. App. R. 53 (C.A.); *Davies v. R.; Cody v. R.* (1937), 57 C.L.R. 170 (Aust. H.C.); *R. v. Jeffries*, [1949] N.Z.L.R. 595 (C.A.); *Alexander v. R.* (1980), 145 C.L.R. 395 (Aust. H.C.); Law Reform Commission of Canada study paper on *Pretrial Eyewitness Identification Procedures, supra,* note 5 at 98-112; *Code of Practice for the Identification of Persons by Police Officers, infra,* Appendix A, para. 2.3.
18   *R. v. Chapman, ibid.*
19   *Ibid.,* at 55, 56.
20   (1985), 18 C.C.C. (3d) 159 at 162 (Ont. C.A.).

previous occasion from a properly conducted line-up in which the
suspect is placed with other persons of similar height, age and general
appearance. In this way, an additional assurance is obtained that the
witness was forced to rely upon his own unaided recollection in
picking out the person whom he claims to have seen on the previous
occasion and was not unconsciously influenced by the fact that when
he identified the suspect he knew that he was viewing a person who
was already under suspicion by the police.

(1) Lineup Procedure

If a lineup is held it must be conducted fairly. A fair lineup is
one where the foils are sufficiently similar to the suspect to create a
fair test.[21] The members of the lineup should not be conspicuously
different from each other in age, build, colour, complexion, dress,
or any other relevant particular.[22]

There are numerous examples in Canada of lineups that were
held by courts to be unfair and therefore afforded little if any
weight. For example, in *R. v. Cosgrove (No.2)*,[23] the witness described her assailant as "tiny" and "short". The appellant was the
shortest and lightest man in the lineup. Mr. Justice Brooke, on
behalf of the Ontario Court of Appeal disapproved of the lineup:[24]

> I agree with the defence that the line-up from which the appellant
> was identified was not a fair one as far as he was concerned. He was a
> short man and to anyone looking for a short man his presence was
> conspicuous as he was the shortest man in the line.

In *R. v. Faryna*,[25] the Manitoba Court of Appeal described the
lineup as "badly constructed" because:

> "... not only did the majority not bear any resemblance to the ac-
> cused, but for the most part, they were police officers dressed in suits or
> sports jackets and differ [sic] considerably in height and weight from
> the accused."

The Quebec Court of Appeal criticized the lineup in *Nepton v.
R.*,[26] where the accused differed from the foils in hair colour,
height and dress. In *R. v. Jones*,[27] the Ontario Court of Appeal was

21   See, generally, Chapter 1, part 4(2)(d).
22   *R. v. Goldhar; R. v. Smokler* (1941), 76 C.C.C. 270 at 272 (Ont. C.A.); see also, *R. v.
      Todish* (1985), 18 C.C.C. (3d) 159 (Ont. C.A.).
23   (1977), 34 C.C.C. (2d) 100 (Ont. C.A.).
24   *Ibid.*, at 104.
25   (1982), 3 C.C.C. (3d) 58 at 70 (Man. C.A.).
26   (1971), 15 C.R.N.S. 145 (Que. C.A.).
27   (1971), 3 C.C.C. (2d) 153 (Ont. C.A.).

critical of a lineup where only one other person bore any resemblance to the accused in age or appearance.[28]

Not only must the lineup participants be chosen fairly, but the
lineup must be conducted in such a manner as to not influence the
selection in any way.[29] The classic statement of this proposition is
found in Lord Alverstone's judgment in *R. v. Dickman*:[30]

> We need hardly say that we deprecate in the strongest manner any
> attempt to point out beforehand to a person coming for the purpose of
> seeing if he could identify another, the person to be identified, and we
> hope that instances of this being done are extremely rare. I desire to say
> that if we thought in any case that justice depended upon the inde-
> pendent identification of the person charged, and that the identifica-
> tion appeared to have been induced by some suggestion or other
> means, we should not hesitate to quash any conviction which fol-
> lowed. The police ought not, either directly or indirectly, to do any-
> thing which might prevent the identification from being absolutely
> independent, and they should be most scrupulous in seeing that it is
> so.

This direction is most commonly violated by exposing the
suspect to the witness in some manner before the lineup takes
place. This might happen innocently or intentionally, but in either
case it weakens the subsequent identification.[31]

Since early in the century the courts have been critical of
allowing a witness to see a photograph of the suspect before
attending a lineup.[32] The evidence of identification is admissable
but it is weakened.[33] The reason is explained in *R. v. Dwyer; R. v.
Ferguson*:[34]

> It is one thing for a police officer, who is in doubt upon the question
> who shall be arrested, to show a photograph to persons in order to
> obtain information or a clue upon that question; it is another thing for a
> police officer to show beforehand to persons, who are afterwards to be
> called as identifying witnesses, photographs of those persons whom
> they are about to be asked to identify. It would be most improper to

---

28   See also, *R. v. Engel* (1981), 9 Man. R. (2d) 279 (C.A.); *R. v. Opalchuk* (1958), 122
      C.C.C. 85 at 91, 92 (Ont. Co. Ct.).
29   *R. v. Goldhar; R. v. Smokler, supra*, note 22; *R. v. Smierciak* (1946), 87 C.C.C. 175 (Ont.
      C.A.).
30   (1910), 5 Cr. App. R. 135 at 142, 143 (C.A.).
31   *R. v. Dickman, ibid.; R. v. Simpson and Kinney* (1959), 124 C.C.C. 129 (Ont. C.A.).
32   *R. v. Watson* (1944), 81 C.C.C. 212 (Ont. C.A.); *R. v. Opalchuk, supra*, note 28; *Sutton v.
      R.* (1969), 9 C.R.N.S. 45 (Ont. C.A.).
33   *R. v. Baldwin* (1944), 82 C.C.C. 15 (Ont. C.A.); *R. v. Jarrett* (1975), 25 C.C.C. (2d) 241
      (N.S.C.A.); *R. v. Kervin* (1974), 26 C.R.N.S. 357 (N.S.C.A.); *R. v. Lanigan* (1984), 53
      N.B.R. (2d) 388 (C.A.).
34   [1925] 2 K.B. 799 at 802 (C.C.A.).

inform a witness beforehand, who was to be called as an identifying witness, by the process of making the features of the accused person familiar to him through a photograph.

Based on this principle, the Ontario Court of Appeal ruled in *Sutton v. R.*,[35] that the conviction could not stand. The accused had appealed on the grounds that the trial judge had not warned the jury of the danger of accepting the lineup identification evidence where the witness had first been shown a photo array containing the picture of the accused. In delivering the judgment for the court, Jessup J.A. stated:[36]

> . . . the authorities are in accord as to the impaired value of an identification witness who has been shown a photograph of an accused before identifying him . . .
>
> [The] jury should have had brought to its attention, with an appropriate cautionary instruction, the fact that [the witness] had viewed a photograph of the appellant and more particularly, if her evidence in that respect was accepted by the jury, that a photograph of the appellant was particularly drawn to her attention; and the jury should have been told to consider all such circumstances.

A lineup may also be suggestive in other ways. For example, it is improper to dress only the suspect in the clothes described by the witness. There is too great a likelihood that the clothes, as opposed to the person, will be identified.[37]

What is the situation if the witness does see the suspect, either in person or by photograph, but fails to recognize the person? Is the subsequent lineup identification tainted? Without doubt, the psychologists would answer the question affirmatively. The face is now familiar because it has been seen recently. In *R. v. Sophonow (No. 1)*,[38] Mr. Justice Philp was very much aware of the possibility that previous exposure to the face, even if it was not immediately recognized, could substantially weaken a subsequent identification. He stated that in such situations the trial judge should alert the jury in the "strongest" of terms as to the possibility of mistaken identification. Similarly, in *R. v. Izzard*,[39] the Ontario Court of Appeal determined that the trial judge had failed to direct himself properly when he did not allude to the fact that the witness had

---

35 (1969), 9 C.R.N.S. 45 (Ont. C.A.).
36 *Ibid.*, at 49, 58.
37 *Sommer v. R.* (1958), 29 C.R. 357 (Que. C.A.); *R. v. Smith and Evans* (1908), 1 Cr. App. R. 203 (C.A.). See also, *R. v. Blackmore* (1970), 2 C.C.C. (2d) 397, affirmed 2 C.C.C. (2d) 514n (S.C.C.)[Ont.].
38 (1984), 12 C.C.C. (3d) 272 at 318, 319, affirmed 17 C.C.C. (3d) 128n (S.C.C.)[Man.].
39 (1990), 54 C.C.C. (3d) 252 (Ont. C.A.).

failed to identify the accused at two photo arrays held prior to the preliminary inquiry.

This however, was not the position taken by the Alberta Court of Appeal in *R. v. Kolnberger*.[40] The court believed that the failure to identify on one occasion would not weaken the subsequent identification. This case may be an example of a situation where intuitive belief and psychological experimentation do not coincide. The witness, of course, would not be aware of the possibility that the person being identified is vaguely familiar because of recent exposure in another forum. It would therefore be important to warn the jury of that possibility as was advocated in *Sophonow* and *Izzard*.

Other than directing that a lineup be "fair", the courts in Canada have understandably not become involved in its technical operation. Decisions as to the number of foils in the lineup or whether to place co-suspects in one lineup, are left to departmental policy.[41] There are no judicial guidelines as to the time for holding a lineup except for the logically obvious one; the earlier the procedure is held, the more confidence one has in its reliability. Courts have expressed the view that it is desirable to photograph or videotape the lineup so that the trier of fact has an independent means to assess the fairness, but the evidence is still admissible if this is not done.[42]

(2) Lineup Participation

There is no statutory authority compelling a person to participate in a lineup. An accused is often wise to consent however, because refusal may open the accused to disadvantages of his or her own making. The authorities are most likely then to turn to other forms of identification such as a photo array or a confrontation. Since a lineup is considered the fairest form of identification, the accused who voluntarily forfeits the benefits of a properly held

---

40   (1970), 1 C.C.C. (2d) 121 at 124 (Alta. C.A.).
41   This is not true in Britain: see Appendix A - *Code of Practice for the Identification of Persons by Police Officers*, Annex A. The Law Reform Commission of Canada study paper on *Pretrial Eyewitness Identification Procedures, supra,* note 5, recommends six foils and no more than one suspect in the lineup. (Rule 505, p. 27).
42   *Nepton v. R.* (1971), 15 C.R.N.S. 145 at 146, *per* Hyde J.A.: "I offer the suggestion that the police should adopt the practice which I have noted in some instances of photographing the line-up so that there could be no dispute as to its composition". The Law Reform Commission study paper makes the same recommendation, *supra,* note 5 at 22.

lineup is then hard pressed to complain about the inadequacies of alternate methods.[43]

The question of whether the police may use force to compel a person into a lineup is largely one of academic interest, since in practical terms an uncooperative suspect can sabotage the proceedings. The question however, might arise as to whether the police could take a hair sample or a foot impression, for example, by force; or, as happened in the Australian case of *R. v. Clune*,[44] force the accused into a room so that the identification witness could view him in a group.

It is clear that these types of actions would not violate the privilege against self-incrimination as that concept is understood in Canada. That privilege has been explained by the Supreme Court of Canada in *Marcoux and Solomon v. R.*:[45]

> American jurisprudence on the Fifth Amendment, which protects a person against being compelled "to be a witness against himself", and Canadian jurisprudence on the privilege against self-incrimination, have followed parallel courses, limiting the application of the privilege to its historic reach, *i.e.*, protection against testimonial compulsion. Such a limitation gives rise to a distinction between coerced oral or documentary disclosure which fall within the privilege, and what has been termed "real or physical" evidence, *i.e.*, physical evidence taken from a person without his consent,which, broadly speaking falls outside the privilege . . .
>
> An accused cannot be forced to disclose any knowledge he may have about an alleged offence and thereby supply proof against himself but (i) *bodily condition*, such as features, exhibited in a court-room or in a police line-up, clothing, fingerprints, photographs, measurements (see the *Identification of Criminals Act*, R.S.C. 1970, c. I-1), and (ii) *conduct* which the accused cannot control, such as compulsion to submit to a search of his clothing for concealed articles or his person for body markings or taking shoe impressions or compulsion to appear in Court do not violate the principle. As *Wigmore*, ... has observed ... "When the person's body, its marks and traits, itself is in issue, there is ordinarily no other or better evidence available for the prosecutor."

---

43 *R. v. Haidley and Alford*, [1984] V.R. 229 (S.C.), *per* Brooking J at 253:
"To one not used to the occasional whimsies of the criminal law it might seem strange that an accused man, having refused the best possible means of identification, should then rest his appeal on the ground that the substitute methods actually used were not as fair as the one he chose to reject ... I should have thought there was much to be said for the robust retort that an accused cannot invoke the discretion to reject admissible evidence by complaining of unfairness he has brought upon himself: self-inflicted unfairness is not unfair."

44 [1982] V.R. 1 (S.C.).

45 (1975), 24 C.C.C. (2d) 1 at 6, 7 (S.C.C.). See also, *R. v. Shortreed* (1990), 54 C.C.C. (3d) 292 (Ont. C.A.).

Knowing that compulsory identification procedures would not violate the privilege against self-incrimination does not answer the question of where the right would come from, if it exists. Since it is not a statutory right (except in the limited situations covered by the Identification of Criminals Act[46]), the only other source for the power is the common law. The question therefore becomes whether the common law authorizes reasonable compulsion to effect an identification.

This is far from a settled question. There is an *obiter* comment in the Supreme Court decision of *Marcoux and Solomon*,[47] that suggests that reasonable compulsion may be used as an incident to the general police power to investigate and arrest. Mr. Justice Dickson (as he then was), speaking for the full court, offered this opinion:[48]

> . . . it should not be overlooked that the application of force to compel an accused or a suspect to take part in a line-up may raise a question as to the limits on the powers of the police in relation to detained persons. Reasonable compulsion to this end is in my opinion an incident to the police power to arrest and investigate, and no more subject to objection than compelling the accused to exhibit his person for observation by a prosecution witness during a trial. The powers of peace officers with respect to persons under arrest were dealt with by the Court of Appeal in England in *Dallison v. Caffery*, [1964] 2 All E.R. 610, where Lord Denning, M.R., stated, at p. 617:
>
> "When a constable has taken into custody a person reasonably suspected of felony, he can do what is reasonable to investigate the matter, and to see whether the suspicions are supported or not by further evidence . . . The constable can put the suspect up on an identification parade to see if he is picked out by witnesses. So long as such measures are taken reasonably, they are an important adjunct to the administration of justice . . . ."

The passage referred to above from *Dallison v. Caffery*,[49] involved a civil suit for false arrest. Lord Denning M.R. did not cite any authority for this statement and the comment was entirely *obiter*. The evidence established that the plaintiff had in fact consented to several hours of investigation to check his alibi, including participating in a lineup.

Dallison v. Caffery and *Marcoux and Solomon* were both discussed by the Supreme Court of Victoria in *R. v. Clune*.[50] In *Clune*,

---

46   R.S.C. 1985, c. I-1.
47   *Supra*, note 45.
48   *Ibid.*, at 7.
49   [1964] 2 All E.R. 610 (C.A.).
50   *Supra*, note 44.

the court had to deal directly with the issue as to whether an accused could be forced into an identification procedure.

The accused, Clune, had refused to participate in a lineup. The police therefore, forced him into a room where they had assembled 18 other men. Clune realized what was happening and he covered his face with his hands, thereby thwarting the identification procedure by calling attention to himself. The Crown wished to call evidence of this attempt to hide in order to draw an inference of consciousness of guilt. Given the fact that, in the jurisdiction of Victoria, evidence could be excluded if it was obtained unfairly, the Supreme Court was required to decide if forcing an accused into a room for the purpose of an identification was lawful.

Pointing out that the passages referred to above in *Dallison v. Caffery* and *Marcoux and Solomon* were *obiter*, the court looked at the purpose of the arrest power and concluded, *per* Crockett J.:[51]

> The power of arrest and detention of the suspected perpetrator of a felony is exercisable only for the purpose of taking the suspect before a magistrate to be dealt with according to law for that felony. The power to arrest cannot be used for the purpose of facilitating police inquiries: *R. v. Banner*, [1970] V.R. 240. Perhaps, if whilst under arrest the suspect consents to be interrogated or to participate in a line-up it may be said that such consent prevents the detention from being misused.

And *per* McGarvie J.:[52]

> An important question in this case is whether the police had the power between the arrest of the applicant and the time he was taken before a justice or magistrates' court to compel him to take part in an identification parade. On general principle the answer would be no. It is difficult to see how legal power to use compulsive force to detain a person for the purpose of bringing him before a justice or magistrates' court as soon as practicable can be used to compel the person against his will to participate in an identification parade.

Thus, the ratio of *Clune* is that there is no common law power to force identification. Absent consent the only right is to take the accused before a magistrate to be dealt with according to law.[53]

---

51   *Ibid.*, at 10, 11.
52   *Ibid.*, at 19.
53   See, Criminal Code, R.S.C. 1985, c. C-46, s. 503 [am. R.S.C. 1985, c. 27 (1st Supp.), s. 77]. The Supreme Court of Canada confirmed in *R. v. Storrey* (1990), 53 C.C.C. (3d) 316 [Ont.], that the police can continue to investigate the crime following an arrest. However, the court did not address whether the accused could be forced to participate in the investigation process. The accused in *Storrey* consented to a post-arrest lineup.

Even if a Canadian court were to find the reasoning in *Clune* persuasive, the issue of remedy would still arise. Absent a constitutional violation, the evidence generated through an unlawful identification procedure would likely be admissible.[54] Thus in *R. v. Nielsen*,[55] the Manitoba Court of Appeal ruled that footprint impressions taken from the accused without consent were admissible.

If an accused does refuse to participate in a lineup or other identification procedure, can the refusal be introduced into evidence at trial? This was the principal issue before the Supreme Court of Canada in *Marcoux and Solomon v. R.*.[56] The accused Marcoux had refused to participate in a lineup so the police had resorted to the less acceptable confrontation method to establish identification. At trial, counsel on behalf of Marcoux had vigorously cross-examined the police on the inadequacies of the identification. The Crown then proved that the method adopted was only resorted to after Marcoux had refused to participate in a lineup. The Supreme Court stated:[57]

> As to the admissibility of evidence of refusal by Marcoux to participate in a line-up, it is only necessary to observe that the trial tactics of defence counsel made this evidence admissible beyond any question; admissible, not for the purpose of proving guilt, but to explain the failure to hold an identification parade and the necessity, as a result, to have [the witness] confront Marcoux, a procedure which counsel for Marcoux so roundly criticized . . .
>
> I should make it clear, however, that I do not think evidence of the offer and refusal of a line-up will be relevant and admissible in every case in which identification of an accused is in issue. Admissibility will depend upon the circumstances of the case. If, at trial, it unfolds that the Crown must explain the omission of a line-up or accept the possibilities of the jury drawing an adverse inference, then in those circumstances it would seem that evidence of refusal is both relevant and admissible. In other circumstances I do not think such evidence should normally be tendered. The danger, as I see it, is that it may impinge on the presumption of innocence, the jury may gain the impression there is a duty on the accused to prove he is innocent.

R. v. Fyfe[58] is an example from the Northwest Territories Court of Appeal where the principle in *Marcoux and Solomon* was applied. The accused refused to supply hair and blood samples. The

---

54   See, generally, Chapter 2, part 6(3)(a). The question of a constitutional violation is discussed in Chapter 4, *infra*.
55   (1984), 16 C.C.C. (3d) 39 (Man. C.A.).
56   *Supra*, note 45.
57   *Ibid.* at 8, 9.
58   (1983), 7 C.C.C. (3d) 284 (N.W.T.C.A.).

court ruled that the accused was acting within his common law rights in so doing and to alert the jury to the refusal would imply an obligation to prove his innocence. As such, the evidence of non-compliance was inadmissible.[59]

On the other hand, it would appear that in most cases where the accused declines to cooperate in a lineup or other method of pre-trial identification, the Crown will be allowed to prove the noncompliance in order to prevent a distorted picture from being presented to the jury. This arises out of the obligation on the trial judge to point out to the jury the inadequacies of the method of identification that was in fact ultimately used.[60] The point was well made by Mr. Justice McGarvie of the Supreme Court of Victoria in *R. v. Clune*:[61]

> . . . the refusal to participate in an identification parade usually leaves the Crown with much less satisfactory evidence of identification than a parade might provide. The deficiency of the other evidence of identification is such, that usually the trial Judge draws the attention of the jury to its unsatisfactory nature as compared with evidence of an identification parade. Because of the obvious deficiencies of most other forms of identification relatively [sic] to an identification parade and their apparent unfairness to the accused, I consider that it would usually be admissible, and usually be a proper exercise of discretion to admit, evidence of a refusal to take part in an identification parade . . .

R. v. Shortreed[62] is a good example of a case where it was necessary to prove the noncompliance. Prior to arrest, the police requested that the accused participate in a lineup or provide a photograph. The accused refused to do either. Subsequently, the police attempted on several occasions to surreptitiously photograph the accused. The accused, however, adopted a number of procedures to thwart the process including wearing hats and sunglasses, driving his car with the sun visor down and refusing to leave his business when he suspected the police were watching him. Finally, the police brought one of the victims to the accused's place of business and she identified him. The accused was then

---

59 See also, *R. v. Gowland* (1979), 45 C.C.C. (2d) 303 (Ont. C.A.), and *Mahoney v. Fielding; Ex parte Fielding*, [1959] Q.S.R. 479 at 484:
    "It is the right of the subject charged with a crime, or about to be charged with a crime, to refuse to assist the prosecution, whether by answering questions or submitting to tests ... [T]he refusal to submit to a blood or urine test is irrelevant and inadmissible. Such evidence is highly prejudicial and is introduced for the improper purpose of suggesting that only a guilty man would refuse a test."
60 See discussion, Jury Instructions, this chapter, part 7.
61 [1982] V.R. 1 (S.C.).
62 (1990), 54 C.C.C. (3d) 292 (Ont. C.A.).

arrested and a photograph was taken. Several other witnesses were then able to identify the accused's picture from a photo array. No in-person lineup was ever done. At trial, the Crown was permitted to adduce the evidence as to the accused's refusal to participate in a lineup and as well as his efforts to avoid having a photograph taken. The Ontario Court of Appeal confirmed the trial judge's decisoin. The court reasoned that regardless of the actual conduct of the defence case, it was inevitable that someone on the jury would criticize the methods of identification ultimately used and would draw an adverse inference from the failure to hold a parade. The evidence of noncompliance was relevant and admissible to explain the police conduct.

Shortreed also dealt with the instructions to be given the jury in a case where refusal to participate in an identification process is proved. The Ontario Court of Appeal indicated that it was incumbent on the trial judge to give the jury an instruction limiting the use to be made of the evidence. According to the court, the evidence of the failure to participate in a lineup or other pre-trial identification procedure could not be used as evidence of guilt or of consciousness of guilt, but could only be used for the limited purpose of explaining the failure to hold a lineup and the need to resort to less satisfactory identification procedures.[63] However, the Supreme Court of Canada appeared to accept a broader use for the evidence in *Marcoux and Solomon*.[64] The court approved an instruction that allowed the jury to determine what significance it would attach to the refusal to participate in a lineup. The implication is that a refusal may be used to prove consciousness of guilt. This particular passage from *Marcoux and Solomon* is not dealt with in *Shortreed*, leaving the law on this point somewhat unclear.

Two conclusions would therefore appear to flow from the case law that has developed with respect to lineups. The first is that the lineup is the fairest identification procedure, but, if refused, the police are entitled to resort to a less satisfactory method. The second is that though the inadequacies of the method ultimately used will be explained to the jury, so in most cases will the decision to refuse. These factors will be relevant to counsel who may be called upon to advise a client as to the benefits and risks of participating or refusing to participate in an identification parade.

---

63   *Ibid.*, at 302. See also *R. v. Clune, supra,* note 61 at 27.

64   (1975), 24 C.C.C. (2d) 1 at 10, affirming 13 C.C.C. (2d) 309. The Supreme Court approved the following instruction: " 'It will be for you to decide on the totality of the evidence what significance you will attach to Mr. Marcoux's refusal to participate in a suggested line-up.' "

4. PHOTOGRAPHS

(1) General Principles

Without doubt the use of photographs to aid in the identification of criminals is not only helpful to the administration of justice, but is often indispensable.[65] The importance of photographs to the system is reflected by the Identification of Criminals Act,[66] which provides for the taking of photographs of any person charged with a hybrid or an indictable offence.[67] The authorities are permitted to use such force as may be necessary to effect the procedure.[68] The constitutionality of the Identification of Criminals Act has been upheld by the Supreme Court of Canada in *R. v. Beare; R. v. Higgins.*[69]

Though photographs are useful to the identification process, they do have several drawbacks. The first is that a photograph cannot display the dynamic cues that may be important in effecting an accurate identification. Photographs cannot display height and they may distort important fine details such as complexion, eye and hair colour, and weight. The use of photographs eliminates the possibility of viewing the suspect's posture, mannerisms and body movements. The second major limitation of photographs is that the identification procedure takes place outside the view of the suspect. The suspect is therefore denied the opportunity to monitor the procedure and to independently assess its fairness. Finally, any reference to photographs at a trial may imply to the jury that the accused has a prior criminal record. The Crown may, by implication, effectively by-pass the prohibition against proving prior criminal conduct by making reference to photographs contained in police records.

It was these difficulties that led both the Devlin Commission[70] and the Law Reform Commission study paper[71] to recommend that the use of photographs be limited to situations where the police have no suspect in mind. Once a suspect has been identified,

65   *R. v. Watson* (1944), 81 C.C.C. 212 (Ont. C.A.).
66   R.S.C. 1985, c. I-1, s. 2 [formerly R.S.C. 1970, c. I-1, s. 2]; SOR/48-412.
67   The Act in fact reads "indictable offence", but s. 34 of the Interpretation Act, R.S.C. 1985, c. I-21, extends the scope of the section.
68   *Supra*, note 66, s. 2(2).
69   (1988), 45 C.C.C. (3d) 57 (S.C.C.).
70   *Report to the Secretary of State for the Home Department of the Departmental Committee on Evidence of Identification in Criminal Cases* (London: H.M.S.O., 1976).
71   *Supra*, note 5.

if the party will cooperate, a lineup should be held. This policy is now reflected by the Code of Practice which governs police investigations in Britain.[72]

The courts have long recognized these difficulties with photographs. A distinction has therefore been drawn between the propriety of asking a person to examine photographs before an arrest has been made to assist in identifying a suspect, and the impropriety of showing photographs to a witness after an arrest.[73] After arrest, the correct procedure is to invite the suspect to participate in a lineup. This point was clearly made by Gibbs C.J., of the High Court of Australia, in *Alexander v. R.*:[74]

> There are, however, two grounds of objection to the proof of identification by means of police photographs. In the first place, the accused will of necessity be absent when the identification is made, and has no means of knowing whether there was any unfairness in the process or whether the witness was convincing in the way in which he made the identification. Secondly, the production in evidence at the trial of photographs coming from the possession of the police is very likely to suggest to the jury that the person photographed had a police record, probably for offences of the kind in question. For these reasons, it is most undesirable that police officers who have arrested a person on a charge of having committed a crime should arrange for potential witnesses to identify that person except at a properly conducted identification parade.

Similarly, if there are multiple identification witnesses, only one should view the pictures. Once there are grounds to arrest a suspect, it is desirable that the remaining witnesses view a lineup.[75]

If a witness does view photographs to help identify a suspect, that person's usefulness at a subsequent identification procedure, be it a lineup or at trial, is reduced. The concern as expressed by the Ontario Court of Appeal in *R. v. Goldhar; R. v. Smokler,* is that the witness will identify the picture as opposed to the face viewed at the scene of the crime:[76]

---

72 See, *infra*, Appendix A.
73 *R. v. Dwyer; R. v. Ferguson,* [1925] 2 K.B. 799 at 802, 803 (C.A.); *Sutton v. R.* (1969), 9 C.R.N.S. 45 (Ont. C.A.); *R. v. Simpson and Kinney* (1959), 124 C.C.C. 129 (Ont. C.A.); *R. v. Watson, supra,* note 65; *R. v. Jarrett* (1975), 25 C.C.C. (2d) 241 (N.S.C.A.); *R. v. Pace* (1976), 16 N.S.R. (2d) 271 (C.A.).
74 (1980), 145 C.L.R. 395 at 400, 401 (Aust. H.C.).
75 *R. v. Lamb* (1980), 71 Cr. App. R. 198 (C.A.). The Law Reform Commission study paper, *supra,* note 5 at 156-58, makes the same recommendation. See, in addition, Annex D of the *Code of Practice,* reproduced in Appendix A.
76 (1944), 76 C.C.C. 270 at 271 (Ont. C.A.). See also, *Re Puerto Rico and Hernandez (No.2)* (1973), 15 C.C.C. (2d) 56 (F.C.A.), and generally, note 73, *supra.*

... while no doubt it is often necessary to assist the police in their search that photographs should be exhibited to some one who may be able to pick out a photograph of the person to be sought for, there is always the risk that thereafter the person who has seen the photograph will have stamped upon his memory the face he has seen in the photograph, rather than the face he saw on the occasion of the crime. The usefulness of such person as a witness may thereafter be seriously impaired ... It is important that trial Judges, as well as the police, should have this in mind.

If photographs are used to make an identification, be it pre-arrest or post-arrest, the evidence of the identification is still admissible. Only the weight to be afforded the evidence is affected.[77]

Whenever photographs are used to aid an identification, it is important to ensure that the procedure followed is fair. The use of a single photograph has been strongly criticized by the courts.[78] The procedure has been termed "irregular" and "unjustified",[79] and the Ontario Court of Appeal has characterized evidence obtained in such a manner as "valueless".[80]

If the police have a suspect, then the pictures used in the photo array must be of people with similar features.[81] If this is not done then the court will place little weight on the identification evidence.[82]

When using a photo array nothing must be done to indicate to the witness the person who is suspected by the police. Thus the photographs should be of a similar type and size so that nothing distinguishes the accused's photographs from the others.[83] The photographs should not be marked in any way,[84] and the police must be careful to ensure that none of their words or actions convey the identity of the suspect.[85] Only one photograph of each person should be in the array. If the accused's picture appears

---

77   *R. v. Baldwin* (1944), 82 C.C.C. 15 (Ont. C.A.); *R. v. Jarrett, supra,* note 73; *R. v. Kolnberger* (1970), 1 C.C.C. (2d) 121 (Alta. C.A.); *R. v. Kervin* (1974), 26 C.R.N.S. 357 (N.S.C.A.); *R. v. Power* (1987), 67 Nfld. & P.E.I.R. 272 (Nfld. T.D.); *R. v. Haidley and Alford,* [1984] V.R. 229 (S.C.).

78   *R. v. Smierciak* (1946), 87 C.C.C. 175 (Ont. C.A.); *R. v. Sutton, supra,* note 73; *R. v. Babb* (1971), 17 C.R.N.S. 366 (B.C.C.A.); *R. v. Richards,* [1964] 2 C.C.C. 19 (B.C.C.A.).

79   *R. v. Babb, ibid.,* at 372.

80   *R. v. Smierciak, supra,* note 78 at 180.

81   *R. v. Faryna* (1982), 3 C.C.C. (3d) 58 (Man. C.A.); *R. v. Pace, supra,* note 73.

82   *Ibid.*

83   *R. v. Sophonow (No. 1)* (1984), 12 C.C.C. (3d) 272 at 319, affirmed 17 C.C.C. (3d) 128n (S.C.C.)[Man.]; *R. v. Zaversnuke* (1982), 17 Man. R. (2d) 130 (Co. Ct.); *R. v. Pace, supra,* note 73.

84   *R. v. Power, supra,* note 77.

85   *R. v. Opalchuk* (1958), 122 C.C.C. 85 (Ont. Co. Ct.).

more often than the others, there is an obvious element of suggestion which taints the procedure.[86]

(2) Admissibility

If photographs are used to establish identification then a dilemma may develop at trial. If evidence of the photographic array is presented, the jury might infer that the police had a picture of the individual because the person had been in trouble with the law on a previous occasion. Most people are familiar with the common practice of photographing arrested persons and collecting those photographs in "mug-shot" files. Reference to the photograph will allow the Crown to prove indirectly that which it cannot prove directly in its case in chief: that is, that the accused has a criminal record or at least is a person of questionable character. If no reference is made to the photograph, this may leave the jury with an incomplete picture. It may be very important to the defence to show that the identification at a lineup or trial may have been influenced by prior exposure to a photograph. In the words of Lord Devlin:[87]

> Defence counsel has the difficult decision to make: is the advantage to be gained from attacking the identification on the ground that the witness had previously seen a photograph worth the risk that the jury may thereby be led to suspect the accused has a record?

In England, the Code of Practice[88] reduces the use of photographs substantially so perhaps the issue does not arise as often as it would in Canada. When it does arise however, the general rule is that the Crown should not produce the photograph as part of its case in chief. The defence should be informed that photographs were shown and counsel for the defence should be left to decide whether any reference to the photographs should be made.[89] If an accused refused a lineup, then the prosecution would be justified in revealing the use of the photographs at first instance. If it does emerge that the police showed a photograph of the accused to a witness, it is a matter for the discretion of the judge whether to direct the jury that they must not be prejudiced by the fact that the police had such a photograph. It may make matters

---

86   *R. v. Pace* (1976), 16 N.S.R. (2d) 271 (C.A.).
87   *Supra*, note 70; para. 2:26.
88   See, *infra*, Appendix A.
89   *R. v. Lamb* (1980), 71 Cr. App. R. 198 at 203, 204 (C.A.).

worse to highlight the fact, and it may be better to make no remark at all.[90]

The law in Canada on this point is not well developed. A reasonable attempt must be made to balance the competing interests. If identification is not a crucial issue in the trial, then fairness would dictate that the Crown make no mention of the photographs at first instance.[91] Other than this basic direction, it would appear that reference to the photographs will usually be allowed[92] and the trial judge will have a discretion as to what, if any, direction to give the jury.[93]

5. CONFRONTATIONS

Confrontation (sometimes referred to as a show-up) as used in this context refers to any situation where the accused is singled out to the witness. It usually entails the witness confronting an accused at the police station, but may involve such other actions as taking the accused back to the scene if he or she is apprehended shortly thereafter, or having the witness see the accused in court during a remand or bail procedure.

Since early in the century the courts have been aware of the frailties associated with an identification made in such circumstances. For example, in the 1908 decision of *R. v. Smith and Evans*, the confrontation was described as the "wrong procedure" and as "unsatisfactory", and the evidence obtained from such a procedure as "valueless".[94] This continues as the prevailing sentiment.[95]

---

90 *R. v. Lawrenson*, [1961] Crim. L.R. 398 (C.A.); *R. v. Watson* (1944), 81 C.C.C. 212 (Ont. C.A.).
91 *R. v. McLaren* (1935), 63 C.C.C. 257 (Alta. C.A.).
92 *R. v. Harrison* (1928), 49 C.C.C. 356 (B.C.C.A.); *R. v. Creemer* (1967), 1 C.R.N.S. 146 (N.S.C.A.). See, however, *R. v. MacLean* (1975), 27 C.C.C. (2d) 57 (B.C. Co. Ct.), where the trial judge refused to admit the photographs because they contained references to previous arrests and convictions.
93 *Supra*, note 90.
94 (1908), 1 Cr. App. R. 203 at 204 (C.A.).
95 *R. v. Todish* (1985), 18 C.C.C. (3d) 159 (Ont. C.A.); *R. v. Gagnon* (1958), 122 C.C.C. 301 (B.C.C.A.); *R. v. Bearbull* (1983), 24 Man. R. (2d) 121 (Co. Ct.); *R. v. Zaversnuke* (1982), 17 Man. R. (2d) 130 (Co. Ct.); *R. v. Winterhalt* (1986), 45 Sask. R. 303 (C.A.); *R. v. Chapman* (1911), 7 Cr. App. R. 53 (C.A.); *R. v. Keane* (1977), 65 Cr. App. R. 247 (C.A.); *Mezzo v. R.*, [1986] 4 W.W.R. 577 (S.C.C.), *per* Wilson J. at 621, 622. See also, Law Reform Commission study paper, *supra*, note 5 at 173-77, and Code of Practice, para. 2.13 and Annex C, reproduced in Appendix A.

It is, however, true that regardless of weakness, the evidence is admissible.[96] The trial judge is duty bound to explain the weakness so that the trier of fact may assess the weight.[97]

The situation may arise where a suspect requests a confrontation in the naïve belief that this procedure will quickly result in his or her exoneration. The police may accede to this request out of a sense of fairness. One case that has considered this scenario is *R. v. Lamb*.[98] In that judgment, the Criminal Court of Appeal disapproved of the police action while understanding the basis for it. The reason the police should not accede to the request is that it imperils the innocent, making them vulnerable to an unfair and suggestive procedure. The guilty may benefit, however, in that adopting the poor procedure weakens any subsequent attempt to obtain persuasive evidence.[99] It is for this reason that the Law Reform Commission study paper recommends that any legislative guidelines ultimately adopted restrict confrontations to urgent situations, such as where a witness is dying, and that confrontations not be undertaken even at the request of the suspect.[100]

6. COMPOSITE SKETCHES

The word composite sketch is used in this context to cover any drawing made by a third party on the instructions of an eyewitness. It would include free-hand portraits, sketches produced through commercial kits, and computer-generated drawings. The common element is that the witness translates the visual memory into words; the artist translates the words into a picture. The process recognizes the limitations of the verbal description and seeks to compensate by creating a two-dimensional representation. As discussed in Chapter 1, the quality of such sketches is generally quite poor.[101]

At trial, the defence may wish a composite sketch to be introduced for the purpose of discrediting the eyewitness. Discrepancies between the drawing and either the description, given at trial or on other occasions, on the one hand, or the actual

---

96   *Ibid.*

97   See, by implication, the judgment of the Supreme Court in *Marcoux and Solomon v. R.* (1975), 24 C.C.C. (2d) 1 (S.C.C.), and the comments concerning same by Wilson J. in *Mezzo v. R., supra*, note 95.

98   *R. v. Lamb* (1980), 71 Cr. App. R. 198 (C.A.).

99   *Supra*, note 5.

100   *Ibid.*, at 173-77.

101   See, generally, Chapter 1, part 4(2)(a).

appearance of the accused on the other, will be relevant to the reliability of the evidence. The law would appear clear that in such circumstances the sketch is admissible under the general rule that allows cross-examination on previous inconsistent statements and identifications.[102]

The Crown may seek to introduce a composite sketch in order to establish the resemblance between it and the accused. There is no Canadian authority on whether the sketch is admissible at the behest of the Crown, except one *obiter dicta, per incuriam* comment in *R. v. Sophonow (No.2)*,[103] suggesting that it is not. There are, however, two Commonwealth cases suggesting the opposite.

The English Court of Appeal considered the matter in *R. v. Cook*.[104] Two arguments were advanced by the appellant in support of the contention that the sketch was inadmissible: (1) it was hearsay; (2) it was a prior consistent statement.

The Court of Appeal considered and rejected both arguments. With respect to the hearsay argument, the reasoning was that the sketch was original evidence introduced by and through the eyewitness. The artist was nothing more than a conduit, translating the witnesses' words into pictures. "The police officer is merely doing what the witness could do if possessing the requisite skill."[105] Since the eyewitness was available to be cross-examined on the quality and accuracy of the sketch, there was no objection to the evidence on the basis of hearsay.

With respect to the second argument, the court's reasoning was that a composite sketch is not a statement but more akin to a photograph:[106]

> Seeing that we do not regard the photofit as a statement at all it cannot come within the description of an earlier consistent statement which, save in exceptional circumstances, cannot ever be admissible in evidence. The true position is in our view that the photograph, the sketch and the photofit are in a class of evidence of their own to which neither the rule against hearsay nor the rule against the admission of an earlier consistent statement applies.

---

102   *R. v. Sophonow (No.2)* (1986), 25 C.C.C. (3d) 415 at 447, leave to appeal to S.C.C. refused 67 N.R. 158 [Man.]; *R. v. Hentschel*, [1988] V.R. 362 at 375 (S.C.).
103   *Ibid.*, at 446, 447.
104   (1987), 84 Cr. App. R. 369 (C.A.). See also, *R. v. Constantinou* (1989), 91 Cr. App. R. 74 (C.A.).
105   *Ibid.*, at 375.
106   *Ibid.*

The reasons in *Cook* were adopted by the Supreme Court of Victoria in *R. v. Hentschel*.[107] Brooking J. succinctly analyzed the problem:[108]

> A woman is raped. She sees her attacker's face. But the eye produces no photograph. Instead an image is, through nerve impulses, formed in the brain. The rape accomplished, the offender goes: he is not so accommodating as to pose for a photograph before taking his leave. If he had violated not a women but a bank he might have left behind him a whole series of pictures taken by the security camera. But the woman's only security camera is her own eyes: the picture is developed in her brain and after her attacker has gone it remains there, stored as a visual memory. Could she but reproduce the face which she sees during the attack and holds still in her mind's eye after it! How is this to be done? The most detailed description is no substitute for the image. She makes a drawing, by her own hand or that of another, which reproduces as best she can the face which is still freshly impressed upon her visual memory. Why, as a matter of common sense or fairness or justice, should it not be placed before a jury as her attempt to re-create photographically, so to speak, the face which she saw? Would any sensible person not regard such a drawing as helpful?

The *Hentschel* judgment reviewed the two arguments in *Cook* and expanded upon them. The Supreme Court of Victoria agreed that there was no reason to reject the composite sketch on the basis of hearsay, as the witness who saw the perpetrator could be cross-examined on the calibre of the sketch. With respect to the prior consistent statement argument, the court stated that out-of-court identifications are admissible as an exception to this general rule.[109] The preparation of a composite sketch was considered a reasonable extension of the more usual fact scenario, where evidence of an out-of-court photo or lineup identification is admitted.[110]

> ... while the rationale and exact limits of the principle whereby evidence of a prior identification is admissible remain to be finally determined, the existence of the principle is undoubted, and if the making of a drawing and its acceptance by the identifying witness as the best representation of the offender that can be made may ... be viewed as in essence the same as the making of an identification from a living person or a photograph, then a basis in principle is found for the reception of evidence of the making of a composite picture.

The American authorities also appear to be moving towards the same conclusion. Though early authorities rejected the

---

107   *Supra*, note 102.
108   *Ibid.*, at 372, 373.
109   *Ibid.*, at 374. See, generally, Chapter 2, part 6(3)(b).
110   *Ibid.*, at 374.

sketches as hearsay,[111] states that now recognize the right to prove out-of-court identifications tend to classify the sketches in the same manner.[112] The protection afforded the defendant is the right to cross-examine the eyewitness on the accuracy and quality of the sketch.

It therefore appears that the prevailing opinion is that composite sketches should be treated in the same manner as any other out-of-court identification. The sketch would therefore be admissible and its weight would be a matter for the trier of fact.

7. JURY INSTRUCTIONS

In addition to the general jury instructions as to the frailties of eyewitness identification, there is also a responsibility on the trial judge to point out the strengths and weaknesses in the methods used to effect a pre-trial identification.[113] This obligation ensures that the jury approaches its tasks with sufficient knowledge and guidance.

R. v. Baldwin,[114] is an example of a case where the witness saw a photograph prior to making an identification. Robertson C.J.O., delivering one of the majority judgments dismissing the appeal, said:[115]

> Evidence procured under such circumstances, while, no doubt, still admissible, has lost much of the weight that otherwise it might have had, and it is the duty of the trial Judge in such circumstances as the present to call the attention of the jury to what has happened, and to properly caution the jury.

In *R. v. Sophonow (No. 1)*,[116] the Manitoba Court of Appeal indicated that the evidence of a witness ought to have been the subject of the "strongest warning", where he failed to make an

---

111 *People v. Turner*, 235 N.E. 2d 317 (Ill. C.A., 1968); *Commonwealth v. McKenna*, 244 N.E. 2d 560 (Mass., 1969); *People v. Jennings*, 257 N.Y.S. 2d 456 (C.A., 1965).

112 *State v. Ginardi*, 268 A. 2d 534 (N.J., 1970), affirmed 273 A. 2d 353 (N.J., 1971); *State v. Grier*, 630 P. 2d 575 (Ariz. App., 1981); *State v. Motta*, 659 P. 2d 745 (Hawaii, 1983).

113 *R. v. Baldwin* (1944), 82 C.C.C. 15 (Ont. C.A.); *Sutton v. R.* (1969), 9 C.R.N.S. 45 (Ont. C.A.); *R. v. Spatola*, [1970] 4 C.C.C. 241 (Ont. C.A.); *R. v. Blackmore* (1970), 2 C.C.C.(2d) 397, affirmed 2 C.C.C. (2d) 514n (S.C.C.) [Ont.]; *R. v. Sophonow (No. 1)* (1984), 12 C.C.C. (3d) 272, affirmed 17 C.C.C. (3d) 128n (S.C.C.)[Man.]; *R. v. Kervin* (1974), 26 C.R.N.S. 357 (N.S.C.A.); *R. v. Lanigan* (1984), 53 N.B.R. (2d) 388 (C.A.); *Davies v. R.; Cody v. R.* (1937), 57 C.L.R. 170 at 182 (Aust. H.C.).

114 *Supra*, note 113.

115 *Ibid.*, at 18.

116 *Supra*, note 113.

identification at a lineup but did make an identification two days later at a confrontation. Another witness in *Sophonow* had failed to make a positive identification when shown photographs but later identified the accused at a lineup. The trial judge advised the jury:[117]

> You will bear . . . his previous identification in mind when you are considering the weight to give to [the witnesses'] act of identification at the line-up . . .

The Manitoba Court of Appeal ruled that this instruction was not sufficient to make the jury aware of the risks attached to the lineup identification.[118]

The details and extent of the instructions with respect to the pre-trial identification procedures will obviously differ with the facts of the case. The jury instruction will be sufficient if it fulfills the goal of providing the jury with the tools that are necessary to adequately assess the quality of the identification procedure.

8. VOICE IDENTIFICATION

A witness is entitled to give evidence of identity based on voice recognition. The weight to be afforded the evidence is an issue for the trier of fact.[119] Some of the factors that might affect weight would be previous familiarity with the voice, the stress and attention level of the witness, any distinctive characteristics of the voice, and length of delay between time of exposure and time of identification.

It would appear that the Supreme Court of Canada, in the decision of *Marcoux and Solomon v. R.*,[120] has implicitly accepted the decision of the United States Supreme Court in *U.S. v. Wade*,[121] to the effect that requiring an accused to provide a voice sample is not a violation of the constitutional protection against self-incrimination. In *Wade*, the accused and all other members of the lineup were required to utter the words alleged to have been said by the bank robber. The United States Supreme Court ruled that

---

117   *Ibid.*, at 320.
118   *Ibid.*
119   *R. v. Murray and Mahoney* (1917), 27 C.C.C. 247 (Alta. C.A.); *R. v. Braumberger* (1967), 62 W.W.R. 285 (B.C.C.A.); *R. v. Hentschel*, [1988] V.R. 362 (S.C.).
120   (1975), 24 C.C.C. (2d) 1 (S.C.C.). See also the *obiter* remarks of Fauteux J. in *Que. (A.G.) v. Bégin*, [1955] S.C.R. 593 at 602.
121   388 U.S. 218 (1967).

this was not a violation of the Fifth Amendment privilege against self-incrimination since,[122] (quoting *Schmerber v. Calif.*)[123]:

> [the privilege] offers no protection against compulsion to submit to fingerprinting, photography, or measurements, to write or speak for identification, to appear in court, to stand, to assume a stance, to walk, or to make a particular gesture.

There is tacit approval for this passage in *Marcoux and Solomon*, and this would be consistent with the Supreme Court's approach to the privilege against self-incrimination which extends to the accused "qua witness and not qua accused".[124] The accused is not being required to testify; only to exhibit the physical characteristics of his or her voice.

In the same manner that visual identification may be wrong, so may voice identification. In fact, voice identification may be even more subject to error than visual identification because of the limited number of distinguishing characteristics and the fact that voices change with variations in mood. It may be very easy to recognize the voice of a famous person, but describing that voice to another may be virtually impossible. The jury may therefore often be asked to accept on "blind faith" the assertion, "that is the voice".

For this reason, jury instructions for voice identification should parallel those for visual identification. There is no Canadian authority specifically on the instructions to accompany a voice identification,[125] but two Australian jurisdictions have considered the issue.

The Supreme Court of Victoria dealt with the matter in *R. v. Hentschel*.[126] Two of the three judges believed that a special warning on the frailties of this type of identification was appropriate but no particular guidelines were given other than the general direction to point out the "dangers and problems".[127]

---

122   *Ibid.*, at 223.

123   384 U.S. 757 at 764 (1966).

124   *Supra*, note 120 at 5.

125   See, however, the dissenting judgment of O'Sullivan J.A., in *R. v. Medvedew* (1979), 43 C.C.C. (2d) 434 (Man. C.A.), where his Lordship suggests that a special warning similar to that in eyewitness cases is necessary.

126   *Supra*, note 119.

127   *Ibid.*, *per* Murphy J. at 364, and *per* Hampel J. at 383*ff*. The judges disagreed in the final result. Murphy J. upheld the conviction (Brooking J. concurring) on the basis of "no miscarriage". Hampel J. would have ordered a new trial on the basis that the jury instructions on the voice identification were insufficient.

The second Australian jurisdiction to have considered the issue is New South Wales. The law in New South Wales is developing in a manner that, it is submitted, will not find favour with Canadian courts. Two Court of Appeal decisions have held that a prerequisite for admissibility of voice identification is that the voice either have been familiar to the witness before the crime, or that it have distinctive features that would lead to an indelible mental impression.[128] The reasoning is that voice identification is said to be so unreliable that an added element is needed before a jury should be invited to consider it. This would not accord with the general principle in Canada that all relevant evidence should be admitted so that the jury might assess its weight.[129] Regardless of this difference in the law, the New South Wales cases do offer suggestions as to jury instructions that would be entirely relevant in Canada. Some of the issues deemed appropriate to cover in the jury instructions are:[130]

1. Was the witness previously familiar with the voice?
2. Is the voice distinctive in any way in such things as tone or expression so as to separate it from other voices?[131]
3. Were the circumstances where the witness identified the voice sufficiently similar to the circumstances where the voice was first heard to lead to the conclusion that the voice would show the same characteristics in both situations?[132]
4. Was the voice disguised?
5. An honest and confident witness may still be mistaken.

Added to this list might be such factors as the witnesses' stress and attention level at the time of the event, and the delay between

128 *R. v. Smith*, [1984] 1 N.S.W.L.R. 462, reversed on other grounds 7 N.S.W.L.R. 444 (C.C.A.); *R. v. Brownlowe* (1986), 7 N.S.W.L.R. 461 (C.A.). For a criticism of these judgments see the opinion of Brooking J. in *R. v. Hentschel, supra*, note 119.
129 *Graat v. R.* (1983), 2 C.C.C. (3d) 365 (S.C.C.).
130 *R. v. Smith* (1987), 7 N.S.W.L.R. 444 (C.C.A.); *R. v. Brownlowe* (1987), 7 N.S.W.L.R. 461 (C.C.A.).
131 Note that if the accused does not testify or a tape recording of the voice is not introduced, the jury cannot independently assess the witnesses' testimony. This would differ from visual identification where the accused's appearance can be compared to the witnesses' description. See, however, *U.S. v. Williams*, 704 F. 2d 315 (6th. Circ., 1983), cert. denied 104 S. Ct. 481, where the right of the trial judge to order the accused to read aloud in court so that the witness could identify the voice was upheld.
132 See, generally, Chapter 1, part 4(2)(e).

the original encounter and the identification procedure. Complete jury instructions such as these will help to educate the jury as to the frailties of the evidence so that the weight may be realistically assessed.

Chapter Four

Constitutional Issues

The purpose of this chapter is to examine some of the questions that are likely to arise in the future concerning the impact of the Canadian Charter of Rights and Freedoms on the identification of criminal suspects. Given the lack of Canadian precedent in the area, no attempt is made to answer any question definitively. Rather the questions are raised and analyzed in terms of policy objectives, first principles of constitutional interpretation, and United States jurisprudence, where applicable.

1. THE RIGHT TO COUNSEL

(1) The Right to Seek Advice

The decision whether or not to participate in a lineup may be a very important decision for a suspect. Taking part may exonerate the person early in the process and thus minimize the interference with liberty. On the other hand, an identification made during a lineup may bolster a witnesses' in-court identification. A decision not to participate may result in a less satisfactory method being employed to effect a pre-trial identification and possibly evidence of the refusal being admitted at trial as evidence of consciousness of guilt.[1]

Given these considerations it is not surprising that the Supreme Court of Canada held, in *R. v. Leclair (sub nom. R. v. Ross)*,[2] that the right to counsel provision of s. 10(*b*) of the Charter of

---

1   *Marcoux and Solomon v. R.* (1975), 24 C.C.C. (2d) 1 (S.C.C.). See, generally, Chapter 3, part 3(2).

2   (1989), 46 C.C.C. (3d) 129 (S.C.C.).

Rights and Freedoms would include the right to consult with and obtain the advice of counsel before making the decision as to whether or not to participate in a lineup.

Leclair and Ross were both advised of their right to counsel and both indicated that they wished to avail themselves of this right. Given their arrest in the early morning hours, both had been unable to reach the counsel of their choice. The police, however, proceeded to assemble a lineup and to insist that both participate, which they did. Mr. Justice Lamer, speaking for the majority, criticized this action:[3]

> The police were mistaken to follow such a procedure. As this court held in *Manninen*,[4] the police have, at least, a duty to cease questioning or otherwise attempting to elicit evidence from the detainee until he has had a reasonable opportunity to retain and instruct counsel. In my view, the right to counsel also means that, once an accused or detained person has asserted that right, the police cannot, in any way, compel the detainee or accused person to make a decision or participate in a process which could ultimately have an adverse effect in the conduct of an eventual trial until that person has had a reasonable opportunity to exercise that right.

Similar comments were made by the Supreme Court in *R. v. Manninen*,[5] in explaining the purpose behind s. 10(*b*) of the Charter:[6]

> The purpose of the right to counsel is to allow the detainee not only to be informed of his rights and obligations under the law but, equally if not more important, to obtain advice as to how to exercise those rights.

These two passages would appear to make it clear that there is a duty on the police to inform the detainee of the right to counsel before undertaking any pre-trial identification technique, including such things as the taking of bodily specimens, obtaining voice or handwriting samples, or conducting a one-on-one confrontation. In accordance with *Leclair*, none of these investigatory processes should take place until after the accused has met with counsel or has waived that right. The right protected by s. 10(*b*) of the Charter is the right to obtain advice, including advice on the legal rights of the authorities. For example, there is arguably no legal right to obtain a hair sample by force,[7] and this would be important information for an accused to have in making a decision as to whether or not to provide same.

---

3   *Ibid.*, at 136.
4   (1987), 34 C.C.C. (3d) 385 (S.C.C.).
5   *Ibid.*
6   *Ibid.*, at 392.
7   See Chapter 3, part 3(2).

One issue left open after *Leclair*[8] is whether there is any duty on the police to inform the detainee of the right to counsel at any subsequent stage in the investigatory process, or if it is sufficient to inform him only once, at the time of arrest or detention. If there is a duty to repeat the information, then, for example, this would have to be done if a lineup was conducted several hours after the arrest.

Certainly a strictly literal interpretation of the Charter implies that this information need be given only once. The Ontario Court of Appeal opted for this interpretation in *R. v. Logan*.[9] The court stated that s. 10(*b*) should be interpreted as "upon arrest or detention", meaning a point in time not a continuum. Therefore, there was no duty to reinform at each critical encounter with the police.[10]

The contrary argument is that the Constitution is to be interpreted using a purposive approach, as sanctioned by the Supreme Court of Canada in *R. v. Big M Drug Mart Ltd.*[11] The meaning of a Charter section is to be ascertained by an analysis of the interest it is meant to protect. If the purpose of s. 10(*b*) is held to entail an attempt to equalize the power between the state and the individual by giving to the individual the option of the knowledge and advice of a trained advocate, then requiring the repetition of s. 10(*b*) would recognize the realities of the situation and the potential vulnerability of the detainee.[12]

This is the prevailing opinion in the United States as represented by cases such as *Rivers v. U.S.*,[13] and *People v. Fowler*.[14] The reasoning is that only by advising the accused of his or her constitutional rights at all critical stages can you be assured that the right is appreciated and any waiver is intelligently given.[15]

---

8   *Supra*, note 2.
9   (1988), 46 C.C.C. (3d) 354 (Ont. C.A.).
10 *Ibid.*, at 381.
11 (1985), 18 C.C.C. (3d) 385 at 423, 424 (S.C.C.).
12 See, *R. v. Nugent* (1988), 42 C.C.C. (3d) 431 at 461, 462 (N.S.C.A.), where the Nova Scotia Court of Appeal stated that in light of the particular circumstances of the case, it was necessary to repeat the warning before conducting a videotaped reconstruction of the crime.
13 400 F. 2d 935 (5th Circ., 1968).
14 461 P. 2d 643 (Calif., 1969).
15 See, in addition, *Long v. U.S.*, 424 F. 2d 799 (D.C. Circ., 1969); *People v. Evans*, 401 N.Y.S. 2d 293 (App. Div., 1978); *State v. Connally*, 243 S.E. 2d 788 (N.C. App., 1978): *contra*, *People v. Redmond*, 407 N.E. 2d 132 (Ill. App., 1980).

(2) The Right to Counsel at Pre-trial Corporeal Identifications

In *Leclair*,[16] the Crown had argued that there was no right to consult counsel before attending a lineup because there was no right to have counsel at the lineup. This reasoning was rejected by the Supreme Court on the basis that advice concerning participation was an important function for counsel. The court specifically left open the question as to whether there is a right to have counsel present at a lineup.[17]

There is nothing preventing an accused from having a lawyer present at a lineup or other pre-trial procedure. Some police forces may voluntarily accede to the request; others may refuse in all circumstances.[18]

There is recognition throughout the world that there is a valuable role for counsel at a lineup. Britain,[19] New Zealand,[20] France[21] and Germany[22] have legislation encoding the right. In the United States it has developed as a constitutional protection.[23] Since there is no legislation on this subject in Canada, the question arises whether the Charter of Rights and Freedoms creates a constitutional right to have one's legal representative at a corporeal identification procedure.

(a) The Role of Counsel

The presence of counsel at an identification procedure is valuable for at least three reasons.

The first reason is that counsel can provide advice to the suspect as to the fairness of the procedure. The value of this type of

---

16 (1989), 46 C.C.C. (3d) 129 (S.C.C.).
17 *Ibid.*, at 137.
18 N. Brooks, *Pretrial Eyewitness Identification Procedures: Police Guidelines* (Ottawa: Law Reform Commission of Canada, 1983), at 85.
19 *Code of Practice for the Identification of Persons by Police Officers*, see, *infra*, Appendix A.
20 Crimes Amendment Act, 1982, S.N.Z., c. 46, s. 344B(2).
21 Code de Procédure Pénale, art. 118 (1959). See D.E. Murray, "The Criminal Lineup at Home and Abroad", [1966] Utah L. Rev. 610 at 624.
22 Murray, *ibid.*
23 See, *infra*, this chapter, part 1(2)(b). Also see American Law Institute, *Model Code of Pre-Arraignment Procedure*, s. 160.3 (1975).

assistance was recognized by the Supreme Court in *Leclair*, where Lamer J., for the majority, stated:[24]

> [The accused] could have been advised, for example, not to participate unless they were given a photograph of the line-up, or not to participate if the others in the line-up were obviously older than themselves.

Though much of the advice could be given before the process begins, that does not detract from the value of allowing a trained advocate to be present during the procedure to help the client assess its ongoing fairness and to give advice if unanticipated issues arise; for example, to advise a client not to don distinctive clothing unless all other members do the same, or to change lineup places if a second witness is to view the parade.

A second argument for allowing counsel to be present is that this may help to eliminate any possibility of suggestion, intentional or otherwise. As explained in Chapter 1, many subtle factors may interact to bias the identification procedure. The mere presence of a lawyer may help to reduce or eliminate this problem and will help to ensure that the procedure is carried out as fairly as possible.

Finally, having counsel present is important so that the line-up process may be reconstructed at trial. Identification evidence obtained through a lineup may be very powerful evidence, capable of influencing trial deliberations, yet the ability to challenge the evidence through cross-examination is limited without a clear picture of what occurred. The witness may be entirely unaware of any of the subtle influences and therefore unable to disclose them at trial. The suspect's lack of knowledge as to the relevant factors, coupled with the stress of the procedure, would generally preclude this person as a reliable historian. If the lineup took place through a one-way mirror, the suspect would be deprived of any opportunity to observe. If there were problems, the lawyer could point them out so they could be corrected immediately, thus enhancing law enforcement. If the fairness of the lineup became an issue at trial, the lawyer would be in a much better position to canvass it.

It is difficult to articulate any reason against having counsel present at a lineup, other than administrative convenience. Even this reason is without substantial foundation since any constitutional right to have counsel present would come with a correlative obligation on the accused and counsel to act with due diligence and not unduly delay the proceedings.[25]

---

24   (1989), 46 C.C.C. (3d) 129 at 137 (S.C.C.).
25   *Tremblay v. R.* (1987), 37 C.C.C. (3d) 565 (S.C.C.).

Even if there is a right to be present, many lawyers would likely not take advantage of the opportunity. First, being present leaves the lawyer vulnerable to being a witness at the trial. Secondly, having a lawyer present may, in fact, increase the credibility of the procedure to the client's detriment. The issue of whether a client chooses to avail himself or herself of the right to have counsel present, however, is irrelevant to the question of whether the Constitution creates the right. If the right exists, it can certainly be waived by a properly informed accused.[26]

(b) The United States Position

On 12th June 1967, the Supreme Court of the United States released three decisions dealing with various aspects of identification evidence.[27] In the first case, *U.S. v. Wade*,[28] the court recognized many of the difficulties and risks associated with pre-trial identification lineups:[29]

> The vagaries of eyewitness identification are well-known; the annals of criminal law are rife with instances of mistaken identification . . . A major factor contributing to the high incidence of miscarriage of justice from mistaken identification has been the degree of suggestion inherent in the manner in which the prosecution presents the suspect to witnesses for pretrial identification . . . Suggestion can be created intentionally or unintentionally in many subtle ways . . .
> But as is the case with secret interrogations, there is serious difficulty in depicting what transpires at lineups and other forms of identification confrontations. "Privacy results in secrecy and this in turn results in a gap in our knowledge as to what in fact goes on . . ."[30] For the same reasons, the defense can seldom reconstruct the manner and mode of lineup identification for judge or jury at trial . . . [N]either witnesses nor lineup participants are apt to be alert for conditions prejudicial to the suspect. And if they were, it would likely be of scant benefit to the suspect since neither witnesses nor lineup participants are likely to be schooled in the detection of suggestive influences. Improper influences may go undetected by a suspect, guilty or not, who experiences the emotional tension which we might expect in one being confronted with potential accusers . . . In short, the accused's inability effectively to reconstruct at trial any unfairness that occurred at the lineup may deprive him of his only opportunity meaningfully to attack the credibility of the witness' courtroom identification.

---

26   *Clarkson v. R.* (1986), 50 C.R. (3d) 289 (S.C.C.).
27   *U.S. v. Wade*, 388 U.S. 218 (1967); *Gilbert v. California*, 388 U.S. 263 (1967); *Stovall v. Denno*, 388 U.S. 293 (1967).
28   *U.S. v. Wade, ibid.*
29   *Ibid.*, at 228-32.
30   Citing *Miranda v. Arizona*, 384 U.S. 436 at 448 (1966).

Having articulated some of the difficulties with pre-trial line-ups, the Supreme Court then went on to clearly establish that the Sixth Amendment, which guarantees the accused "the right . . . to have the assistance of counsel for his defense", would include the right to have legal assistance at pre-trial lineups:[31]

> Since it appears that there is grave potential for prejudice, inten-tional or not, in the pretrial lineup, which may not be capable of reconstruction at trial, and since presence of counsel itself can often avert prejudice and assure meaningful confrontation at trial, there can be little doubt that for Wade the post-indictment lineup was a critical stage of the prosecution at which he was "as much entitled to such aid [of counsel] . . . as at the trial itself."[32] . . . No substantial countervailing policy considerations have been advanced against the requirement of the presence of counsel.
>
> In our view counsel can hardly impede legitimate law enforce-ment; on the contrary, for the reasons expressed, law enforcement may be assisted by preventing the infiltration of taint in the prosecu-tion's identification evidence. That result cannot help the guilty avoid conviction but can only help assure that the right man is brought to justice.

The *Wade* decision is clear. There is a constitutional right in the United States to have counsel at pre-trial lineups. In the second case decided the same day, *Gilbert v. California*,[33] the court con-cluded that the identical right existed for one-on-one confronta-tions. The reason articulated by the court in both cases was that the presence of counsel helps to minimize the risk of convictions resulting from mistaken identification, by reducing the likelihood of improper suggestion and by providing the suspect with an effective means to challenge the identification at trial.

The decisions of *U.S. v. Wade* and *Gilbert v. California* were limited five years later, by *Kirby v. Illinois*,[34] to corporeal identifica-tions occurring after the institution of formal criminal proceedings. In *Kirby*, the issue was whether a confrontation done shortly after arrest and before the institution of charges, could be undertaken without requiring the presence of counsel. Based entirely on an historical analysis of the United States Constitution, the court found that the right to counsel, as protected by the Sixth and Fourteenth Amendments, "attaches only at or after the time that adversary judicial proceedings have been initiated against [the accused]."[35] Police investigations done before this stage do not

---

31   *U.S. v. Wade, supra,* note 27 at 236-38.
32   Citing *Powell v. Alabama*, 287 U.S. 45 at 57 (1932).
33   *Supra,* note 27.
34   406 U.S. 682 (1972).
35   *Ibid.,* at 688.

attract the right to counsel provisions of *Wade*, as this is not a "critical stage of the prosecution".[36] The majority opinion was the subject of a strong dissent,[37] based on the argument that the frailties of a lineup procedure are the same whether the lineup takes place before or after the laying of formal charges.[38] The effect of *Kirby* is to allow the police to conduct any pre-trial identification outside of the purview of counsel simply by delaying the institution of formal charges.[39]

(c) Predicting a Canadian Response

If there is a constitutional right to have counsel present at a lineup, it must be found either in s. 7 or s. 10(*b*) of the Charter.

By virtue of s. 7, any governmental action involving an individual's liberty must be carried out in a fundamentally just manner. During a pre-trial lineup a person's liberty may be at stake, since, as pointed out by the Supreme Court in *Leclair*,[40] the evidence obtained through the lineup may be critical to the outcome of the case. Though s. 7 has not created an absolute right to counsel in all circumstances, it does appear clear that s. 7 would at least include a right to counsel where such person is necessary to help an accused to present a case adequately.[41] It could be argued that the evidence potentially generated by the lineup may be so integral to the outcome of the trial itself that counsel should be present. Only if counsel observes the process may an effective challenge to the evidence be undertaken at trial.[42]

However the right to counsel under s. 7 cannot be that broad, or counsel could claim a right to observe interviews with potential witnesses on the basis that what is said may be integral to the outcome of the trial. The critical nature of the proceeding to the

---

36   *Ibid.*, at 690.
37   *Per* Brennan, Douglas and Marshall JJ.
38   For criticism of the majority opinion see: L. Taylor, *Eyewitness Identification* (Michie Co., 1982), at 147; C.A. Pulaski, "*Neil v. Biggers*: The Supreme Court Dismantles the *Wade* Trilogy's Due Process Protection" (1974), 26 Stan. L. Rev. 1097; W.W. Sherwood, "The Erosion of Constitutional Safeguards in the Area of Eyewitness Identification", (1987) 30 Howard L.J. 439; J.D. Grano, "*Kirby, Biggers* and *Ash*: Do Any Constitutional Safeguards Remain Against the Danger of Convicting the Innocent?" (1974), 72 Mich. L. Rev. 719.
39   Taylor, *ibid.*, at 148; Pulaski, *ibid.*, at 1103.
40   (1989), 46 C.C.C. (3d) 129 at 137 (S.C.C.).
41   *Re Howard and Presiding Officer of Inmate Disciplinary Ct. of Stony Mountain Inst.* (1985), 19 C.C.C. (3d) 195 (F.C.A.), appeal to S.C. dismissed as moot (1988) 41 C.C.C. (3d) 287; *R. v. Rowbotham* (1988), 63 C.R. (3d) 113 at 174 (Ont. C.A.).
42   The same argument could be made under s. 11(*d*) of the Charter.

outcome of the trial is but one factor to consider. The second factor is that there must be a role for counsel. Traditionally, the role of counsel is to give advice and to receive instructions. If there is a need for one of these functions to be performed at a stage critical to the outcome of the trial, then it may be fundamentally unjust not to allow for the presence of counsel. Since a lawyer may be able to give valuable advice at a lineup and a lineup may be critical to the outcome, it could be argued that under s. 7 there is a right to have counsel present.

A similar argument may be made pursuant to s. 10(*b*) of the Charter. The section speaks of the right to "retain" counsel and, as stated by the Ontario Court of Appeal in *R. v. Logan*,[43] "retain" has a connotation of continuity. Having engaged counsel, it follows that there is an ongoing relationship and the right to seek advice whenever there is a legitimate reason for doing so.[44]

This argument would parallel that accepted by the United States Supreme Court in *U.S. v. Wade*.[45] In that case the right to counsel was held not to extend to scientific pre-trial identification techniques such as the taking of blood or hair samples[46] because, even though the results could be critical to the outcome of the trial, there was no effective role for counsel at the time of the actual test. The right to counsel applied at lineups however, because there was a valuable role for that person to perform during the actual procedure.[47]

As discussed earlier,[48] there are generally three roles suggested as being performed by counsel at a lineup.

1. Counsel can provide advice to the client on how a fair procedure should be conducted.
2. Counsel can point out potentially suggestive procedures.
3. Counsel can serve as the accused's eyes and ears and therefore be better able to reproduce the event at trial.

It might be argued that the first of these functions can be performed before the lineup commences and that the second and third are just as effectively performed by a videotape machine. The first response fails to recognize that assessing fairness is an ongoing function. The accused can be unfairly singled out by the body

---

43 (1989), 46 C.C.C. (3d) 354 (Ont. C.A.).
44 *Ibid.*, at 381.
45 388 U.S. 218 (1967)
46 *Ibid.*, at 227.
47 See, generally, this chapter, part 1(2)(b).
48 See, generally, this chapter, part 1(2)(a).

language or eye movements of the foils. On viewing the line, counsel could ask that one of the foils be cautioned or dismissed, if that person's actions are inappropriate. A request by the witness that a particular member of the line speak certain words, perform certain actions, or don distinctive clothing, may raise issues as to how this may be done fairly. The suspect cannot call a halt to the proceeding to seek advice from an absent lawyer without completely destroying the integrity of the process. Therefore it makes eminent sense for counsel to be in the room so as to be able to react to issues as they arise.

Counsel could also serve as an observer. A videotape can do this as well and one would hope that the videotaping of lineups soon becomes standard procedure. Videotapes, however, only expose problems after the fact. The administration of justice is better served if any disputes as to procedure are resolved in advance. The suspect deserves the right to establish his or her innocence at the earliest opportunity and this will be possible if the lineup is properly conducted. It does the innocent person little good to wait months or even years to expose the problems of a suggestive lineup at trial.

Would the presence of defence counsel disrupt the procedure? It is difficult to imagine how. The witness would know only that another person was observing the procedure. It would be inappropriate to introduce the person as defence counsel since this would imply that one person in the line was the suspect. It is a better practice not to alert the witness that there is a definite suspect present.[49] The defence counsel may wish to interview the witness after the fact, but since there is no property in witnesses and adequate disclosure may already have resulted in the name and previous statements being shared, this would rarely if ever create a difficulty.

The above analysis would suggest that a lineup is a critical stage in the proceedings because it could have a profound effect on the outcome of the trial. There is a role for counsel to play in giving advice to the client on the conduct of the procedure. There is no convincing countervailing argument that having counsel present would interfere with the administration of justice. Sections 7 and 10(*b*) of the Charter may be interpreted to allow for counsel to be present following arrest or detention,[50] if:

---

49   See, *supra*, Chapter 1, part 4(2)(d).
50   Note that this is substantially earlier in the process than that which exists in the United States by virtue of *Kirby v. Illinois, supra*, note 34, and accompanying text. The Charter mandates the "start time" as the point of arrest or detention.

1. counsel's presence is requested at a stage critical to the outcome of the trial; and
2. there is an issue on which counsel can provide advice.

Since both criteria are met for post-detention lineups and confrontations, it would follow that the right to have counsel present at these procedures is sanctioned by the Constitution.

(3) The Right to Counsel at Photo Arrays

Photographs are a valuable tool in the investigation of crime. Quite often photograph or "mug-shot" identifications provide police with their only lead as to the identity of a suspect. A right to counsel at this early stage, however, would be entirely impractical, since representation would need to be afforded to each person whose picture was displayed. In some cases the police do have a suspect in mind, but do not have reasonable and probable grounds to arrest. Counsel at this stage is still impractical since, assuming the person can be located, notifying the person pre-arrest to obtain counsel may result in that person fleeing the jurisdiction or destroying evidence.

If there is a constitutional right to counsel at photo arrays, the only logical time for it to attach is at the time of arrest or initial detention. This event "triggers" the rights under s. 10 of the Charter. Though s. 7 rights may attach earlier generally, with respect to identification procedures any earlier point in time is impractical. The question therefore becomes whether there is a constitutional right, pursuant to ss. 7 and 10(*b*) of the Charter, to have counsel present at post-detention or post-arrest photographic arrays.

(a) The United States Position

By virtue of *U.S. v. Wade*,[51] *Gilbert v. California*,[52] and *Kirby v. Illinois*,[53] the United States Supreme Court established that there was a right to counsel at post-indictment corporeal identifications. In *U.S. v. Ash*,[54] the court was asked to extend this right to counsel protection to post-indictment photographic arrays. The majority

---

51 *Supra*, note 27, and accompanying text.
52 *Ibid.*
53 *Supra*, note 34, and accompanying text.
54 413 U.S. 300 (1973).

ruled that the Sixth Amendment protection did not extend to this right.

The majority decision[55] concentrated on the historical role of counsel as a "spokesman for, or advisor to, the accused".[56] In *Wade*, the court had found that the accused needed advice during a lineup. The court had also stated that the presence of counsel was important at lineups because they could be suggestive and difficult to reproduce at trial. In *Ash*, the majority explained *Wade* by stating that the first reason had been the deciding factor and that the second and third reasons were simply additional benefits that the accused gained as a result of requiring counsel to give advice:[57]

> Although Wade did discuss possibilities for suggestion and the difficulty for reconstructing suggestivity, this discussion occurred only after the Court had concluded that the lineup constituted a trial-like confrontation, requiring the "Assistance of Counsel" to preserve the adversary process by compensating for advantages of the prosecuting authorities.

The main criterion therefore, as to whether counsel could be present at a pre-trial step, was whether the accused needed advice and assistance. "Since the accused himself is not present at the time of the photographic display . . . no possibility arises that the accused might be misled by his lack of familiarity with the law or overpowered by his professional adversary."[58] Therefore, reasoned the court, there was no constitutional right to have counsel present to observe the conduct of a photo array.

The majority decision in *Ash* was the subject of a strong dissent.[59] The basis of the dissent was that the dangers of misidentification by photo array were equal to those by lineup:[60]

> [T]he photographs . . . cannot in any sense reveal to defense counsel the more subtle, and therefore more dangerous, suggestiveness that might derive from the manner in which the photographs were displayed or any accompanying comments or gestures . . .
>
> . . . the accused himself is not even present at the photographic identification, thereby reducing the likelihood that irregularities in the procedure will ever come to light . . .

---

55   *Per* Blackman J. (Burger C.J., White, Powell and Rehnquist JJ., concurring): Stewart J. concurring in separate reasons.
56   *Supra*, note 54 at 312.
57   *Supra*, note 54 at 314.
58   *Supra*, note 54 at 317.
59   *Per* Brennan, Douglas and Marshall JJ.
60   *Supra*, note 54 at 335, 336.

Thus, the difficulties of reconstructing at trial an uncounseled photographic display are at least equal to, and possibly greater than, those involved in reconstructing an uncounseled lineup.

(b) Predicting A Canadian Response

The Law Reform Commission study paper[61] recommends in favour of counsel at photographic arrays for the same reasons as the dissenting judges in *U.S. v. Ash*:[62]

1. There is a potential for suggestion.
2. There are no foils, therefore fewer, if any, neutral observers.
3. The suspect is not present.
4. The photo array procedure is difficult to reconstruct at trial.
5. Once an identification is made from a photograph, the witness is unlikely to retract it.

The paper points out that there is no countervailing argument in proceeding in the absence of counsel, since witnesses will have to be notified and appointments set, thus providing an opportunity to notify counsel.[63]

The recommendations to the Law Reform Commission are recommendations for legislation. The policy that Parliament may eventually wish to implement through legislative change is not necessarily open to judges who are duty bound to interpret the Constitution. There may very well be a need for lawyers at photo arrays, but whether the Constitution may be interpreted to provide for them is problematic.

Section 10(*b*) of the Charter provides for the right to "retain" and "instruct" counsel. Traditionally, counsel has been retained to give advice and to carry on the case on the instructions of the client. Thus the majority in *Ash* spoke of counsel's role as a "spokesman" and "advisor".[64] The critical difference between a lineup and a photo array is the presence of the accused, because only if the accused is present will there be a need for advice. It is true that there are additional benefits to be gained from the presence of counsel at a lineup; primarily the enhanced ability to recreate the event at trial. This, however, is simply a gratuitous benefit that flows from the primary role of counsel as advisor to the accused.

---

61   *Supra*, note 18 at 77-88.
62   *Supra*, note 54.
63   *Supra*, note 18 at 79.
64   *Supra*, note 54 at 312.

Does s. 7 of the Charter expand the role of counsel? At a photo array counsel would presumably fill two functions. The first would be to give advice to the police on how the process should be conducted. It would be stretching the concept of fundamental justice far beyond logical limits to suggest that the accused has a constitutional right to supervise police investigations where the accused is not even present. The accused's historical and constitutional right is to challenge the quality of those investigations in court.

The second role would be as an observer. Mere presence would eliminate or reduce bias and would aid in reconstruction of the process at trial. Without doubt this would be of great value and would be a useful legislative change. It is, however, submitted that this is not an aspect of fundamental justice. It is not a basic tenet or principle of our justice process[65] that the accused be allowed to observe and monitor the investigation and preparation of the case to be presented in court. It is true that the photo array process may be biased and manipulated, but so may any interview with a witness. The questioning technique can plant suggestions and distort memories.[66] One would be hard pressed to argue that there is a constitutional right to monitor Crown interviews with witnesses. Section 7 of the Charter gives the accused the right to challenge the evidence at trial, but it is submitted that it goes no further than that.

An argument was advanced above[67] that there was a Constitutional right to counsel at a lineup because two criteria were met:

1. The lineup was a critical stage in the outcome of the trial; and
2. There was an issue on which counsel could provide advice.

Photo arrays meet the first criterion. The evidence generated is as critical to the outcome of a trial as is the lineup. The second of the criteria is not met. There is no advice to be given the client. The role of observer, though without doubt valuable, is not a traditional role for counsel. It is arguably not a role contemplated by either s. 7 or s. 10(*b*) of the Charter. If there is to be a right to counsel at pre-trial photo arrays it will have to come via Parliament and not via the courts.

---

65   *Ref. re s. 94(2) of Motor Vehicle Act (B.C.)* (1985), 23 C.C.C. (3d) 289 at 309 (S.C.C.).
66   See, generally, Chapter 1, part 3.
67   See, generally, this chapter, part 1(2)(c).

2. FUNDAMENTAL JUSTICE

Certain identification procedures may be so suggestive that a question is raised as to whether the evidence generated is too unreliable to be admitted in court. The possibility that identification evidence could be excluded on the basis of a violation of constitutional principles was recognized by Wilson J., joined by Chief Justice Dickson, in her separate but concurring judgment in *Mezzo v. R.*[68] Her Ladyship acknowledged that a motion could be made at trial to exclude the lineup evidence in *Mezzo* on the basis of "constitutional fairness".[69] Though no Canadian court has had the opportunity to consider this argument in detail, it is a well developed principle of American constitutional law.

(1) The United States Position

The United States Supreme Court first addressed the issue of the fairness of pre-trial identification procedures in *Stovall v. Denno*,[70] the third case of 12th June 1967 trilogy of *Wade-Gilbert-Stovall*.[71] The court set forth general principles of what would constitute an unfair procedure or, in the language of the Fourteenth Amendment to the United States Constitution, what would amount to a violation of due process.

Stovall involved a hospital confrontation, made necessary by the serious medical condition of the victim. The Supreme Court acknowledged a right to challenge pre-trial identifications that were "so unnecessarily suggestive" as to be "conducive to irreparable mistaken identification".[72] Lacking a section equivalent to s. 24 of the Charter of Rights and Freedoms, the United States Supreme Court attempted to articulate a constitutional principle that did not result in a *per se* exclusionary rule. The court concluded therefore, that a violation of due process depended on the "totality of the circumstances", and that given the facts of *Stovall* a hospital confrontation was "imperative".[73] Thus the court created a "totality of circumstances" balancing test to determine if a pre-trial

---

68 [1986] 4 W.W.R. 577 (S.C.C.).
69 *Ibid.*, at 623.
70 *Stovall v. Denno*, 388 U.S. 293 (1967).
71 *U.S. v. Wade*, 388 U.S. 218 (1967); *Gilbert v. California*, 388 U.S. 263 (1967); *Stovall v. Denno*, 388 U.S. 293 (1967).
72 *Supra*, note 70 at 302.
73 *Ibid.*

procedure was constitutional. One factor to be considered was the exigency of the situation; in an emergency a suggestive procedure would be countenanced. The contrary position would also hold true; absent compelling circumstances there would be no justification for suggestive pre-trial identification procedures.

Nine months after *Stovall,* in *Simmons v. U.S.,*[74] the Supreme Court considered a due process objection to an in-court (dock) identification that the petitioner alleged had been irreparably tainted by a very suggestive out-of-court pre-trial photographic procedure.

Following a bank robbery, police obtained snapshots of Simmons from a relative and showed these photos to bank employees. The petitioner argued that his constitutional rights to due process were violated by this procedure and that the in-court identification should be suppressed. The government made no attempt to admit the pre-trial identification evidence. The dispute was over the issue of whether the bank employees should be allowed to make an in-court identification.[75]

The Supreme Court stated that the applicable test was whether the "identification procedure was so impermissibly suggestive to give rise to a very substantial likelihood of irreparable misidentification".[76] The court stated that it was applying the test in *Stovall,* albeit in slightly different words. However, the court went on to consider factors never discussed in *Stovall.* A new question emerged; given the facts of the case, how likely is it that the identification is wrong? On the facts of *Simmons,* the court concluded that, given the lack of disguise, the excellent lighting conditions and the time period for observation, the identification was probably correct.[77] Therefore the in-court identification of Simmons by the bank employees was permissible.

The effect of *Simmons* was unclear.[78] *Stovall* had set up a balancing test. In assessing the constitutionality of a police-conducted pre-trial identification procedure, the first question was whether the procedure employed was suggestive and conducive to irreparable misidentification.[79] If it was, the second question was whether it was necessary in the circumstances.[80] Nowhere in

---

74   390 U.S. 377 (1968).
75   *Ibid.,* at 382.
76   *Ibid.,* at 384.
77   *Ibid.,* at 385.
78   Pulaski, *supra,* note 38.
79   Supra, note 70 at 302.
80   *Ibid.*

Stovall was the question raised as to whether the identification was probably correct. This, however, was relevant in *Simmons* but the court did not appear to acknowledge that the test had been altered.

In a later Supreme Court case, Marshall J., in a dissenting opinion, attempted to explain the apparent differences in *Stovall* and *Simmons*.[81] The interpretation offered was that *Stovall* was concerned with the admissibility of out-of-court pre-trial identifications, whereas *Simmons* involved the admissibility of the in-court identification. The question in *Simmons* was; given the fact that the pre-trial procedure was suggestive and unnecessary, should the witness be allowed to make an in-court identification? Marshall J. stated that when this question is considered, the quality of the original observation becomes highly relevant.[82] It is not relevant to the question of the admissibility of the out-of-court identification. When that issue is before the court, the only concern is whether the procedure was suggestive and, if so, whether it was necessary.[83]

The Marshall analysis was after the fact, but certainly helps to explain *Stovall*, *Simmons*, and the next two Supreme Court cases on the point, *Foster v. California*,[84] and *Coleman v. Alabama*.[85]

Foster v. California is the only United States Supreme Court decision that has excluded pre-trial identification evidence on the basis of a violation of due process. On arrest, Foster was placed in a three-man lineup. He was the tallest of the three and was wearing a leather jacket similar to that worn by the robber. The eyewitness could not make a positive identification but "thought" that Foster could be the man. He therefore asked to speak to Foster and this was arranged. Even after this one-on-one confrontation, the witness was still unable to make an identification. Several days later a second lineup was arranged. There were five people in this lineup, but Foster was the only person who had been in both. This time the eyewitness made a positive identification. At trial the witness testified about the pre-trial procedures and then made an in-court identification.

The first question for the Supreme Court was whether the procedures followed by the police were suggestive and conducive

---

81   See the dissenting opinion of Marshall J., in *Manson v. Brathwaite*, 432 U.S. 98 (1977), at 121-23.
82   *Ibid.*, at 122.
83   *Ibid.*
84   394 U.S. 440 (1969).
85   399 U.S. 1 (1970).

to irreparable mistaken identification, in accordance with the test in *Stovall*.[86] The court had no difficulty in concluding that the procedures followed were improper. In effect, said the court, "the pretrial confrontations clearly were so arranged as to make the resulting identifications virtually inevitable."[87]

The second question from the *Stovall* test was, given the "totality of the circumstances", was there a violation of due process?[88] The court found no basis to justify the police procedures and therefore concluded that there was a due process violation. The out-of-court identification was therefore ruled inadmissible. The court then turned to the in-court identification and, applying *Simmons*, ruled that since the original observation was poor, the in-court identification was also inadmissible.

In *Coleman v. Alabama*,[89] the issue was the admissibility of the in-court identification.[90] The plurality applied *Simmons* and ruled that the in-court identification did not stem from the allegedly suggestive lineup. The witness testified that he got a good view of his assailant and identified him as soon as he saw him at the police station. The court found that this constituted an independent basis for the in-court identification and therefore the identification was reliable.[91] The in-court identification was therefore ruled admissible.

The penultimate decision from the United States Supreme Court on this issue is *Neil v. Biggers*.[92] Any ambiguity in the *Stovall* and *Simmons* decisions was laid to rest by the court. The court implicitly overruled *Stovall*, and determined that the standards for admissibility should be the same for in-court and out-of-court identifications.[93] The balancing test of *Stovall* was gone, replaced by a pure reliability test:[94]

> It is the likelihood of misidentification which violates a defendant's right to due process . . . We turn, then, to the central question, whether under the "totality of the circumstances" the identification was reliable even though the confrontation procedure was suggestive. As indicated by our cases, the factors to be considered in evaluating the

---

86   *Supra*, note 84 at 442.
87   *Supra*, note 84 at 443.
88   *Supra*, note 84 at 442.
89   *Supra*, note 85.
90   *Supra*, note 85 at 4.
91   *Supra*, note 85 at 5.
92   409 U.S. 188 (1972).
93   *Ibid.*, at 198.
94   *Ibid.*, at 198, 199.

likelihood of misidentification include the opportunity of the witness to view the criminal at the time of the crime, the witness' degree of attention, the accuracy of the witness' prior description of the criminal, the level of certainty demonstrated by the witness at the confrontation, and the length of time between the crime and the confrontation.[95]

Following *Neil v. Biggers*, the sole focus was the reliability of the identification. As long as there was some reasonable opportunity to observe the offender, the techniques used to obtain the pre-trial identification were no longer in issue.[96]

The most recent treatment of this topic by the United States Supreme Court was in *Manson v. Brathwaite*.[97] The case involved the purchase of heroin by an undercover police officer. Shortly after the sale the officer returned to the police station. He described the vendor to other officers, but could not identify him. Another officer thought the description fitted the accused Brathwaite. He obtained a picture which was subsequently identified by the undercover officer. Brathwaite was arrested two months later. At the trial, held eight months after the sale, the evidence concerning the photo identification was admitted. The officer also made a positive in-court identification. Brathwaite appealed, arguing that the identification evidence was inadmissible as it was obtained in a manner that violated due process.

The United States Supreme Court confirmed its earlier position in *Neil v. Biggers*. Reliability was held to be the "linchpin" in determining if there was a due process violation.[98] According to the court, factors that influenced reliability were the opportunity of the witness to view the perpetrator at the time of the crime, the degree of attention, the accuracy of the prior description, the level of confidence, and the time lapse between the crime and the first opportunity to make an identification.[99] Unless it could be said that there was a substantial likelihood of misidentification, the evidence was for the jury to weigh.[100] If the identification was reliable it could be bolstered by evidence of a pre-trial identification re-

---

95   This list of factors was compiled by the court without the aid of any psychological evidence. The literature does not support two of the factors mentioned. The accuracy of the witnesses' prior description and the level of certainty are poor indicators of the reliability of the identification. See, generally, *supra*, Chapter 1, part 5.

96   Grano, Pulaski and Sherwood, *supra*, note 38. Also see W.W. Sherwood, "Recent Developments, Identification: Unnecessary Suggestiveness May Not Violate Due Process" (1973), 73 Colum. L. Rev. 1168.

97   432 U.S. 98 (1977).

98   *Ibid.*, at 114.

99   *Ibid.*, at 114. See note 95, *supra*.

100   *Ibid.*, at 116.

gardless of whether the pre-trial identification was obtained in a suggestive manner. The jury could then assess the impact of the pre-trial procedures.[101]

There is a ten year gap between *Stovall v. Denno*[102] and *Manson v. Brathwaite*.[103] The United States Supreme Court appears to have changed its position over those years. The court moved from a test that looked at whether the most reliable pre-trial identification process available in the circumstances was used, to a test that looked at whether the identification at trial was reliable. The problem with the "reliability" test is that it ignores the inherent unreliability of eyewitness identification and the difficulties faced in exposing its limits at trial. If there is to be a constitutional guarantee, its purpose should be to ensure that the police preserve, as far as possible, the original memory and do nothing within reason to contaminate it. Once contaminated it is virtually impossible to assess the reliability of the identification. A reliability test for unreliable evidence seems a contradiction. One factor that seems to have caused the shift from the "totality of circumstances" test in *Stovall* to the reliability test in *Brathwaite* is the lack of flexibility as to the admissibility of the evidence. In *Manson v. Brathwaite* the Supreme Court rejected a *per se* exclusionary rule because, argued the court, it interferes with the jury process, it is a poor deterrent in influencing police practices, and inflexibility does not promote justice.[104] The development of a similar constitutional principle in Canada may be aided by the two-stage approach mandated by s. 24 of the Charter. This section creates the flexibility that the United States Supreme Court wanted as the governing principle in that jurisdiction.

(2) Predicting a Canadian Response

The identification of an individual as the person allegedly responsible for a crime may be one of the most important steps in the criminal process. Once a perpetrator is identified the entire system is activated to determine if the individual so identified is legally responsible for the crime. The pre-trial identification process creates evidence which may be admitted at trial to prove criminal liability. Yet the process is fraught with difficulty. It is an

101   *Ibid.*, at 114.
102   388 U.S. 293 (1967).
103   *Supra*, note 97.
104   *Ibid.*, at 112, 113.

unreliable process to begin with. The selection may be biased by suggestion, intentional or otherwise.[105] Once a selection is made, the witness is unlikely to retract the identification, whether it was made under fair or unfair conditions in the first place.[106] The process takes place in relative privacy. The process is difficult to reconstruct at trial and the effectiveness of cross-examination is blunted by the witnesses' own inability to separate original from supplanted memory.[107] Assessing a witnesses' truthfulness is a very difficult task, since the usual indicators of demeanour and confidence are of little if any use.[108] Jurors may be hard pressed to understand the significance of evidence concerning suggestive techniques, leaving the accused virtually without remedy against an assertion, "that is the man".[109]

Section 7 of the Charter of Rights and Freedoms ensures that no individual is deprived of life, liberty and security of the person, except in accordance with the principles of fundamental justice. An analysis of s. 7 involves two steps. First there must be a finding that there has been a deprivation of "life, liberty and security of the person", and secondly that the deprivation is contrary to the principles of fundamental justice.[110] There are three distinct elements to s. 7, "life", "liberty" and "security of the person", and each must be given independent meaning and protection by the courts.[111]

The *Charter* contemplates that the criminal investigatory process will be subject to constitutional review. Search and seizure powers are specifically recognized, but the umbrella effect of s. 7[112] would appear to make the entire gambit of pre-trial procedures that can ultimately affect liberty open to Charter review. Pre-trial identification procedures interfere with liberty because the process is designed to generate information significant to the criminal process. An identification may provide the reasonable and probable grounds to effect an arrest. It may produce the evidence critical to the jury verdict. What happens outside the courtroom may virtually determine the outcome of the trial. As

---

105   See, generally, *supra*, Chapter 1, part 3.
106   See, generally, *supra*, Chapter 1, part 5(1).
107   See, generally, *supra*, Chapter 1, part 3.
108   See, generally, *supra*, Chapter 1, part 5.
109   See, generally, *supra*, Chapter 1, part 6(1).
110   *R. v. Beare; R. v. Higgins* (1988), 45 C.C.C. (3d) 57 at 69 (S.C.C.).
111   *Re Singh and Min. of Employment & Immigration* (1985), 17 D.L.R. (4th) 422 at 458 (S.C.C.).
112   *Ref. re s. 94(2) of Motor Vehicle Act (B.C.)* (1985), 23 C.C.C. (3d) 289 (S.C.C.).

such the liberty of an individual may be affected by this information. It follows, therefore, that the information must be obtained in accordance with the principles of fundamental justice.

Principles of fundamental justice are to be found in the basic tenets and values of our judicial system.[113] Protecting against the conviction of the innocent is certainly basic to the Canadian legal system. Identification evidence obtained through improper and suggestive techniques increases the likelihood of misidentification and thus may result in the wrongful conviction of the innocent. The system should operate to reduce the likelihood of this event. Any pre-trial identification procedure should be as accurate and as risk free as possible.

Section 7 would therefore appear to mandate that pre-trial identifications be conducted in a manner that will reduce the possibility of misidentification. The risk will be minimized if the least suggestive technique available is used to effect the identification. In *Neil v. Biggers*,[114] the Supreme Court of the United States stated:[115]

> ... the primary evil to be avoided is "a very substantial likelihood of misidentification" ... Suggestive confrontations are disapproved because they increase the likelihood of misidentification, and unnecessarily suggestive ones are condemned for the further reason that the increased chance of misidentification is gratuitous.

It is virtually impossible to have a risk free pre-trial identification procedure. What the United States Supreme Court opposed was increasing the risk unnecessarily and gratuitously. The Canadian system of justice, which is dedicated to protecting the innocent, should similarly not tolerate unnecessary and gratuitous risks.

Section 7 of the Charter provides that the state may deprive someone of their liberty so long as it does so in accordance with principles of fundamental justice. It is submitted that fundamental justice should require that the most reliable technique available in the circumstances be employed. Less reliable techniques increase the risk of misidentification and are therefore incompatible with the basic tenets of our system. There are only two reasons for using an unnecessarily suggestive technique. The first is unwillingness on the part of the police to reduce the risk of misidentification. The second is a desire to fix the image of the person suspected into the

---

113 *Ibid.*
114 409 U.S. 188 (1972).
115 *Ibid.*, at 198.

mind of the witness so as to bolster a case.[116] No system based on principles of fundamental justice would be able to tolerate such improper motives.

It would follow from this that once a suspect has been arrested or detained a properly conducted lineup should be employed as long as the suspect consents and there are no other serious impediments.[117] This is the most reliable technique available. Failure to hold a properly conducted lineup would result in a *prima facie* breach of the Constitution. What is entailed in a "properly conducted" lineup will develop over time but, at a minimum, it would require a sufficient number of people of similar build, appearance, and dress to effect a fair test of the witnesses' memory.

If the suspect was to refuse a lineup, and if the suspect was aware of the consequences of that decision, this would constitute a waiver of the constitutional protection afforded by s. 7.[118] The police would then be free to use whatever was appropriate in the circumstances. In England, if a suspect refuses a lineup, the police are entitled to use a group identification, video identification or showup as long as the suspect is first notified that these are the consequences of a refusal.[119]

If the police did not have the grounds to effect an arrest, then the police would be required to use the most reliable procedure available in the circumstances. For example, a properly conducted photo array is probably mandated when the police have a suspect but require an identification before making an arrest. What is to be done in other situations will depend on the circumstances. The governing principle remains constant; in order to reduce the risk of misidentification, the most reliable pre-trial identification technique available in the circumstances is to be employed.

3. ARBITRARY ARREST OR DETENTION

An arrest or detention made in violation of s. 9 of the Charter may precede a pre-trial identification procedure. For example, an accused who is arbitrarily arrested may be placed in a lineup or his or her picture may be taken and subsequently identified by a witness. The evidence generated following the unconstitutional

---

116 Sherwood, *supra*, note 38 at 748.
117 An example of an impediment that would justify a departure from this general rule would be the serious medical condition of the witness.
118 *Clarkson v. R.* (1986), 25 C.C.C. (3d) 207 (S.C.C.).
119 *Code of Practice,* see, *infra,* Appendix A.

arrest may be inadmissable at trial. As the Ontario Court of Appeal stated in *R. v. Duguay:*[120]

> It is repugnant to our concept of the administration of criminal justice and to the rights of citizens in a free and democratic society, to make them subject to arbitrary arrest for investigative purposes.

The identification evidence obtained following a s. 9 Charter violation would meet the first criterion of s. 24. It would be "obtained in a manner that infringed" the Charter as that phrase has been interpreted. In *R. v. Strachan,*[121] the Supreme Court indicated that the first criterion of s. 24(2) would be satisfied if the violation of the Charter preceded the discovery of the evidence and was not too remote. Identification evidence following an arbitrary arrest or detention would usually satisfy that requirement. Whether the evidence of the pre-trial identification would be excluded at trial would depend on whether the admission of the evidence would bring the administration of justice into disrepute.

4. REMEDIES

(1) Violation of the Right to Counsel

In *R. v. Leclair,*[122] the Supreme Court determined that failure to provide a reasonable opportunity to consult with counsel, prior to participating in a lineup, was a violation of s. 10(*b*) of the Charter of Rights and Freedoms. By virtue of the structure of the Charter, the next question considered by the court was whether the lineup evidence should have been excluded at trial. The court therefore examined the factors, which had been identified in *Collins v. R.*[123] as useful, to decide the issue of whether the system is better served by the admission or exclusion of the evidence.

The first factor considered by the court in *Leclair* was the nature of the evidence. The court has on several occasions drawn a distinction between "real" evidence and "intangible" evidence such as statements.[124] The evidence generated through a lineup is intangible opinion evidence. The court determined that conscripting the accused to create this form of evidence could render the

---

120   (1985), 18 C.C.C. (3d) 289 at 298, affirmed 46 C.C.C. (3d) 1 (S.C.C.)[Ont.].
121   (1989), 46 C.C.C. (3d) 479 (S.C.C.).
122   (1989), 46 C.C.C. (3d) 129 (S.C.C.).
123   (1987), 33 C.C.C. (3d) 1 (S.C.C.).
124   *Collins v. R., ibid.; R. v. Manninen* (1987), 34 C.C.C. (3d) 385 (S.C.C.); *R. v. Strachan, supra,* note 121.

trial process unfair.[125] Secondly, the court looked at the fact that there was no urgency and that the lineup procedure could have been held later in the day. Based on these factors, the court determined that the admission of the evidence would bring the administration of justice into disrepute. Accordingly, the court ruled that the evidence should have been excluded at trial.

If there is a constitutional right to have counsel present at a lineup,[126] then there would be no reason to distinguish between a violation of this right and the situation covered by *Leclair*. The critical factor going to the fairness of the trial is the intangible nature of the evidence. The accused, in the words of *Leclair*, is conscripted against himself since he is used as a means of creating evidence.[127] This evidence can ultimately affect the fairness of the trial and therefore should be excluded. It would therefore appear that though the accused has the onus of proof under s. 24(2),[128] the onus may be fairly easy to overcome when the violation of the right to counsel leads to pre-trial eyewitness identification evidence.

(2) Violation of the Right to Fundamental Justice

It has been argued above[129] that the use of unnecessarily suggestive pre-trial identification techniques is a violation of the accused's rights pursuant to s. 7 of the Charter. If this is so, then the issue arises as to whether the evidence of identification obtained from an unnecessarily suggestive pre-trial identification should be excluded at trial. This question would need to be determined with reference to s. 24(2) of the Charter and the interpretive guidelines set out by the Supreme Court in *Collins v. R.*.[130]

The effect of the evidence on the fairness of the trial is a prime consideration of *Collins*. As Lamer J. stated:[131]

> . . . the purpose of s. 24(2) is to prevent having the administration of justice brought into *further disrepute* by the admission of the evidence in the proceedings. This further disrepute will result from the admission of evidence that would deprive the accused of a fair hearing, or

---

125 *Supra*, note 122 at 139, 140.
126 See discussion this chapter, part 1(2)(c).
127 *Supra*, note 122 at 140.
128 *Supra*, note 123 at 16.
129 See this chapter, part 2(2).
130 *Supra*, note 123.
131 *Supra*, note 123 at 16, 17.

from judicial condonation of unacceptable conduct by the investigatory and prosecutorial agencies.

If there is a constitutional protection that would mandate the use of the fairest possible pre-trial identification technique, its *raison d'être* is to prevent untrustworthy evidence. A violation of this constitutional guarantee would mean that the reliability of the evidence generated is suspect. Unreliable evidence could clearly affect the fairness of the trial and should therefore be excluded.

Another factor that the Supreme Court considered in *Collins* was the seriousness of the Charter violation. In this regard Lamer J. stated:[132]

> I should add, that the availability of other investigatory techniques and the fact that the evidence could have been obtained without the violation of the Charter tend to render the Charter violation more serious . . . [F]ailure to proceed properly when that option was open to [the authorities] tends to indicate a blatant disregard for the Charter, which is a factor supporting the exclusion of the evidence.

The argument advanced is that s. 7 requires the police to use the most reliable technique available in the circumstances. Thus, for example, a hospital confrontation would be acceptable if the witness was in a critical condition, and a photo array would be acceptable if the police did not have reasonable and probable grounds to effect an arrest. The purpose of the rule is to ensure the most reliable identification, given the circumstances. Therefore a violation of s. 7 means that there was a more reliable investigatory technique that was not used. To allow the evidence to be admitted when improper and suggestive techniques are used would amount to judicial condonation of unacceptable conduct by the authorities.[133]

Finally, the court in *Collins* indicated that it is necessary to consider any disrepute that may result from the exclusion of the evidence.[134] On this issue Lamer J. stated:[135]

> . . . it must be emphasized that even though the inquiry under s. 24(2) will necessarily focus on the specific prosecution, it is the long-term consequences of regular admission or exclusion of this type of evidence on the repute of the administration of justice which must be considered.

Section 24 of the Charter clearly contemplates the ability to consider each case on its facts and to take into account special or

---

132 *Supra*, note 123 at 20.
133 *Collins v. R., supra*, note 123 at 16, 17. See, note 131, *supra*, and accompanying text.
134 *Supra*, note 123 at 17.
135 *Ibid*.

unusual circumstances. It may very well be that failure to use the most reliable identification procedure in a particular case should not result in the exclusion of the evidence. For example, if a person was held hostage for several days it might not bring the administration of justice into disrepute to allow an identification from a single photograph to be admitted. But in the classic "fleeting" glance case, it can certainly be argued that the administration of justice is better served by the development of high standards for pre-trial identification that will reduce the risk of the wrongful conviction of the innocent. If this results in evidence being excluded in the individual prosecution, that is arguably not too high a price to pay for improved standards of practice in this area.

(3) Excluding Dock Identifications

A pre-trial eyewitness identification done in violation of the Constitution gives rise to two separate evidentiary questions. The first question on the admissibility of the pre-trial identification is dealt with above.[136] The second question that arises is whether the witness should be allowed to make an in-court identification. Psychological experimentation would lead to a concern that suggestive pre-trial identification procedures may have contaminated the original memory and therefore the evidence is no longer trustworthy.

Any argument that the dock identification could be excluded would have to be made pursuant to s. 24(2) of the Charter.[137] In order for s. 24(2) to apply, the evidence under consideration must be "obtained in a manner that infringed or denied any rights or freedoms guaranteed" by the Charter.

The meaning of this phrase was considered by the Supreme Court of Canada in *R. v. Strachan.*[138] Chief Justice Dickson offered this assessment:[139]

> . . . [T]he first inquiry under s. 24(2) would be to determine whether a Charter violation occurred in the course of obtaining the evidence. A temporal link between the infringement of the Charter and the discovery of the evidence figures prominently in this assessment, particularly when the Charter violation and the discovery of the evidence occur in

---

136 This chapter, parts 4(1) and 4(2).
137 *R. v. Therens* (1985), 18 C.C.C. (3d) 481 (S.C.C.); *Collins v. R.* (1987), 33 C.C.C. (3d) 1 (S.C.C.).
138 (1988), 46 C.C.C. (3d) 479 (S.C.C.).
139 *Ibid.*, at 498, 499.

the course of a single transaction. The presence of a temporal connection is not however, determinative. Situations will arise where evidence, though obtained following the breach of a Charter right, will be too remote from the violation to be "obtained in a manner" that infringed the Charter.

This passage directs an inquiry into how the evidence was "obtained". Arguably the in-court identification offered at trial is not "obtained" following a Charter breach. An improper identification technique may influence the quality of the evidence, but the observation of the criminal was made in advance of any police involvement. The contrary argument is that the original memory has been supplanted by the pre-trial procedure and that the dock identification is directly obtained from the unconstitutional actions.

This dilemma is not easily resolved. If the original observation was made under good conditions and the pre-trial procedure has not unduly biased it (for example, failure to provide counsel prior to a fair lineup), then it may be proper to admit the dock identification on the grounds that the evidence existed prior to the Charter breach. On the other hand, if the pre-trial actions have so contaminated the original observation as to render it entirely unreliable, then the proper course would be to exclude both the out-of-court and in-court identifications. The dock identification could be said to have been obtained following a Charter breach and to allow patently unreliable evidence to be tendered would bring the administration of justice into further disrepute.[140]

If the dock identification is admitted, but the pre-trial procedure is suppressed, the accused would be entitled, by virtue of the common law,[141] to a special warning in the jury charge. The jury would have to be warned that there is no evidence of any pre-trial identification and a proper police investigation should have included such steps. The Crown may be left with a case where the only evidence of identification is a dock identification made several years after the crime. It may be unsafe to convict on such evidence.

The *Charter of Rights and Freedoms* is certainly not a complete answer to the frailties of eyewitness identification evidence. It may provide some arguments for the exclusion of evidence garnered

---

140   *Collins v. R., supra*, note 137.
141   See, *infra*, Chapter 3, parts 1 and 7.

during pre-trial identifications. The main impact that the Charter may have in this area is to encourage the use of better quality identification techniques so as to reduce the likelihood of the misidentification of the innocent.

Chapter Five

Scientific Means of Identification

One of the most important methods used to establish the identity of the perpetrator of a crime is the analysis of physiological and biological material. This material is either unique to the individual or is at least capable of excluding a vast portion of the general public as possible donors. This chapter examines some of the most common types of physiological and biological material · encountered at a criminal trial, in order to review the extent to which the material may be used to establish the identity of the perpetrator. The last topic in the chapter looks at the admissibility of opinions derived from scientific tests which have yet to gain general acceptability in the scientific community.

1. DNA PROFILING[1]

The basic unit of life is the cell.[2] The cell contains DNA (deoxyribonucleic acid) which carries in it the individual's genetic information.[3] Each strand of DNA is made up of groups of atoms called nucleotides. There are four different nucleotides in DNA,[4] and these are strung together like a chain.[5] DNA is made up of two of these chains held together in a double helix structure.[6]

Sequences of DNA nucleotides comprise the 23 pairs of chromosomes in each human cell; one full set of 23 chromosomes

---

1   The authors are indebted to Barry D. Gaudette, Chief Scientist, Molecular Genetics Section, Central Forensic Laboratory, R.C.M.P. Headquarters, Ottawa, Canada, for his extensive assistance in preparing this section.
2   J.D. Watson *et al.*, *Molecular Biology of the Gene*, 4th ed. (Menlo Park, Calif.: Benjamin/Cummings, 1987), at 4.
3   *Ibid.*, at 240.
4   *Ibid.*, at 75.
5   *Ibid.*, at 74.
6   *Ibid.*

having been inherited from each parent.[7] Particular sequences of nucleotides, located in particular positions on particular chromosomes comprise the genes, the fundamental units of heredity.[8]

Human DNA consists of approximately three billion pairs of nucleotides.[9] The vast preponderance of the sequence is identical for all people; reflecting that we generally have two arms, two legs, etc. It is estimated however, that approximately three million pairs of nucleotides are unique to the individual (with the exception of identical twins), accounting for the great variation among people.[10]

DNA is found in all nucleated cells in the body.[11] These include white blood cells, semen, skin tissue, and hair roots.[12] They do not include fingernails and hair shafts. Saliva is not made up of nucleated cells either, but there may be sufficient cells from the lining of the mouth in the saliva to provide a DNA sample. Each person's DNA complement is exactly replicated in every cell, so any sample provides equivalent DNA information.

DNA profiling[13] is a process by which the DNA is examined through a method called restriction fragment length polymorphism analysis (R.F.L.P.). Once the DNA is extracted from the forensic sample it is cut into fragments by restriction enzymes which are designed to chemically cut the DNA at targeted locations.[14] The pieces of DNA that are targeted by the enzyme "scissors" are those that are variable among individuals and those that are polymorphic, that is, those that have the greatest number of variants in the population. The fragments are then separated according to length by a process known as electrophoresis.[15] This process involves placing the fragments along one end of a tray containing agarose gel. An electric current is then passed through the gel causing the DNA, which is negatively charged, to move. The shorter, lighter fragments move faster than the larger, heavier

---

7   L.T. Kirby, *DNA Fingerprinting* (New York: Stockton Press, 1990), at 8.

8   *Supra*, note 2 at 78.

9   V.W. Weedn, "DNA Profiling" (1989), 1 Expert Evidence Reporter 61.

10   *Ibid.*, at 62.

11   *Supra*, note 7 at 55.

12   *Ibid.*, at 55*ff.*

13   The process is sometimes called "DNA fingerprinting." The term "DNA profiling" is to be preferred. Unlike fingerprints, DNA analysis does not positively identify an individual. Instead it is used to positively exclude an individual or to establish a probability of common origin.

14   B. Gaudette, "DNA Typing: A New Service to Canadian Police" (1990), 52 RCMP Gaz. 1.

15   *Ibid.*

ones and when the process is complete the fragments are single-stranded and are arranged in lanes on the gel according to molecular weight.[16] Following this separation, the DNA is transferred to a nylon membrane where it is immobilized.[17]

The next step involves "hybridizing" the DNA with radioactively labelled molecular "probes". Though the DNA is now arranged according to weight on the gel, it cannot be seen. The probes are designed to attach themselves to a complementary piece of DNA. The pieces targeted by the probes can then be visualized through a photographic process whereby the radioactive sample creates an image on an x-ray film. This x-ray is called an autoradiograph.

There are a number of probes available on the commercial market, each designed to target a different locus on the DNA. The more probes one uses, the more genetic information one obtains. The RCMP has determined that it will use five "single-locus" probes in the tests conducted in its laboratories.[18] These probes are designed to attach to five specific loci on the DNA. Following hybridization it is possible to visualize the genetic material inherited from each parent at that particular locus.

The autoradiograph produced during a DNA profiling test looks somewhat like the picture of a railway track with irregularly spaced ties. The position of the black bands indicates how far the DNA fragment moved when the electric current was passed through it. A single-locus probe, such as that used by the RCMP, will usually show two bands. Each band represents the genetic material (allele) inherited at that location from each parent. If two bands appear, the person is said to be heterozygous at that locus, meaning that the person inherited different genetic material from each parent. If only one band appears, the person is said to be homozygous at that locus, meaning the same allele was inherited from each parent. If there is enough genetic material in the forensic sample to use all five probes, an RCMP test will reveal up to ten bits of information on the person's genetic code.

Any properly conducted DNA profile should also involve the use of a "control probe" to ensure that the test has been properly done. The RCMP laboratory presently runs two control probes on every sample. The first control probe is a sex specific probe which is designed to attach to a specific location on the Y chromosome,

---

16   *Supra*, note 7 at 96, 97, 143, 144.
17   *Ibid.*, at 101.
18   Conversation with B. Gaudette, *supra*, note 1.

found only in the male population. There would be no reaction to this probe in an uncontaminated sample from a female. In a male, one band would be produced as all males are monomorphic at this locus, meaning the allele is inherited from one parent, in this case the father. The DNA fragment that is targeted by this probe is common to all males, meaning that if the test has been done correctly, the band should be at the same location in all trials.

As a further control, RCMP laboratories will run another monomorphic probe that targets a locus that is identical in all of the population. If the test has been done correctly, this control probe will produce a band at the same location in all cases. Conversely, if the band is not at the correct location the results of the test must be rejected or at least scrutinized with extreme care.

One of the most common problems with DNA profiling is a phenomenon called band shifting. Band shifting is caused when the DNA fragments in one lane of the electrophoresis gel travel across the gel more rapidly than identical fragments in a second lane.[19] This might be caused by unequal amounts of DNA in each lane, contaminated DNA, or problems with the gel.[20] It is estimated that band shifting occurs in about 30% of forensic cases.[21] It is possible to determine if band shifting has occurred by examining the bands produced by the control probes. If they are not in the correct location, band shifting is a likely explanation.

If band shifting is detected then it may be appropriate to repeat the test. In the forensic context, however, this may not be possible. All of the DNA material found at the crime scene may have been used up in the first test. Another possibility is to apply a correction factor to the test results. The correction factor is determined by calculating the amount of shift in the control bands and applying it to all the bands. This assumes that all bands have shifted equally. This assumption has not been subjected to rigorous scientific testing and may therefore lead to erroneous results.

Once the autoradiograph has been produced (and corrected if band shifting has occurred), it is possible to compare it to the graph produced from a known sample. If the bands are not in the same place, the samples must have come from different individuals. If the bands correspond it is important to know what percentage of the population would produce this particular genetic profile.

19   *Supra*, note 7 at 119.
20   *Supra*, note 7 at 123.
21   *Supra*, note 7 at 119.

The first step in the statistical analysis is the development of a population profile. This involves subjecting the DNA from a random sample of people to the probe and determining the percentage of people whose allele falls at a particular molecular weight. Theoretically, there is an infinite variation. In practice, the weights fall within a range. In the same manner that one could determine the percentage of adults who were under five feet tall, five feet to six feet, and over six feet, a profile concerning each allele can be constructed. The profile indicates the percentage of the population whose allele falls within a particular range. In practice, the RCMP has chosen to divide the molecular weight scale into 26 arbitrary divisions or "bins". The present RCMP data base contains DNA profiles from approximately 1300 individuals.

If the alleles are statistically independent it is possible to calculate the percentage of people who have the same profile. This is done by means of a genetic principle called the Hardy-Weinberg law.[22] A population is said to be in Hardy-Weinberg equilibrium if the mating is entirely random. This means that the alleles are being shuffled at random and the presence of one is independent of another. One can therefore calculate the frequency of the "genotype" or the particular pair of alleles for a specific locus by multiplying the frequency of each allele and doubling it (because one has the same probability of inheriting each allele from both parents).

If there is sufficient genetic material, the RCMP forensic laboratories will be using five probes which will provide information concerning five genotypes typically made up of two alleles each. This has the potential to provide a highly significant calculation as to probability of common origin.

The statistical analysis however must be approached with caution. The statistical analysis is based on an assumption of random mating which promotes gene exchange throughout the population. In reality, however, we do not have fully random mating. Reproductive isolation may be caused by such things as geography, religion or custom. It may be necessary to create data bases for population subsets so as to more accurately reflect the true nature of gene exchange. The general data base may be entirely inapplicable to a particular subset of the population.

DNA profiling certainly has the potential to serve an important and beneficial role in the criminal justice system. If the test is

---

22   D.P. Doolittle, *Population Genetics: Basic Principles* (Berlin, New York: Springer-Verlag, 1987), at 2-11.

done according to rigorous standards, if the results are accurately interpreted, and if the statistical analysis is based on valid population data, then there is no better test to identify a criminal or exonerate a suspect. If these standards are not adhered to, without doubt there is a potential for injustice.

2. BODY FLUIDS

(1) Blood

Blood is a complex body fluid containing more than 160 antigens, 150 serum proteins, and 250 cellular enzymes.[23] Given a large enough blood sample and unlimited funds it would be possible to analyze blood so as to establish biochemical individuality.[24] At a practical level however, the forensic serologist is limited in the amount of information that can be extracted from blood. A genetic marker is only valuable to the serologist if it is easily extracted; if it is robust in the sense that it will survive drying and other hazards associated with the unsterile environment of a crime scene; and if the analysis of the marker involves a simple procedure whereby an individual may be assigned to one category or another without ambiguity.[25] These practical considerations mean that the average forensic laboratory is generally equipped to analyze approximately ten genetic markers. As DNA profiling becomes more prevalent, however, the traditional role for the forensic serologist will largely disappear. More exacting information may be obtained from a DNA profile then can ever be obtained from a traditional serological test.

The most well known genetic marker is the ABO antigen system. The ABO system has traditionally occupied an important place in the forensic laboratory due to the stability and hardiness of the ABO markers.[26] In addition to the ABO system, the other genetic markers (antigens, serum proteins and cellular enzymes) most commonly used in forensic examination are phosphoglucomutase (PGM); adenylate kinase (AK); acid phosphatase

---

23   H.C. Lee, "Identification and Grouping of Bloodstains", as found in R. Saferstein (ed.), *Forensic Science Handbook* (Prentice-Hall Inc., 1982), at 268.
24   G.F. Sensabaugh, "Biochemical Markers of Individuality", as found in Saferstein, *ibid.*, at 339.
25   *Ibid.*, at 342.
26   *Ibid.*, at 345.

(ACP or EAP); haptoglobin (HP); esterase D (ESD); glyoxalase I (GLO I); and adenosine deaminase (ADA).

The various genetic markers do not appear with equal frequency within the population. There are numerous population studies of frequency distribution which show virtual correlation when there has been random mating.[27] However, if this premise is not true the statistic is inapplicable. For example, the Amish community in the United States exhibits appreciable differences in gene frequencies from the general population.[28]

The genetic markers found in blood are statistically independent of one another in the same way that every toss of a coin is independent of the one before.[29] This means that the probability of any combination of markers being found in one person's blood can be calculated by multiplying the individual probabilities together. The resulting statistic does not uniquely identify the individual; others in the population will have the same phenotypic combination. However, if sufficient systems are analyzed it may be possible to reduce the probability of random match to a very small number.

The forensic serologist may also be able to give some indication of the age of a blood stain. As blood ages it changes in colour from scarlet to dull brown due to the breakdown of haemoglobin into haematin.[30] The approximate age of fresh blood can therefore be determined if it can be established that haemoglobin has not yet turned into haemin crystals.[31] Once this process has been completed however, it is virtually impossible to determine the age of a blood stain. Factors such as heat, light, temperature and humidity can profoundly affect the speed at which blood ages.[32]

(2) Semen and Saliva

Approximately 80% of the population are secretors. A secretor is an individual who has the ABO blood grouping antigens in certain body fluids such as semen, vaginal secretions and saliva.[33]

---

27   *Ibid.*, at 392.
28   *Ibid.*
29   B. Fisher, A. Svensson & O. Wendel, *Techniques of Crime Scene Investigation*, 4th ed. (Lausanne: Elsevier, 1987), at 202.
30   A.A. Moessens, F.E. Inbau & J.E. Starrs, *Scientific Evidence in Criminal Cases*, 3rd ed.(Mineola, N.Y.: Foundation Press, 1986), at 350.
31   *Ibid.*
32   *Ibid.*
33   *Supra*, note 29 at 205.

The ABO typing can therefore be extracted from these fluids. All individuals have a variety of other genetic markers in body fluids, although not all of these markers have forensic application.[34] Semen for example, undergoes significant dilution in the vagina and thus only the hardiest markers are potentially available for typing.[35] Phosphoglucomutase (PGM) is one marker that can generally be typed in semen.[36] Caution, however, must be exercised since this marker is sometimes found in vaginal fluids and therefore the sample may be contaminated.[37] Adenylate kinase (AK), esterase D (ESD) and glyoxalase (GLO) are present in semen in concentrations that are generally borderline for routine detection. If the sample is large enough it may be possible to obtain typing information.[38]

Saliva also contains a number of genetic markers over and above the ABO marker found in the body fluids of secretors. For the most part the markers in saliva are unique to saliva and are not found in other body fluids. How well these markers survive has not really been investigated and therefore there is not a great deal of forensic information that is routinely extracted from saliva samples.[39]

3. HAIR ANALYSIS

A characteristic of the mammalian species is the presence of hair.[40] Hair grows out of an organ known as a hair follicle which is located in the skin.[41] The root is the portion in the follicle and its enlarged base is termed the bulb.[42] The portion of the hair above the skin is termed the shaft.[43] Hair is composed of a chain of proteins called keratins.[44] As these keratin cells harden they are

---

34   *Supra*, note 24 at 381.
35   *Ibid.*
36   *Ibid.*
37   *Ibid.*
38   Baechtel, "The Identification and Individualization of Semen Stains", as found in R. Saferstein (ed.), *Forensic Science Handbook*, Vol. 2 (Prentice Hall Inc., 1988), at 373.
39   *Supra*, note 24 at 381.
40   A.A. Moessens, F.E. Inbau & J.E. Starrs, *Scientific Evidence in Criminal Cases*, 3rd ed. (Mineola, N.Y.: Foundation Press, 1986), at 477.
41   R. Bisbing, "The Forensic Identification and Association of Human Hair", as found in R. Saferstein (ed.), *Forensic Science Handbook* (Prentice-Hall Inc., 1982), at 187.
42   *Ibid.*
43   *Ibid.*
44   *Ibid.*

pushed from the follicle which results in hair growth outward from the root end.[45]

A microscopic examination of a hair shaft reveals that it is composed of three layers. The outer layer is called the cuticle. It is composed of thin translucent scales that act as a protective coating.[46] The middle layer is called the cortex. It is this layer that contains the pigment granules (also called melanin granules) that are responsible for hair colour.[47] The inner layer is called the medulla. It contains air bubbles, some pigment cells and cellular debris.[48] A pencil provides a good model for understanding hair structure. The eraser and metal casing can be compared to the root system; the graphite core can represent the medulla; the wooden casing, the cortex; and the painted surface, the cuticle. Like a pencil, a hair may be cut sharply or rounded with use. If not properly cared for a pencil, like a hair, may be broken or frayed.[49]

The main methodology for the comparison of a known and unknown hair sample is through the use of macroscopic and microscopic investigation. The forensic examiner compares the characteristics of the known and unknown samples. This process is complicated by the fact that no two hair specimens from one person are identical in every detail.[50] Head hair, for example, actively grows for a period of two to six years before being shed. There are considerable microscopic differences between young actively growing hair and dead hair.[51]

The variation in microscopic characteristics among the hairs of one person means that an analysis of a known sample requires a sufficient number of hairs in order to adequately represent the range of characteristics exhibited by that person.[52] An *ad hoc* committee composed of a number of international forensic hair examiners has suggested that 20 hairs from each of five locations on the scalp (centre, front, back, and both sides) should be obtained by a combination of combing and pulling.[53] The committee

---

45   *Supra*, note 40.
46   S. Seta, H. Sato & B. Miyake, "Forensic Hair Investigation", as found in *Forensic Science Progress*, Vol. 2 (Berlin; New York: Springer-Verlag, 1988), at 57-59.
47   *Ibid.*, at 60-62.
48   *Supra*, notes 40 and 41.
49   *Supra*, note 41 at 188.
50   H. Deadman, "Human Hair Comparisons Based on Microscopic Characteristics", as found in *Proceedings of the International Symposium on Forensic Hair Comparisons* (U.S. Government Publishing Office, 1985), at 45, 46.
51   *Ibid.*
52   *Ibid.*
53   *Ibid.*, at 47.

further recommended that a pubic hair sample consist of at least 30 hairs pulled and combed from different spots of the pubic area.[54] These hairs can then be examined in order to obtain a representative sample.

Once a known sample is obtained, the subjective part of the process begins. Hair comparison involves the study of characteristics. It requires the examiner to differentiate typical and atypical features and to determine if a difference can be explained by natural variation.[55] Since it is a subjective science, the quality of the analysis is directly related to the skill and professionalism of the examiner.

A fundamental dissimilarity between the known and unknown sample means that the hair did not originate from one source. It is, however, universally accepted that general microscopic comparison of hair does not allow for a unique association of the unknown sample with one individual. Though hair varies a great deal, it is (at least at a microscopic level) not unique. Therefore if there are no dissimilarities and significant similarities, the most that can be stated is that the questioned hairs are consistent with having originated from the same person as the known sample.[56] An *ad hoc* committee of forensic hair analysts has recommended that "consistency" should be reported only if there is a "strong association" between the known and unknown samples.[57]

If there are insufficient criteria to establish "consistency" and there are no dissimilarities, then no conclusion can be given as to whether the questioned and known hairs are of common origin. Statements such as the hair "could have come from" the suspect, or the suspect "cannot be eliminated" as a source, should be approached with caution.[58] It is important to explore with the examiner the meaning of this ambiguous language. If there were insufficient microscopic features to come to a firm conclusion, then the test should be reported as inconclusive.

If a known and unknown hair sample match in all particulars, two possibilities exist, either they came from the same source or there is a coincidental match. At the present time there are insuffi-

---

54   *Ibid.*
55   *Supra*, note 40 at 486.
56   B. Gaudette, "Strong Negative Conclusions in Hair Comparison — A Rare Event" (1985), 18 Can. Soc. Forensic Sci. J. 32.
57   Committee on Forensic Hair Comparisons, "Report Writing, Conclusions and Court Testimony", as found in *Proceedings of the International Symposium on Forensic Hair Comparisons* (U.S. Government Publishing Office, 1985), at 108.
58   *Ibid.*

cient population statistics to know the probability of either occurrence.[59] A particular hair morphology might occur in a significant segment of the population. Until a standardized data base is collected (as exists, for example, with blood) no meaningful statistics can be given.

4. BITE MARKS

Bite marks are unique to the individual.[60] Properly preserved and analyzed, a bite mark can provide persuasive evidence linking the accused to the crime. Bite marks are most commonly found on the skin of the victim; usually the breast, neck, arm or thigh.[61] Occasionally the victim may inflict a bite mark injury on an assailant. Sometimes bite marks will be found in other media such as food or chewing gum.

The first part of a successful bite mark comparison requires that the unknown mark be properly recorded and preserved. Photographs are vital but must be carefully done. Photographs taken from an angle for example, cause distortion which makes interpretation very difficult. The American Board of Forensic Odontology has suggested that all bite marks be photographed with a circular scale placed in the photo. This will permit calculation of the photographic angle so that a correction can be made before analysis is undertaken.[62] It is also possible to make three-dimensional representations of the bite mark by placing dental materials in the skin abrasions which harden into a mould.[63]

The quality of a bite mark analysis is very much dependent on the medium in which the mark is left. A controlled laboratory study showed that 98.8% of matches were correct when the sample bite marks were made in wax. This fell to 76% when the bite marks were made in pig skin which had been used to simulate human skin.[64] A limited study found only 66% reliability among

---

59   C.G.G. Aitken & J. Robertson, "A Contribution to the Discussion of Probabilities of Human Hair Comparisons" (1987), 32 J. Forensic Sci. 684.

60   R. Rawson *et al.*, "Statistical Evidence for the Individuality of the Human Dentition" (1984), 29 J. Forensic Sci. 245; R.F. Sognnaes *et al.*, "Computer Comparison of Bite Mark Patterns in Identical Twins" (1982), 105 J. Amer. Dental Assn. 449.

61   G. Gustafson, *Forensic Odontology* (Lausanne: Elsevier, 1966), at 141, 142.

62   R. Rawson *et al.*, "Analysis of Photographic Distortion in Bite Marks: A Report of the Bite Mark Guidelines Committee" (1986), 31 J. Forensic Sci. 1261.

63   B.W. Benson *et al.*, "Bite Mark Impressions: A Review of Techniques and Materials" (1988), 33 J. Forensic Sci. 1238.

64   D.K. Whittaker, "Some Laboratory Studies on the Accuracy of Bite Mark Comparison" (1975), 25 Int. Dental J. 166.

experienced odontologists who examined bite marks in dog skin.[65] For the purposes of the criminal justice system, these studies are somewhat alarming. They signify a substantially high error rate even when the marks were made under ideal laboratory conditions and examination took place immediately.[66]

The errors arise because the bite mark is distorted in human skin. Human skin is extremely elastic. It distorts with the pressure and with the sucking action that may accompany a bite.[67] Marks on a corpse may be distorted due to shrinkage caused by water loss.[68] In addition, sufficient detail may simply not be obtained to allow for an accurate identification or may be obliterated by bruising.[69] It has been suggested that there must be clear marks from at least four or five teeth before an identification should be undertaken.[70]

The difficulties with bite mark analysis have been recognized by forensic odontologists. In 1984 the American Board of Forensic Odontology adopted a protocol for bite mark analysis in order to attempt to standardize a scientific approach to the topic.[71] The purpose was to develop a common system so that the analysts could more accurately and consistently describe and compare the mark pattern.[72] A scoring system was developed which assigns a high point value for unusual and unique features, and a low one for usual or ordinary features.[73] Only if the score is high can there may any confidence that the mark can be individualized.[74] The authors of the protocol acknowledge that such a system is not perfect but suggest it might serve as an aid in making comparisons.[75] One thing that is strongly recommended by leading researchers in the area is that a positive identification be indepen-

65   R. Rawson *et al.*, "Reliability of the Scoring System of the American Board of Forensic Odontology for Human Bite Marks" (1986), 31 J. Forensic Sci. 1235.
66   *Supra*, note 64.
67   I.M. Sopher, *Forensic Dentistry* (Springfield, Ill.: Thomas, 1976), at 137.
68   *Supra*, note 61 at 145.
69   *Ibid.*, at 144.
70   A.J. Ligthelm & F.A. de Wet, "Registration of Bite Marks: A Preliminary Report" (1983), 1 J. Forensic Odonto-Stomatology 19 at 24.
71   American Board of Forensic Odontology, "Guidelines for Bite Mark Analysis" (1986), 112 J. Amer. Dental Assn. 383; also see Rawson *et al.*, *supra*, note 65.
72   *Ibid.*
73   *Ibid.*
74   *Ibid.*
75   G.L. Vale *et al.*, "Discussion of the Reliability of the Scoring System of the American Board of Forensic Odontology for Human Bite Marks" (1988), 33 J. Forensic Sci. 20.

dently confirmed by more than one qualified dental forensic scientist.[76] This recognizes the difficulties posed by bite mark analysis.

5. FINGERPRINTS

During the mid-nineteenth century, a British civil servant working in India began to use fingerprints as a means to prevent impersonation. At the same time a Scottish doctor working in Japan also became interested in the analysis of fingerprints and postulated the hypothesis that fingerprints are unique. The hypothesis proved correct and by the early part of the twentieth century fingerprint analysis had become an invaluable tool of virtually all police departments.[77]

A fingerprint is the impression left by the friction skin ridges found on the palmar side of the fingers and thumb. The same type of friction ridges can be found on the palm of the hand and on the soles of the feet. The friction ridges contain sweat pores through which perspiration is exuded. The perspiration attracts oil from other parts of the skin and small bits of dirt. This residue is deposited in the impression of the ridge pattern whenever the finger (or palm or sole) touches a relatively smooth surface. This impression is referred to as a latent print. In addition to latent prints, there are two other manners in which fingerprints are formed. If the finger is pressed into certain substances such as wax, fresh paint, tar or putty, a negative impression of the friction ridge pattern will be created. Prints in such media are referred to as plastic prints. Prints classed as visible prints will be formed if the finger is covered with a foreign substance such as blood or ink and then comes in contact with a smooth surface.[78]

The practical use of fingerprints for law enforcement derives from three universally accepted principles:

1. The friction ridge pattern that develops during the foetal stage remains unchanged during life (except for permanent scarring, which in itself creates a unique characteristic).

---

76 R. Rawson *et al.*, *supra*, note 65; Ligthelm & de Wit, *supra*, note 70; L.T. Johnson & D. Cadle, "Bite Mark Evidence: Recognition, Preservation, Analysis, and Courtroom Presentation" (1989), 55, No. 3, N.Y. State Dental J. 38 at 41.

77 *Supra*, note 30 at 416, 417.

78 R.D.Olsen, *Scott's Fingerprint Mechanics* (Springfield, Ill.: Thomas, 1978), at 5-15 and 111-117.

ERRATUM —
CORRECTION NOT TRUE

2. The pattern is unique to the individual (except for
    identical twins).
3. Though the ridge patterns are unique, their overall
    patterns have sufficient similarities to allow for a sys-
    tematic classification process.

The fingerprint expert has two main roles. The first is to successfully retrieve the print, and the second is to determine its origin.

There are numerous methods available to develop and retrieve latent prints. These vary from the common fingerprint powder through to the use of laser beams.[79] Once the print is retrieved the expert is then charged with comparing the known and unknown prints. Since this is a qualitative science, the accuracy of the process will be based largely on the expertise of the observer. For example, a print made on a curved surface such as a doorknob may not appear identical to a print made by the same finger on a flat surface such as a fingerprint card.[80] Another difficulty in fingerprint analysis is that caused by latent print "reversal". In an ordinary case, fingerprint powder adheres to the perspiration deposited from the pores located on the top of the ridges. In a "reversal" situation, the powder outlines the furrows, not the ridges. This occurs when great pressure is placed on the hands when they come in contact with an object. The pressure compresses the ridges and allows the perspiration to flow into the furrows. The fingerprint powder then outlines the furrows. This problem can be further complicated if uneven pressure causes a "partial reversal", resulting in a print where some of the powdered areas are ridges and other furrows.[81]

The ultimate responsibility of the fingerprint examiner is to determine if the observed characteristics agree and there are no unexplainable dissimilarities.[82] By tradition, though not from empirical study, fingerprint examiners in Canada will generally require ten points of similarity without any unexplainable dissimilarities before they will render an opinion as to identity. Dissimilarities may be caused by the flexibility in the skin, excessive pressure and movement during contact which may create distortions.[83]

---

79   W. Clements, *The Study of Latent Fingerprints* (Springfield, Ill.: Thomas, 1987), at 49
       and 74-77.
80   *Supra*, note 78 at 27.
81   *Supra*, note 79 at 82-84.
82   *Ibid.*
83   *Supra*, note 79 at 112.

Latent prints are affected by temperature and humidity. High temperature and low humidity cause evaporation which will dry out the print. If an item with a print on it is taken from a cold location and put in a warm place, condensation may form which could destroy the print. Rain and strong sunlight may have similar effects.[84] The passage of time alone will not destroy a print. If latent prints are subjected to ideal environmental conditions they may last indefinitely.[85]

A single fingerprint found at a crime scene may be sufficient to justify a conviction unless an innocent explanation for the print is offered.[86] Thus a print on a window was held sufficient to justify a conviction for break and enter, absent any reasonable explanation for its presence.[87] A print, however, may not be sufficient to establish legal possession. Legal possession requires control and a fingerprint merely establishes that the person handled the object. Additional evidence raising an inference of control will be necessary before a conviction for possession can result.[88]

6. NEW TECHNIQUES — A CAUTIONARY NOTE

The issue before the court in the case of *R. v. Medvedew*[89] was the admissibility of opinion evidence based on spectrographic analysis, commonly called voiceprint analysis. The majority of the Manitoba Court of Appeal ruled that the evidence was admissible and that the conflicting scientific opinions as to the reliability of the technique went to weight, not admissibility. A strong dissent authored by O'Sullivan J.A., argued in favour of a preliminary threshold for admissibility which would require that a new technique be generally accepted in the scientific community before it be admissible in a trial.

Shortly after the *Medvedew* decision, a study commissioned by the Federal Bureau of Investigation and performed by the United States National Research Council was released.[90] The

---

84 *Supra*, note 78 at 123.
85 *Supra*, note 78 at 123, 124.
86 *R. v. Keller* (1970), 1 C.C.C. (2d) 360 (Sask. C.A.); *R. v. MacFadden* (1981), 60 C.C.C. (2d) 305 (B.C.C.A.).
87 *R. v. Christopherson*, [1986] B.C.W.L.D. 4005 (C.A.), 10th September 1986.
88 *R. v. Breau* (1987), 33 C.C.C. (3d) 354 (N.B.C.A.); *R. v. Kuhn (No.1)* (1974), 15 C.C.C.(2d) 17 (Sask. C.A.).
89 (1979), 43 C.C.C. (2d) 434 (Man. C.A.).
90 R.H. Bolt, "On the Theory and Practice of Voice Identification" (Washington D.C.: National Academy of Sciences, 1979).

study concluded that spectrographic analysis was unreliable. Based on this study the technique has fallen into disuse except as an investigatory tool.

The *Medvedew* experience provides a practical example of the danger of accepting new scientific procedures that have not been subjected to the rigours of peer review and independent verification. It seems inappropriate to ask a jury to weigh conflicting scientific opinion on the validity of a new technique. That exercise belongs in the research laboratory, not in the courtroom.

In the United States, the general test for determining the admissibility of expert evidence in the case of a newly developed scientific technique, is that set out by the Court of Appeals for the District of Columbia in *Frye v. U.S.*:[91]

> Just when a scientific principle or discovery crosses the line between the experimental and demonstrable stages is difficult to define. Somewhere in this twilight zone the evidential force of the principle must be recognized, and while courts will go a long way in admitting expert testimony deduced from a well-recognized scientific principle or discovery, the thing from which the deduction is made must be sufficiently established to have gained general acceptance in the field in which it belongs.

This test does not require absolute certainty of result or unanimity of scientific opinion.[92] Rather it requires that the principles and procedures be generally accepted as reliable and accurate.[93] Conflicting testimony concerning the conclusions to be drawn by the experts, so long as they are based on generally accepted and reliable scientific principle, will normally affect the weight of the evidence as opposed to its admissibility.[94]

There are several recent United States decisions that have subjected DNA profiling to a *Frye* analysis.[95] There have not been any serious challenges to the technique itself. It has its origins in medical genetic research and is well accepted in the scientific community. The challenges have been directed at examining whether the laboratories properly performed the accepted scientific tests. There are two reported decisions that have rejected the DNA results because the laboratory did not comply with quality

---

91   293 F. 1013 at 1014 (D.C., 1923).
92   *U.S. v. Baller*, 519 F. 2d 463 at 466 (4th Circ., 1975).
93   *U.S. v. Franks*, 511 F. 2d 25 (6th Circ., 1975).
94   *Ibid.*
95   *Andrews v. Florida*, 533 So. 2d 841 (Fla. App., 1988); *Cobey v. Maryland*, 559 A. 2d 391 (Md. App., 1989); *Spencer v. Commonwealth*, 384 S.E. 2d 775 (Va., 1989); *People v. Castro*, 545 N.Y.S. 2d 985 (1989); *State v. Schwartz*, 447 N.W. 2d 422 (Minn., 1989).

control guidelines.[96] Arguably this is an issue of weight as opposed to admissibility. The American experience suggests that evidence from DNA profiling will soon be admitted routinely. The Canadian experience will probably be the same.

---

96   *People v. Castro, ibid.; State v. Schwartz, ibid.*

Chapter Six

Identity and Similar Fact Evidence

1. INTRODUCTION

The law relating to similar fact evidence has been described as a "pitted battlefield".[1] Given this description, the fear of unexploded shells makes one very cautious before gingerly treading into the area. As a result, this chapter is written with some trepidation.

"Similar fact" is the phrase used to describe evidence of discreditable conduct on the part of the accused at times other than those directly involved in the case before the court.[2] This chapter will first discuss the development of the general principles relating to this type of evidence. It will then deal with the use of this type of evidence as a means of proving identity. Finally, the related area of using evidence of disposition to prove identity will be discussed.

2. GENERAL PRINCIPLES

(1) From *Makin* to *Boardman*

The obvious starting point of any discussion of similar fact evidence is the case of *Makin v. A.G. for New South Wales*.[3] The Makins were charged with the murder of a baby boy who had been given permanently into their care by his mother. This baby was found buried in the back yard of the house that had been occupied by them at the relevant time. The issue before the court was the admissibility of evidence of the fact that three other babies' bodies

---

1   Lord Hailsham in *Boardman v. D.P.P.* (1974), 60 Cr. App. R. 165 at 176 (H.L.).
2   *R. v. Robertson* (1987), 58 C.R. (3d) 28 at 45 (S.C.C.). This conduct need not constitute a criminal offence. See also, *R. v. Butler* (1987), 84 Cr. App. R. 12 (C.A.).
3   [1894] A.C. 57 (P.C.).

were found buried in the same yard, and that nine other babies' bodies were found buried in the yards of two previous residences of the accuseds. In addition the court had to determine whether the evidence of four other women, that they had placed their babies into the Makins' care under similar arrangements, was admissible.

The court held that both classes of evidence were admissible. The principles upon which such admissibility was based are set out in the following classic and oft quoted statement of Lord Herschel:[4]

> It is undoubtedly not competent for the prosecution to adduce evidence tending to shew that the accused has been guilty of criminal acts other than those covered by the indictment, for the purpose of leading to the conclusion that the accused is likely from his criminal conduct or character to have committed the offence for which he is being tried. On the other hand, the mere fact that the evidence adduced tends to shew the commission of other crimes does not render it inadmissible if it be relevant to an issue before the jury, and it may be so relevant if it bears upon the question whether the acts alleged to constitute the crime charged in the indictment were designed or accidental, or to rebut a defence which would be otherwise be open to the accused.

The gist of this statement is that evidence of other criminal acts is admissible if it is relevant for a purpose other than to show that the accused is a person of bad character. However, Lord Herschell was prophetic when, immediately following the above statement, he asserted that:[5]

> The statement of these general principles is easy, but it is obvious that it may often be very difficult to draw the line and to decide whether a particular piece of evidence is on the one side or the other.

In an attempt to simplify this problem, the judiciary created a number of categories or pigeon-holes of relevant purposes. Examples of these categories are rebutting the defence of accident or involuntary conduct, rebutting the defence of ignorance or mistake of fact, proof of identity, proof of intent and rebutting the defence of innocent association.[6]

The House of Lords re-examined these principles in *Boardman v. D.P.P.*[7] In that case, the headmaster of a boarding school was charged with two sexual offences involving two of his male students. The evidence was that he approached each of these students in their bed at night and eventually suggested that they

---

4   *Ibid.*, at 65.
5   *Ibid.*, at 65.
6   See, *Cross on Evidence*, 5th ed. (London: Butterworth's, 1979), at 382-93.
7   *Supra*, note 1.

engage in homosexual conduct with him. The conduct was such that they played the active part and he the passive. The issue was whether the evidence relating to the incident with one pupil was admissible in relation to the other and *vice versa*; that is, could the stories be mutually corroborative? In holding that this evidence was admissible for that purpose, the court attempted to refine the principles originally set out in *Makin.* In implicitly rejecting the use of categories as the basis of admissibility, the various judges used the following language to set out the principles upon which admissibility of similar fact evidence was to be founded:

> But there may be cases where a judge, having both limbs of Lord Herschell's famous proposition in mind, considers that the interests of justice (of which the interests of fairness form so fundamental a component) make it proper that he should permit a jury when considering the evidence on a charge concerning one fact or set of facts to consider the evidence concerning another fact or set of facts if between the two there is such a close or *striking similarity* or such an underlying unity that probative force could fairly be yielded.[8]

> The basic principle must be that the admission of similar fact evidence (of the kind now in question) is exceptional and requires a strong degree of probative force. This probative force is derived, if at all, from the circumstance that the facts testified to by the several witnesses bear to each other such a *striking similarity* that they must, when judged by experience and common sense, either be all true, or have arisen from a cause common to the witnesses or from pure coincidence. The jury may, therefore, properly be asked to judge whether the right conclusion is that all are true, so that each story is supported by the other(s).[9]

> The test is . . . whether there is "such an underlying unity between the offences as to make coincidence an affront to common sense" or . . . "If the jury is precluded by some rule of law from taking the view that something is coincidence which is against all probabilities if the accused person is innocent, then it would seem to be a doctrine of law which prevents a jury from using what looks like common sense."[10]

> There are two further points of a general character that I would add. The "striking resemblances" or "unusual features", or whatever phrase is considered appropriate, to ignore which would affront common sense, may be either in the objective facts . . . or they may constitute a *striking similarity* in the accounts by witnesses of disputed transactions.[11]

> I think that one needs to find very *striking peculiarities* common to the two stories to justify the admission of one to support the other.[12]

---

8   *Ibid.*, at 172 *per* Lord Morris.
9   *Ibid.*, at 174, 175 *per* Lord Wilberforce.
10   *Ibid.*, at 181, 182 *per* Lord Hailsham.
11   *Ibid.*, at 182.
12   *Ibid.*, at 187 *per* Lord Cross.

It has, however, never been doubted that if the crime charged is committed in a uniquely or *strikingly similar* manner to other crimes committed by the accused, the manner in which the other crimes were committed may by evidence upon which a jury could reasonably conclude that the accused was guilty of the crime charged.[13][italics added]

The use of the phrase "strikingly similar"[14] indicates that the court was of the view that the degree of probative value of the proffered evidence was the key to admissibility. In order tó overcome the deleterious effects of similar fact evidence[15] a high degree of probative value was required before evidence of this type was admitted.[16] However, subsequent decisions in both Canada and England have moved away from this standard.

(2) Similar Fact After *Boardman*

(a) Canada

The Supreme Court of Canada re-examined some of the approaches to similar fact evidence in *Sweitzer v. R.*[17]. Although the issue in this case was identity, a recognized category of admissibility, the court stated that these categories, although useful, were only illustrative of the general rule set out in *Makin*.[18] Although not dealing directly with the concept of striking similarity, McIntyre J. implicitly rejected it by stating the following principle:[19]

---

13   *Ibid.*, at 189 *per* Lord Salmon.

14   The phrase was first used in *R. v. Sims*, [1946] 1 All E.R. 697 (C.A.).

15   The policy reasons behind the rule forbidding this type of evidence to show the character of the accused were put in the following way in *Wigmore on Evidence*, Tillers revision, vol. IA (1983), para. 58.2, at 1212 : "It may almost be said that it is because of the indubitable relevancy of specific bad acts of showing the character of the accused that such evidence is excluded. It is objectionable not because it has no appreciable probative value but because it has too much. The natural and inevitable tendency of the tribunal — whether judge or jury — is to give excessive weight to the vicious record of crime thus exhibited and either allow it to bear too strongly on the present charge or to take the proof of it as justifying a condemnation, irrespective of the accused's guilt of the present charge."

16   Two of the judges felt that the facts in this case were borderline at best: Lord Wilberforce, *supra*, note 7 at 175, and Lord Cross, *supra*, note 7 at 188.

17   (1982), 29 C.R. (3d) 97 (S.C.C.).

18   *Ibid.*, at 102.

19   *Ibid.*, at 101. In *R. v. Carpenter* (1982), 31 C.R. (3d) 261 (Ont. C.A.), the court held that striking similarity was not the test when the issue was accident, although it might be when the issue is identity.

The general principle described by Lord Herschell may be and should be applied in all cases where similar fact evidence is tendered, and its admissibility will depend upon the probative effect of the evidence, balanced against the prejudice caused to the accused by its admission . . .

The test of the probative value of the evidence balanced against the prejudicial effect of its admission was specifically endorsed by the same court in *R. v. Robertson.*[20] In that case Wilson J. enunciated the following proposition:[21]

> A general statement of the exclusionary rule is that evidence of the accused's discreditable conduct on past occasions, tendered to show his bad disposition, is inadmissible unless it is so probative of an issue or issues in the case as to outweigh the prejudice caused.

She then went on to specifically reject the notion of similarity as a controlling factor in determining admissibility She stated:[22]

> The degree of probative value required varies with prejudicial effect of the admission of the evidence. The probative value of the evidence may increase if there is a degree of similarity in circumstances and proximity in time and place. However, admissibility does not turn on such a striking similarity . . .

This test does not require that the evidence have a high degree of probative value as a pre-condition of admissibility. The facts in *Robertson* are illustrative of this proposition. Robertson was charged with sexual assault. It was alleged that he went to the complainant's apartment and, after gaining entry by a ruse, he asked her to sleep with him. When she refused, he struck her and then sexually assaulted her. The similar fact evidence in question was that of the complainant's roommate. She stated that the accused had, on a previous occasion, made a physical approach to her and asked her to sleep with him. When she refused, he apparently did no more than briefly put his arm around her. However, he repeatedly refused to leave and later when walking with the roommate pinned her against a wall and told her that he could never love her, he could only hurt her.

Wilson J. held that although the evidence was not of great probative value, it was nevertheless admissible. Since the accused desisted when the roomate rejected his advances the evidence was capable of both a sinister and innocent interpretation. Accordingly, its admission would cause very little prejudice. In the result,

---

20   (1987), 58 C.R. (3d) 28 (S.C.C.). See also, *R. v. Green* (1988), 62 C.R. (3d) 398 (S.C.C.).
21   *Ibid.*, at 45.
22   *Ibid.*, at 47.

it seems that a low degree of probative value is not in itself a sufficient reason to exclude similar fact evidence. It will only be excluded if the prejudicial effect of the evidence outweighs whatever probative value the evidence has.[23]

This rule has been criticized by Kerans J.A., speaking for a unanimous Alberta Court of Appeal, in *R. v. Wood*.[24] In that case he stated:

> Were the issue open to me, I would hesitate to endorse a rule that requires the trial judge to assess the degree of possible prejudicial effect and then balance it against the probative force of the evidence. First, quantification of the intangible and elusive impact of prejudice is extremely difficult and open to the suggestion of artifice. For example, in *Robertson*, one juror might not think ill at all of the accused because he was guilty of a crude and rude seduction attempt. Another might be outraged. Secondly, to compare the degree of likelihood of "forbidden" reasoning to the probative force of the evidence is to compare apples to oranges. I would have preferred to say, as I believe, did Lord Wilberforce, that *any* true propensity evidence triggers the need, as a condition to admissibility, that it have *compelling* probative force. Any real possibility of an unjust verdict should keep the evidence out unless the evidence is so compelling as to be almost determinative of guilt, in which case it would be unjust of the accused to take advantage of his biography to keep it out. As Lord Cross said in *Boardman* . . . that would be " . . . an affront to common sense".

In order to complete the picture the subsequent Supreme Court of Canada decision in *R. v. Morin*[25] must be dealt with. In that case the issue was whether psychiatric evidence that the accused had certain abnormal traits in common with the perpetrator of the crime was admissible in evidence. In determining this issue, Sopinka J., for a court unanimous on this point, discussed the general principles applicable to similar fact evidence. He stated:[26]

> In similar fact cases it is not sufficient to establish that the accused is a member of an abnormal group with the same propensities as the perpetrator. There must be some further distinguishing feature . . . The tendered evidence must tend to show that there is some striking similarity between the manner in which the perpetrator committed the criminal act and such evidence.

He then set out the following proposition:

---

23   This test has been applied in *R. v. Leaney* (1987), 38 C.C.C. (3d) 263, reversed in part 50 C.C.C. (3d) 289 (S.C.C.)[Alta.]; *R. v. Wood* (1987), 39 C.C.C. (3d) 212 (Alta. C.A.); *R. v. C.(M.H.)*, 46 C.C.C. (3d) 142 (B.C.C.A.).
24   *Ibid.*, at 223, 224.
25   (1988), 66 C.R. (3d) 1 (S.C.C.).
26   *Ibid.*, at 23.

> Apart from the requirement that the proffered evidence tend to show that the accused shared some distinctive feature with the perpetrator, such evidence will be excluded if its prejudicial effect overbears its probative value.

It would seem that a two stage test is being enunciated; the first stage being the existence of a striking similarity, and the second stage being that the prejudicial effect of the evidence not outweigh its probative value. As a result, it could be argued that this case is contradictory to *Robertson* in that it accepts striking similarity as a pre-condition to admissibility of similar fact evidence. However, it must be remembered that this case was not about the discreditable conduct of the accused. As a result, it is not a similar fact case in the true sense of the term. Rather, it is a case dealing with the disposition of the accused in its purest form.[27] Consequently, the principles enunciated in *Morin* may not be applicable to true similar fact cases. As well, given that *Robertson* is not cited in Sopinka J.'s judgment, it is highly unlikely that the court intended to change its previous pronouncement.

Also, the test in *Robertson* was subsequently confirmed by the Supreme Court in *R. v. D.(L.E.)*.[28] In that case, the admissibility of similar fact evidence was based on balancing probative value against prejudicial effect.

In the result, notwithstanding *Morin*, the test for admissibility of similar fact evidence in Canada seems to be the simple but nebulous one of balancing the probative value of the evidence with its prejudicial effect. If the former outweighs the latter the evidence is admissible, while if the reverse is true the evidence is excluded.

(b) England

The Court of Appeal has not adopted the phrase "strikingly similar" as the basis for determining the admissibility of similar fact evidence. The phrase has been described as merely a label to describe the underlying concept of positive probative value. In *R. v. Scarrott*,[29] Scarman L.J. put the proposition in this way:

> I now come to the one comment which this Court would make on the statement of general principle made by Lord Salmon. Hallowed

---

27   For a more detailed discussion of this form of evidence see, *infra*, this chapter, part 5.
28   (1989), 71 C.R. (3d) 1 (S.C.C.). See also, *R. v. B.(C.R.)*, [1990] 3 W.W.R. 385 (S.C.C.).
29   (1977), 65 Cr. App. R. 125 at 129, 130 (C.A.). See also, *R. v. Rance; R. v. Herron* (1975), 62 Cr. App. R. 118 (C.A.); *R. v. Shore* (1988), 89 Cr. App. R. 32 (C.A.).

though by now the phrase "strikingly similar" is . . . it is no more than a label. Like all labels it can mislead; it is a possible passport to error. It is, we repeat, only a label and it is not to be confused with the substance of the law which it labels.

Positive probative value is what the law requires, if similar fact evidence is to be admissible. Such probative value is not provided by the mere repetition of similar facts; there has to be some feature or features in the evidence sought to be adduced which provides a link — an underlying link as it has been called in some of the cases. The existence of such a link is not to be inferred from the mere similarity of facts which are themselves so common place that they can provide no sure ground for saying that they point to the commission by the accused of the offence under consideration.

The court did not expand on the meaning of positive pro-bative value. The phrase "strikingly similar" connotes a high degree of probative value, the phrase "positive probative value" does not necessarily lead to the same conclusion. In *R. v. Lunt*,[30] the court seemed to enunciate the proposition that the nature of positive probative value may vary with the nature of the issue. In this case they suggested that the following guidelines applied in cases where similar fact evidence was an issue.[31]

"(1) As a general rule the prosecution may not adduce evidence tending to show that the accused has been guilty of criminal acts other than those charged against him, or that the accused has a propensity to commit crimes of the kind charged. (2) Notwithstanding the general rule, however, evidence is admissible as 'similar fact' evidence if, but only if, it goes beyond showing a tendency to commit crimes of the kind charged and is positively probative in regard to the crime charged . . . (3) In order to decide whether the evidence is positively probative in regard to the crime charged it is first necessary to identify the issue to which the evidence is directed. Thus the evidence may be put forward, for example, to support an identification (where unusual points of similarity of appearance of method can be relevant and positively probative), or to prove intention, or to rebut a possible defence of accident or innocent association. In these several examples the answer to the question of what is positively probative may vary. (4) Once the issue has been identified the question will be: will the 'similar fact' evidence be positively probative, in the sense of assisting the jury to reach a conclusion on that issue on some ground other than the accused's bad character or disposition to commit the sort of crime with which he is charged? 'If the evidence of similar facts will not assist the jury to this end, it is irrelevant and inadmissible' . . . (5) If the evidence is positively probative in the foregoing sense the judge will neverthe-less have a discretion to exclude it if it 'would probably have a preju-dicial influence on the minds of the jury which would be out of proportion to its true evidential value'. . ."

30   (1986), 85 Cr. App. R. 244 (C.A.).
31   *Ibid.*, at 244, 245. See also, *R. v. Shore, supra*, note 29.

As a result, the best that can be said is that positive probative value means relevant evidence that shows more than bad character or disposition. Although not quite as nebulous as the Canadian test, it connotes a test that will not necessarily require that similar fact evidence have a high degree of probative value before it is admitted into evidence.

The balancing of probative value and prejudicial effect also plays a part in determining the ultimate admissibility of similar fact evidence in England. However, the balancing exercise is not determinative of the issue. Similar fact evidence that has positive probative value is admissible as a matter of law. However, even evidence meeting the above standard is subject to a discretion residing in the trial judge to exclude the evidence if its probative value is outweighed by its prejudicial effect.[32] In England this power is discretionary, whereas in Canada such evidence would be excluded as a matter of law.

(c) Australia

The High Court of Australia has stated that similar fact evidence will only be admitted if it has strong probative force. The reasons for this test and not some lesser one were put in the following way by Gibbs C.J., in *Perry v. R.*:[33]

> With all respect, it is not right to treat evidence which tends to show the commission by the accused of other criminal acts in the same way as any other circumstantial evidence. In the first place, as I have already said, a jury might place too much weight on the fact that the accused had a criminal tendency. Secondly, evidence of this kind will often raise difficult and doubtful questions as to whether the accused had in fact been guilty of other criminal acts, and may distract the jury from the vital issues in the case. It is therefore not enough that the evidence should be only technically relevant (otherwise than as showing a propensity); it must be really material; it must have strong probative force.

He also expressly stated that the discretion to exclude evidence because prejudicial effect outweighed probative value only came into play if the evidence was held to be admissible as a matter of law. This two step test is the same as in England.

---

32   See, generally, *supra*, Chapter 2, part 6(3)(a).
33   (1982), 44 A.L.R. 449 at 453, 454 (Aust. H.C.). This holding was re-affirmed in *Sutton v. R.* (1984), 51 A.L.R. 435 (Aust. H.C.).

Therefore, in Australia the test of admissibility is more stringent than in either Canada or England. It is only in that jurisdiction that the spirit of the reasoning in *Boardman* is still followed.

(3) Pre-conditions of Admissibility

In order for evidence of similar facts to be admitted there must be some link between the person who was involved in the similar fact evidence and the accused. An example of this principle in operation is the case of *Sweitzer v. R.*[34] In that case, the accused was initially charged with 15 counts of rape. As a result of an order severing the various counts he was tried on only one count. At the trial, the Crown successfully put into evidence the facts of the 14 other counts as well as the facts surrounding another incident which did not result in charges being laid. In 11 of these 15 incidents, there was no evidence identifying the accused as the perpetrator. As a result, the court held that these 11 incidents ought not to have been admitted. McIntyre J. put his reasons for this holding in the following way:[35]

> Before evidence may be admitted as evidence of similar facts, there must be a link between the allegedly similar facts and the accused. In other words, there must be some evidence upon which the trier of fact can make a proper finding that the similar facts to be relied upon were in fact the acts of the accused, for it is clear that, if they were not his own but those of another, they have no relevance to the matters at issue under the indictment.

The strength of the evidence required to link the accused with the evidence of similar facts is not clear. The language in *Sweitzer* seems to indicate that the test of admissibility is the same as that used by a trial judge in determining whether to withdraw a case from the jury.[36] Other cases have used phrases such as the evidence need not be conclusive[37] and only must be capable of supporting an inference that the offences were committed by one person.[38]

On the other hand, some cases have taken the position that the standard is equivalent to the civil standard of proof and that in order to be admissible the evidence must be such that it is

34   (1982), 29 C.R. (3d) 97 (S.C.C.); see also, *Harris v. D.P.P.*, [1952] A.C. 694 (H.L.).
35   *Ibid.*, at 102.
36   See, *supra*, Chapter 2, part 6(2).
37   *R. v. Ross*, [1979] 6 W.W.R. 435, affirmed [1980] 5 W.W.R. 261 (B.C.C.A.).
38   *R. v. Simpson* (1977), 35 C.C.C. (2d) 337 (Ont. C.A.).

"likely"[39] or "probable"[40] that the offences were committed by the same person.

Therefore, although there has to be a link between the accused and the perpetrator of the similar acts as a pre-condition of admissibility, the strength of that link is uncertain.

As well, since the weight to be given to the similar fact evidence is a question for the finder of fact, the evidence can be admitted even if there is a serious question as to whether or not the facts presented are true.[41] The questions of weight regarding the similar fact evidence are part of the fact finding function and not the question of admissibility.

In addition it seems clear that if the similar fact evidence constitutes a criminal offence, and the accused has been tried and acquitted of that criminal offence, evidence of that offence is not admissible under the guise of similar fact evidence. This was the situation in *R. v. Goodman*.[42] In that case the accused was charged with rape and the Crown sought to adduce evidence that the accused had raped another woman in similar circumstances. The accused had been tried and acquitted by a jury of the earlier offence. Galligan J. held that this evidence was not admissible. In so doing he followed the English case of *G.(an infant) v. Coltart*.[43] This holding was obviously one based on a concern for the finality of a jury verdict. In the latter case, Widgery L.J. put the reasons for the decision as follows:[44]

> If an accused charged with a criminal offence is acquitted by a court of competent jurisdiction, it seems to me clear that the prosecution on a subsequent charge brought against that accused cannot seek to prove that he was guilty of the first charge, contrary to the verdict of the court on that charge, in order to obtain the benefit of any conclusion which might flow from such guilt.

Although an older case, *R. v. Ollis*,[45] came to the opposite conclusion, it is unlikely that it will be followed by a contemporary court.

---

39   *R. v. Morris* (1969), 54 Cr. App. R. 69 (C.A.); *R. v. Naum* (1973), 22 C.R.N.S. 193 (Ont. H.C.).
40   *R. v. Lawson* (1971), 14 C.R.N.S. 377 (Alta. C.A.); *R. v. Mitchell* (1989), 70 C.R. (3d) 71 (Ont. C.A.).
41   *R. v. Rance; R. v. Herron* (1975), 62 Cr. App. R. 118 (C.A.).
42   (1982), 9 C.C.C. (3d) 285 (Ont. H.C.).
43   [1967] 1 All E.R. 271 (C.A.).
44   *Ibid.*, at 276.
45   [1900] 2 Q.B. 758 (C.C.R.).

3. SIMILAR FACTS AS PROOF OF IDENTITY

(1) General Principles

Evidence of similar facts has long been admitted on the question of identity. In fact, similar fact evidence may be the only evidence admitted at trial on the issue of identity.[46] An early case setting out this proposition was that of *Thompson v. R.*[47] In that case, the accused was charged with committing acts of gross indecency with two boys. The evidence was that these acts were committed on 16th March. The perpetrator arranged to meet the boys on 19th March. On the latter date, the accused came in contact with the boys but gave them some money and told them to go away. The accused had an explanation for his actions but the boys testified that he had done this because he had recognized a police officer who was accompanying them. The issue in the case was whether the accused was the man who had committed the acts of gross indecency with the boys on 16th March. The accused presented an alibi for that date.

The contested evidence consisted of powder puffs that were found in the accused's possession at the time of his arrest and photographs of naked boys in various positions.

The court held that this evidence was admissible on the question of identity as it tended to show that the accused had the same abnormal propensities as the person who committed the acts of gross indecency with the two boys. Although this case is not strictly a case involving discreditable conduct, it is an early example of the use of evidence reflecting upon an accused's character to prove identity.

A prime example of the use of similar fact evidence to prove identity is *R. v. Straffen*.[48] In that case the accused had previously been found unfit to stand trial for the murder of two young girls. He subsequently escaped from his place of confinement and during the time he was at large another young girl was killed. The accused denied being the killer. Other than the fact that he seemed to have some knowledge of the fact that a young girl had been killed when he had no outside means of obtaining that knowledge, there was no evidence connecting the accused with the killing. The Crown sought to admit evidence of the two previous killings. The

---

46   *R. v. Seguin* (1982), 31 C.R. (3d) 271 (Ont. C.A.).
47   [1918] A.C. 221 (H.L.).
48   [1952] 2 All E.R. 657 (C.A.).

similarities between these killings and the instant one were that each of the young girls was strangled without apparent motive, none of them were sexually molested, and, although the bodies could have easily been hidden, all of the bodies were left where they could be found easily. The court held that these similar traits permitted the admission of this evidence in accordance with the principles set out in *Makin* and *Thompson*.

The reasons supporting the use of such evidence to prove identity were set out in the following manner by Lord Goddard L.C.J. in the case of *R. v. Sims*:[49]

> So also where there is an issue of as to identity of the accused, we think that evidence is admissible of a series of similar acts done by him to other persons, because, while one witness to one act might be mistaken in identifying him, it is unlikely that a number of witnesses identifying the same person in relation to a series of acts with the self-same characteristics would all be mistaken. In all these cases, the evidence of other acts may tend to show the accused to be of bad disposition, but it also shows something more.

Although a number of earlier cases seemed to indicate that similar fact evidence was not admissible on the question of identity,[50] it is clear that this evidence is admissible in Canada. In *R. v. Bird*,[51] the accused was charged with extorting sexual intercourse from the complainant. The evidence was that he had called the complainant in the middle of the day and impersonated a friend of the family. The gist of the allegation against him was that he told the complainant that if she did not have sexual intercourse with a man who would come see her, indecent pictures of her husband and another woman would be circulated. A man identified as the accused appeared and the act took place. It was a somewhat unusual event as the man left both his clothes and his glasses on during the incident. The Crown sought to introduce the evidence of two other women. One of them testified that she received a telephone call from a man, whom she believed to be a friend. This man related a story whose culmination was that the witness would have to have intercourse with another man in order to retrieve indecent pictures taken of the friend and another woman. The caller intimated that he would commit suicide unless this was done. A man she identified as the accused appeared at her door and they had intercourse. Again, the man did not take off his glasses or clothes.

49   [1946] 1 All E.R. 697 (C.A.).
50   *Brunet v. R.* (1928), 50 C.C.C. 1 (S.C.C.); *R. v. Campbell* (1946), 86 C.C.C. 410 (B.C.C.A.); *Holmes v. R.* (1949), 95 C.C.C. 73 (Que. C.A.).
51   [1970] 3 C.C.C. 340 (B.C.C.A.).

The second situation was different. A man called a home and spoke to an 18-year-old girl living there. He stated that he was a doctor and had to speak to her about her mother. He told the girl that the mother had a venereal disease and that he was afraid that it would be communicated to her. He then came to her house and, under the pretence of conducting a medical examination, asked to examine her vagina. When she refused, the person left.

Although the first incident was in substance, if not in detail, identical to the circumstances of the offence, the second was significantly different. Notwithstanding this difference, the court held that the evidence of both incidents was admissible as a "unique brand or hallmark".[52] This consisted of the fact that the man sought sexual gratification from women by contacting them in the middle of the day and relating a far-fetched story to accomplish his purpose. As a result, this evidence was admissible to confirm the identification of the accused by the complainant.

The use of similar fact evidence as proof of identity was approved by the Supreme Court of Canada in *Alward v. R.*[53] In that case, the allegation was that the accused had gone to a hotel room, knocked on the door, forced entry, and robbed the occupant, beating him in the process. As a result of this beating the man died. The court held that evidence relating to the robbery of two other individuals in their hotel rooms carried out the next day was admissible. The accused also gained entry into these hotel rooms by means of a ruse and subsequently robbed the occupants. In holding that the evidence was admissible on the question of identity, the court stated:[54]

> In view of the circumstances that the three incidents were so very close in time and the robberies were carried out in such a startlingly similar manner, I am of the opinion that evidence on the other two incidents was admissible within the jurisprudence . . .

The admissibility of similar fact evidence is peculiarly dependent on the individual facts of a case. In cases involving identity it is difficult to determine in advance which evidence will be admitted[55] and which will be excluded.[56] However there is a

---

52   *Ibid.*, at 345.
53   (1977), 39 C.R.N.S. 281 (S.C.C.).
54   *Ibid.*, at 309.
55   For example, in *R. v. Giovannone* (1960), 45 Cr. App. R. 31 (C.A.), evidence that the accused played the same role in other similar frauds was admitted as evidence to show he was the person who played the role in the case before the court. In *R. v. Grimaldi (No.2)*, [1979] 1 W.W.R. 554, leave to appeal to S.C.C. dismissed 14 A.R. 360, evidence of the fact that the accused had offered three separate women a ride home

body of authority for the proposition that in cases involving identity a higher standard is required than in other cases involving similar fact evidence.
Cross has put the proposition in the following way:[57]

> It is in such cases that the courts require the very strongest evidence of similarity, indeed peculiarity, of technique because the evidence must by itself be so compelling as to be the equivalent of a signature, or the discovery of the accused's fingerprints in each separate connection.

Although a number of cases accepted the principle that similar fact evidence on the issue of identity required a higher standard of admissibility or some unique characteristic,[58] these cases were decided prior to the Supreme Court of Canada's decision in *R. v. Robertson*.[59] As discussed above, this decision seemed to lower the standard of admissibility in similar fact cases generally. This issue was considered in *R. v. Wood*.[60] In that case the accused was charged with a murder in Calgary. The victim had been killed by means of a ligature, sexually mutilated, and left on the street. At the trial, evidence was admitted that the accused had subsequently killed another woman in Toronto by means of a ligature, and that the woman had been sexually mutilated albeit in a different manner from the woman in Calgary. The Alberta Court of Appeal ruled that this evidence ought not to have been admitted. In so doing, the court held that if evidence is to be admitted on the question of identity it must be said that:[61]

---

and then threatened to kill them if they did not comply with his sexual demands was admissible to prove that the accused was the perpetrator in all of the instances.

56   For example, in *R. v. Willett* (1972), 10 C.C.C. (2d) 36 (Ont. C.A.), evidence that the accused was found in the residence of another woman after having broken in was not admissible on a charge of rape where the perpetrator had broken into the residence in order to commit the offence. In *R. v. Demyen (No.2)* (1976), 31 C.C.C. (2d) 383 (Sask. C.A.), evidence that the accused had previously assaulted a child of the woman with whom he was living was held not to be admissible on a charge of murdering the child, of the same sex and age, of a woman whom he had married. In *R. v. Leaney* (1987), 38 C.C.C. (3d) 263 (Alta. C.A.), evidence that the accused had committed a break and enter was not admissible on a charge of robbery, which had taken place six hours earlier.

57   *Cross on Evidence*, 6th ed. (London: Butterworth's,1985), at 323.

58   *R. v. McNamara (No.1)* (1981), 56 C.C.C. (2d) 193 at 288, affirmed 19 C.C.C. (3d) 1 (S.C.C.) [Ont.]; *R. v. Craig* (1982), 1 C.C.C. (3d) 416 at 419 (B.C.C.A.); *R. v. Carpenter*, (1982), 31 C.R. (3d) 261 at 267 (Ont. C.A.). In *R. v. Dickinson* (1984), 40 C.R. (3d) 384 at 389 (Ont. C.A.), Martin J.A. stated: "The degree of similarity required to give similar fact evidence the high degree of probative force required will, however, vary according to the other evidence in the case and the issues raised by the evidence."

59   (1987), 58 C.R. (3d) 28 (S.C.C.). See, *supra*, this chapter, part 2 (2)(a).

60   (1987), 39 C.C.C. (3d) 212 (Alta. C.A.).

61   *Ibid.*, at 218.

. . . the methodology for the two crimes was not only similar but also so unique that it could fairly be said that whoever did one likely did the other.

The court held that the evidence in this case was not so unique and as a result its prejudicial value was so high that a strong degree of probative force would be required before it was admissible. The court combined the language of uniqueness with the concept of probative force and prejudicial value. It seemed to be saying that when the issue was identity, similarity equivalent to uniqueness must be established in order to overcome the prejudicial value occasioned by this type of evidence. Whether or not this reasoning is followed by other courts remains to be seen. If it is, it is a movement toward a specific test of admissibility and a movement away from the generalized test of balancing probative value with prejudicial effect enunciated in *Robertson*.

(2) The Charge to the Jury

The contents of the charge to the jury in cases involving similar fact evidence were recently outlined by Sopinka J. for the majority of the Supreme Court of Canada in the case of *R. v. D.(L.E.).*[62] The purpose of the charge was to minimize the three inherent prejudicial effects of similar fact evidence. These effects are:[63]

> The first is that the jury, if it accepts that the accused committed the prior "bad acts", may therefore assume that the accused is a "bad person" who is likely to be guilty of the offence charged . . .
> The second effect on the jury might be a tendency for the jury to punish the accused for past misconduct by finding that accused guilty of the offence charged. The third danger is that the jury might become confused as it concentrates on resolving whether the accused actually committed the similar acts. The jury members' attention is deflected from the main purpose of their deliberations, which is the transaction charged. Having resolved the first matter, there is a danger that they will substitute their verdict on that matter for their verdict on the issue which they are in fact trying.

In order to minimize these dangers:[64]

> The jury should be instructed that if it accepts the evidence of the similar acts, that evidence is relevant for the limited purpose for which it was admitted. The jury must be specifically warned that it is not to

---

62   (1989), 71 C.R. (3d) 1 (S.C.C.).
63   *Ibid.*, at 20, 21.
64   *Ibid.*, at 21.

rely on the evidence as proof that the accused is the sort of person who would commit the offence charged and on that basis infer that the accused is in fact guilty of the offence charged.

The nature of the charge to the jury in cases involving similar fact evidence when the issue is identity was outlined by the Ontario Court of Appeal in *R. v. Simpson.*[65] Martin J.A.stated:

> First, the trial Judge should caution the jury that they are not to use the evidence on one count in order to infer that the accused is a person whose character or disposition is such that he is likely to have committed the offence or offences charged in the other count or counts. The trial Judge should then instruct the jury that they are entitled to find from the evidence, although they are not required to do so, that the offences charged have characteristics in common that are so similar that it is likely that they were committed by one person, but that it is entirely for them whether such an inference should be made. The trial Judge should then refer the jury to the similarities in the circumstances of the offences. The jury should be further instructed that if they conclude that the offences charged were likely committed by one person then the evidence on each count may assist them in deciding whether the accused committed the offence charged in the other count or counts. If, however, they do not draw the inference that the offences were likely committed by one person, they should, in reaching a decision on any count, consider only the evidence on that count and put out of their minds the evidence on any other count or counts. Finally, it is of the utmost importance that the trial Judge should make it clear to the jury that the accused must not be convicted on any count unless they are satisfied beyond a reasonable doubt that he is guilty of that offence.

Although this charge deals with a situation where the similar facts form the basis for other charges in the same indictment, it would be equally applicable in other cases.

4. THE USE OF SIMILAR FACTS BY THE ACCUSED

Evidence of similar facts can be of assistance to the accused in two ways. Firstly, if the accused can show that he was not the perpetrator of any one of the incidents relied upon by the prosecution as evidence of similar facts, doubt would be cast on the whole of the prosecution case.[66] An interesting example of that process took place in *R. v. Parent.*[67] In that case, the accused was charged with offences relating to eight sexual assaults. These assaults

65   (1977), 35 C.C.C. (2d) 337 at 346, 347 (Ont. C.A.). See also, *R. v. Mitchell* (1989), 70 C.R. (3d) 71 (Ont. C.A.).
66   *R. v. Pickard*, [1960] Crim. L.R. 125.
67   (1988), 46 C.C.C. (3d) 414 (Alta. Q.B.).

202 Identification Evidence

contained a number of similarities and the Crown was going to rely on similar fact evidence to identify the accused as the guilty party. However, during the course of the trial, evidence was given by an expert in genetics who had done tests using DNA fingerprinting.[68] The results of his tests were such that the accused was absolutely eliminated as the perpetrator of three of the sexual assaults. Absent other evidence, the accused was acquitted of all of the remaining counts save one. In the result, evidence casting doubt upon the accused's participation in a similar fact event may, but will not necessarily, result in an acquittal.

Secondly, the accused may choose to adduce evidence of crimes committed in a similar manner to the transaction before the court in order to show that he or she was not the perpetrator of these other events. It would then be argued that this evidence creates a doubt about the accused's participation in the events before the court.

A good example is the case of Adolph Beck.[69] Beck was tried on ten counts of fraud in 1896. These frauds were performed in a highly unusual manner. At the trial, Beck's counsel tried to show that a series of almost identical offences were committed in 1877 and that Beck was not the perpetrator of these earlier frauds. Had he been permitted to do so, counsel would have shown that documents written by the perpetrator in 1877 were in the same handwriting as those written by the culprit in 1896. As it could be proved that Beck had been in Peru from 1873 to 1884, it would then be argued that since he could not have committed the 1877 offences he could not be guilty of the 1896 offences. Unfortunately, the trial judge did not permit this evidence to be adduced. This ruling was criticized by the Committee of Inquiry into the Beck case which stated that it resulted in a miscarriage of justice.[70]

Similarly, in the Australian case of *R. v. Clune*,[71] the Supreme Court of Victoria held that the trial judge ought not to have prevented counsel from trying to show that a robbery similar to the one before the court had taken place while the accused was in custody.

This process was carried further in the case of *R. v. A.(G.J.)*.[72] In that case, the accused was charged with sexually assaulting his

---

68   See, *supra*, Chapter 5.
69   See, E.R. Watson, *The Trial of Adolph Beck* (London: Butterworth's, 1924), and, *supra*, Chapter 2, part 2(1).
70   *Ibid.*, at 257, 258.
71   [1982] V.R. 1 (S.C.).
72   (1989), 70 C.R. (3d) 298 (B.C. Co. Ct.).

young niece. The trial judge permitted the accused to adduce evidence that the child's father, the accused's brother, had sexually assaulted his sisters when they were approximately the same age as the complainant. These assaults were committed in a strikingly similar manner to that complained of by the child.

The legal principles calling for the exclusion of similar fact evidence are based upon the fact that such evidence is prejudicial to the accused. Once the accused chooses to adduce such evidence, this concern disappears. As a result, the only significant impediment to admissibility is relevance.

Therefore the accused can adduce evidence either through cross-examination, or by calling witnesses to show that he or she did not commit a similar act, in order to cast doubt on the Crown's allegations in the case before the court.

5. PROPENSITY AND IDENTITY

(1) Evidence by the Prosecution: From *Thompson* to *Morin.*

The principles governing similar fact evidence have been applied to those cases where the prosecution seeks to prove identity, not by means of the accused's previous actions, but by evidence relating to his or her disposition or propensity. *R. v. Thompson*[73] is a classic case involving this type of evidence. The finding of the powder puffs and photographs showed that the accused was a person with an "abnormal propensity" of the same kind as that of the perpetrator and could be used to bolster the other identification evidence in the case. Although it is highly likely that if the facts of this case were to be put before a court today, the result would be different,[74] the principle enunciated still

---

73 [1918] A.C. 221 (H.L.).
74 In *R. v. Morris* (1969), 54 Cr. App. R. 69 (C.A.), Widgery L.J., in referring to *Thompson*, stated: " ... it may very well be that, if similar facts arose today, a different conclusion would be reached."
    In *R. v. Troughton*, [1983] 1 W.W.R. 673 (Man. C.A), the court held that magazines depicting young boys with exposed genitalia were not admissible to prove identity when the allegation was one of indecent assault on young boys. Similarly, in *R. v. Taylor* (1982), 66 C.C.C. (2d) 437 (Ont. C.A.), the court held that on a charge of indecent assault on a male it was improper to cross-examine the accused on whether or not he was a practising homosexual.

remains. Evidence of abnormal propensity is admissible to prove identity.[75]

In *R. v. Morris*,[76] the accused was charged with the murder of a young girl. At the same time he pleaded guilty to a charge of indecently assaulting another young girl. Indecent photographs of the second young girl were found in the accused's home. Although there was no force used to obtain the photographs, the court held that they were admissible to prove the identity of the murderer since the bodily position of the murdered girl was similar to some of the positions depicted in the photographs. The principle upon which this evidence was admissible was put in the following way:[77]

> In this case to render the evidence of the photographs admissible, it is not enough for the Crown to show that they indicate a tendency on the part of the applicant to sexual deviation. The Crown in order to make the evidence admissible must go further and show that there is a sufficient similarity between the applicant's conduct when the photographs were taken, and the conduct of the murder, to give a real and positive indication that they were one and the same man. It is not necessary to show that the circumstances are so similar that the same man *must* have been concerned in each case. The admissibility of the evidence depends on whether the similarities are sufficient to show that the applicant and the murderer have common characteristics which are so unusual that it is likely that they are one and the same man.

Another form of evidence of propensity is expert psychiatric or psychological evidence regarding the accused. The principles surrounding the admissibility of this type of evidence to prove identity were set out by the Supreme Court of Canada in *R. v. Morin*.[78] In that case, the primary issue was the identity of the murderer of a young girl. However, the accused took the position that if it could be proved that he did commit the murder, he was insane at the time. When cross-examining one of the defence psychiatrists Crown counsel brought out the point that the accused suffered from a psychiatric illness but only a small percentage of persons having this illness would have been capable of committing the offence in the abnormal fashion in which it was committed. On the facts of this case, the court held that the trial judge was correct when he told the jury that they ought to ignore this

---

75   In *R. v. Twomey*, [1971] Crim. L.R. 277 (C.A.), the court held that evidence that the accused was an aggressive homosexual was properly admitted.

76   *Supra*, note 74.

77   *Ibid.*, at 80.

78   (1988), 66 C.R. (3d) 1 (S.C.C.).

evidence on the question of identity. Nevertheless, Sopinka J. went on to hold that evidence of propensity was admissible at the behest of the prosecution. He stated that the admissibility of this evidence was governed by the following principles:[79]

> . . . when the prosecution tenders expert psychiatric evidence, the trial judge must determine whether it is relevant to an issue in the case, apart from its tendency to show propensity. If it is relevant to another issue (e.g. identity), it must then be determined whether its probative value on that issue outweighs its prejudicial effect on the propensity question. In sum, if the evidence's *sole* relevance or *primary* relevance is to show disposition, then the evidence must be excluded.

The court adopted the same general principles for the admissibility of this type of evidence as evidence of conduct on the part of the accused which constitutes similar fact evidence. That is the probative value of the evidence on some issue other than propensity must outweigh its prejudicial effect.

However, Sopinka J. put a higher standard on this type of evidence when the issue was identity. He stated:[80]

> In my opinion, in order to be relevant on the issue of identity the evidence must tend to show that the accused shared a distinctive unusual behavioural trait with the perpetrator of the crime. The trait must be sufficiently distinctive that it operates as a badge or mark identifying the perpetrator.
>
> Conversely, the fact that the accused is a member of an abnormal group some of the members of which have the unusual behavioural characteristics shown to have been possessed by the perpetrator is not sufficient. In some cases, it may, however, be shown that all members of the group have the distinctive unusual characteristics. If a reasonable inference can be drawn that the accused has those traits, then the evidence is relevant, subject to the trial judge's obligation to exclude if its prejudicial effect outweighs its probative value. The greater number of persons in society having these tendencies, the less relevant the evidence on the issue of identity and the more likely that its prejudicial effect predominates over its probative value.

In the result, propensity evidence tendered by the prosecution, including expert evidence, is admissible on the issue of identity if it involves a distinctive and unusual trait and its probative value outweighs its prejudicial effect.

(2) Evidence by the Accused

Evidence of propensity presented by the accused can be used to demonstrate one of two propositions. First, that the accused's

---

79   *Ibid.*, at 26.
80   *Ibid.*, at 26, 27.

character is such that he or she did not have the propensity to commit the offence before the court or second, that another person who is in some way linked to the offence had the propensity to commit the crime.

The first proposition is illustrated by the case of *R. v. Lupien.*[81] In that case the accused was charged with attempted gross indecency with a transvestite. Although he was found in an extremely compromising position by the police, his defence was that he believed that the person he was with was a woman. In order to support this defence, he wanted to call a psychiatrist to testify that he had a certain kind of defence mechanism that made him react violently against any homosexual activity. This evidence, if accepted, would bolster the accused's contention that he did not engage in such activity. The majority of the Supreme Court of Canada[82] held that this evidence ought to have been admitted at the trial as relevant to the issues before the court.

However, it seems that only unusual personality traits on the part of the actual perpetrator will come within the parameters of this rule. In *R. v. Robertson,*[83] the accused, who was charged with committing a brutal murder, wanted to present psychiatric testimony to the effect that a propensity for violence was not part of his psychological make-up. Martin J.A. held that the evidence of the accused's disposition would only be admissible in the following circumstances:[84]

> Evidence that the offence had distinctive features which identified the perpetrator as a person possessing unusual personality traits constituting him a member of an unusual and limited class of persons would render admissible evidence that the accused did not possess the personality characteristics of the class of persons to which the perpetrator of the crime belonged.

In the result the evidence was not admissible for the following reasons:[85]

> In my view, psychiatric evidence with respect to disposition or its absence is admissible on behalf of the defence, if relevant to an issue in

---

81   [1970] 2 C.C.C. 193 (S.C.C.).
82   Ritchie J. (Spence J. concurring) held that the evidence ought to have been admitted and as a result a new trial should be ordered. Hall J. agreed with them on this point but held that there was no substantial wrong or miscarriage of justice occasioned by refusing to admit the evidence. Martland J. (Judson J. concurring) held that the evidence ought not to have been admitted. In the result, the accused won the battle but lost the war.
83   (1975), 21 C.C.C. (2d) 385 (Ont. C.A.).
84   *Ibid.,* at 423.
85   *Ibid.,* at 429, 430.

the case, where the disposition in question constitutes a characteristic feature of an abnormal group falling within the range of study of the psychiatrist, and from whom the jury can, therefore, receive appreciable assistance with respect to a matter outside the knowledge of persons who have not made a special study of the subject. A *mere* disposition for violence, however is not so uncommon as to constitute a feature characteristic of an abnormal group falling within the special field of study of the psychiatrist and permitting psychiatric evidence to be given of the absence of such disposition in the accused.

The requirement that the accused's disposition contain some distinctive or unusual trait seems to be the same whether the disposition of the accused is put into issue by the defence or the prosecution. This requirement is somewhat less stringent when the accused wishes to lead evidence regarding the disposition of a third person in order to show that it was more probable that that person committed the offence before the court.

In *McMillan v. R.*,[86] the accused was charged with killing his child. He led psychiatric evidence to show that his wife had a psychopathic personality disturbance with brain damage. The psychiatrist gave the opinion that, given the nature of this disturbance, she was a danger to the child. This evidence was held to be admissible to show that the wife was a more probable perpetrator than the accused. The death of the child in this case did not have any unusual characteristics.[87] As a result, simply showing that the wife had an abnormal personality was sufficient. The court adopted the following reasoning from the Privy Council decision of *Lowery v. R.*[88]:

> "It is, we think, one thing to say that such evidence is excluded when tendered by the Crown in proof of guilt, but quite another to say that it is excluded when tendered by the accused in disproof of his own guilt. We see no reason of policy or fairness which justifies or requires the exclusion of evidence relevant to prove the innocence of an accused person."

---

86   (1977), 33 C.C.C. (2d) 360, affirming 23 C.C.C. (2d) 160 (S.C.C.)[Ont.].
87   The argument that the evidence was only admissible if the crime could only have been committed by a person with an abnormal personality was specifically rejected by the Ontario Court of Appeal, *ibid.*, at 173. Martin J.A. stated: "I do not consider that because the crime under consideration was not one that could only be committed by a person with a special or abnormal propensity, psychiatric evidence with respect to Mrs. McMillan's disposition was, therefore, inadmissible in the circumstances of this case."
      It is of interest to note that Martin J.A.'s statement in *Robertson, supra*, note 83 at 423, is not discussed.
88   [1974] A.C. 85 at 102 (P.C.), *per* Lord Morris of Borth-y-Gest.

Evidence of the disposition of third parties can be led by means other than expert opinion evidence. For example, in *R. v. Kendall and McKay*,[89] both accused were charged with murder. The killing took place in the victim's bathtub and death was caused by numerous knife wounds. Each accused blamed the other for the killing. The issue in the case was whether Kendall ought to have been able to adduce the evidence of a woman who would state that on another occasion she had been violently attacked by McKay. She would testify that she was repeatedly assaulted from 8:00 p.m. until daylight, made to go into a bathtub where she was punched until the water turned red and threatened with a knife when she tried to escape.

The court held that although the prosecution could not have led this evidence, it was admissible on the part of Kendall to show that McKay had a disposition to commit crimes of violence and was likely to have committed the offence. The only pre-condition to the admissibility of this evidence was that it was relevant.

In the result, evidence led by the accused as to his own disposition may require that the crime have been committed by a person with an unusual or distinctive personality. In most cases, this would require psychiatric evidence to be adduced. However, if the accused wishes to lead evidence that a third party has the disposition or propensity to commit the offence, this propensity or disposition need not be distinctive. This disposition can be proved by utilizing experts or through lay witnesses. However, a precondition to the admissibility of evidence of a third person's disposition is that there must be some other evidence linking that person to the offence.[90]

---

89   (1987), 35 C.C.C. (3d) 105 (Ont. C.A.).
90   *R. v. McMillan, supra*, note 86; *R. v. Williams* (1985), 44 C.R. (3d) 351 (Ont. C.A.).

Chapter Seven

Alibi Evidence

Alibi defences do not enjoy a great reputation in the legal community. Although the court will direct the jury to the contrary, there is concern that the jury will try the accused on the alibi and not upon the issue in the trial.[1] As one leading counsel indicated:[2]

> The weakness or failure of the defence in establishing its theory is made the criterion, and not the guilt or innocence of the person charged.

Lord Devlin offered this observation:[3]

> Experienced advocates think that there must be many cases in which a jury resolves its doubts about the identity by its disbelief of the alibi: if he was not the man, why does he lie about where he was?

It is a simple truism that some alibis are impossible to establish definitively. "I was home in bed, alone" is one. The *Virag* case, which is one of the cases that led to the Devlin Inquiry, is another good example. Virag's alibi was that he was at a gambling club. Many of the people there were of poor character and would have made poor witnesses. Any that could remember his appearance could not establish the date. The story was true, but Lord Devlin conceded that it was, "improbable that conclusive proof of it would have been obtainable".[4] Failure to prove the alibi left the trial judge and the jury believing it must be false.[5]

These difficulties with alibi defences mean that there may be practical and tactical decisions to be made before mounting the

---

1   G.A. Martin, Q.C., *Evidence: Special Lectures of the Law Society of Upper Canada* (Toronto: De Boo, 1955), at 18.

2   E.F.B. Johnston, "Evidence of Accused Persons", [1931] 4 D.L.R. 1 at 6.

3   *Report to the Secretary of State for the Home Department of the Departmental Committee on Evidence of Identification in Criminal Cases (Devlin Report)* (London: H.M.S.O., 1976), para. 3.114.

4   *Ibid.*, para. 3.115.

5   *Ibid.*, para. 3.116.

defence. In order to try to create the fairest legal framework in which to present the defence, the law, in the words of the Devlin Inquiry, must be applied and developed in such a way as to prevent the alibi evidence from being undervalued in the eyes of the jury.[6]

1. DEFINITION

The word "alibi" derives from the Latin adverb for "elsewhere".[7] An alibi is thus an assertion by the accused that he · or she was at a particular place or in a particular area at the critical time and therefore was not at the place where the offence was alleged to have been committed. It is the counterpart of the evidence of identification, or, as Lord Devlin described it, "Identification evidence and alibi evidence are . . . opposite sides of the same coin."[8]

There is occasionally some confusion over whether a defence of alibi has been raised. For example, in *R. v. Gottschall*,[9] the accused, at her trial for murder, testified that her brother was responsible for the crime. The trial judge charged the jury that they could take into account the failure of the accused to make a timely disclosure of her "alibi".[10] The Nova Scotia Court of Appeal stated that this was not an alibi as the accused was not asserting that she was elsewhere. Further, the court said that no comment should have been made about failure to disclose the story at an earlier time. To do so was to imply an obligation to disclose one's defence to the police when clearly no such obligation exists. [11]

Several English cases have dealt with the definition of "alibi" since statutory obligations of disclosure only apply to true alibis.[12] The Criminal Court of Appeal has made it clear that an alibi is an assertion as to the accused's whereabouts at the time of the crime.[13] Thus, stated the court:[14]

---

6   *Ibid.*, para. 1.2.
7   *Black's Law Dictionary*, 4th ed. (St. Paul: West Publishing Co., 1968); *Jowitt's Dictionary of English Law*, 2nd ed. (London: Sweet & Maxwell, 1977).
8   *Supra*, note 3, para. 1.2.
9   (1983), 10 C.C.C. (3d) 447 (N.S.C.A.). See, in addition, *R. v. Cavanagh* (1976), 33 C.C.C. (2d) 134 (Ont. C.A.); *R. v. Sgambelluri* (1978), 43 C.C.C. (2d) 496, leave to appeal to S.C.C. refused 43 C.C.C. (2d) 496n [Ont.]; *R. v. Handleman* (1980), 57 C.C.C. (2d) 242 (Ont. C.A.).
10   See Timely Disclosure of Alibi, *infra*, this chapter, part 4.
11   *R. v. Handleman, supra*, note 9.
12   Criminal Justice Act, 1967 (Eng.), c. 80, s. 11.
13   *R. v. Lewis* (1969), 53 Cr. App. R. 76 (C.A.).
14   *Ibid.*, at 81.

... if the accused is charged with a robbery which is alleged to have been committed on a Monday, and part of the evidence against him is that he was seen on the Tuesday driving a van which contained the stolen goods, he may tender evidence of alibi relating to the Tuesday without giving notice under the section.

This principle was applied by the Criminal Court of Appeal in *R. v. Hassan*.[15] The accused called evidence in an attempt to rebut Crown evidence as to his whereabouts on a date not directly relevant to the crime. The Criminal Court of Appeal agreed that this was not alibi as the accused was simply contradicting a particular piece of evidence. There was no assertion that he was elsewhere at the time of the crime.

2. PROVING AN ALIBI

(1) The Accused

Despite some early law to the contrary,[16] it is clear that the accused can be the only witness in support of an alibi.[17] In fact an alibi may be placed in evidence through the accused's statement without any defence evidence being called.[18]

If the accused does testify the court cannot direct the defence as to the order of calling witnesses and more particularly cannot direct that the accused be called first.[19] As a practical matter however, it is often advisable to call the accused first (or perhaps after character witnesses have set a favourable climate) so as to avoid any adverse inference that the accused has tailored his or her evidence to that of a previous witness.[20] It is unclear what, if any, instruction the jury should be given if the accused fails to testify first. The Ontario Court of Appeal appears to imply in *R. v. Archer*,[21] that it would be proper to inform the jury that an adverse inference was open to them. Similarly, in *R. v. Smuk*,[22] McFarlane J.A. (Tysoe J.A. concurring), of the British Columbia Court of Appeal, stated that this was a factor that was properly considered

15 (1970), 54 Cr. App. R. 56 (C.A.).
16 *R. v. Miller* (1923), 40 C.C.C. 130 (B.C.C.A.).
17 *Russell v. R.* (1936), 67 C.C.C. 28 (S.C.C.).
18 *R. v. Foll* (1957), 118 C.C.C. 43 (Man. C.A.).
19 *R. v. Sparre* (1977), 37 C.C.C. (2d) 495 (Ont. Co. Ct.), citing *R. v. Angelantoni* (1975), 28 C.C.C. (2d) 179 (Ont. C.A.), and *R. v. Smuk* (1971), 3 C.C.C. (2d) 457 (B.C.C.A.).
20 *Dobberthien v. R.* (1974), 18 C.C.C. (2d) 449 (S.C.C.).
21 (1974), 26 C.R.N.S. 225 (Ont. C.A.).
22 *Supra*, note 19.

by the trier of fact, and Branca J.A. stated that it was a fact germane to the issue of credibility. Since it is a relevant factor, it would appear quite proper to bring the issue to the attention of the jury.

(2) Failure of the Accused or an Alibi Witness to Testify

There is no obligation on the accused to testify in support of an alibi.[23] Often, however it will be, in the words of Hodgins J.A. of the Ontario Court of Appeal, "patent to both judge and jury that under those circumstances the alibi has a hollow sound. It is not that of the accused but of his friends".[24]

There are many factors that influence the accused's decision on whether or not to testify. One factor is the presence or absence of a criminal record since s. 12 of the Canada Evidence Act,[25] allows the accused to be cross-examined on the record. The importance of this factor may be somewhat reduced by the Supreme Court decision of *R. v. Corbett*.[26] In that case the court held that s. 12 did not contravene the provisions of the Charter. A majority of the court furthur held that the trial judge retained a discretion to refuse cross-examination on past record. Among the most important factors to be taken into account in exercising the discretion are the nature of the convictions and their remoteness from or nearness to the charge before the court. Very similar crimes and crimes that happened many years before could be excluded to avoid undue prejudice. Arguably, therefore, the accused's decision to testify should no longer be so readily decided on a fear of impeachment based on prior convictions.

Section 4(6) of the Canada Evidence Act provides that the failure of the person charged or the spouse of that person to testify shall not be made the subject of comment by the judge or counsel for the prosecution. The purpose of the section is to prevent the right not to testify being presented to the jury in a manner that would imply that silence is being used as a cloak to hide guilt.[27]

---

23   *R. v. Sophonow (No.2)* (1986), 25 C.C.C. (3d) 415 at 456, leave to appeal to S.C.C. refused 67 N.R. 158 [Man.].

24   *Steinberg v. R.*, [1931] 4 D.L.R. 8 (S.C.C.), reproducing Ont. C.A. decision at 27.

25   R.S.C. 1985, c. C-5.

26   (1988), 64 C.R. (3d) 1 (S.C.C.).

27   *McConnell v. R.* (1968), 4 C.R.N.S. 269 (S.C.C.); *R. v. Potvin* (1989), 68 C.R. (3d) 193 at 242 (S.C.C.).

Just as it is improper to comment on the failure of the accused to testify, it is equally improper to give a direction that precludes the jury from taking into consideration the fact that the accused has failed to support the alibi by his or her own testimony.[28] A direction to the jury that no adverse inference should be drawn from the failure of the accused to testify was held by the majority of the Supreme Court of Canada to be improper in *Vezeau v. R.*,[29] because "[t]he failure of an accused person, who relies upon an alibi, to testify and thus submit himself to cross-examination is a matter of importance in considering the validity of that defence".[30] The combined effect of s. 4(6) of the Canada Evidence Act and *Vezeau* is that failure of the accused or a spouse to testify in support of an alibi is to be treated in the charge to the jury with silence.

The constitutionality of s. 4(6) of the Canada Evidence Act was recently considered by the Ontario Court of Appeal in *R. v. Boss*.[31] The appellant's primary argument was that *Vezeau* was no longer good law, and that s. 4(6) virtually compelled the accused to be a witness, contrary to ss. 7, 11(*c*) and 11(*d*) of the Charter. The appellant argued that the trial judge should be required to instruct the jury that no adverse inference should be drawn from the accused's failure to testify. The Ontario Court of Appeal rejected this argument and ruled that there was no constitutional right for an instruction that would prohibit the drawing of an adverse inference. The court's reasoning was that s. 4(6) created no legal obligation to testify, just a tactical one, and this did not amount to a constitutional violation. There was no violation of the presumption of innocence since the onus of proof remained on the Crown whether the accused testified or not.

The strength of an alibi may also be affected by failure to call a witness one might reasonably expect to be called. However, this issue must be approached with caution, since there may be many reasons why counsel might choose not to call a witness who was in a position to corroborate the alibi.[32] The person may be of disreputable character, may have a poor memory of the event, or be generally uncooperative. Absent additional information, it would

---

28   *Vezeau v. R.* (1976), 34 C.R.N.S. 309 (S.C.C.).
29   *Ibid.*
30   *Ibid.*, at 317.
31   (1989), 68 C.R. (3d) 123 (Ont. C.A.).
32   *R. v. Zehr* (1980), 54 C.C.C. (2d) 65 (Ont. C.A.); *R. v. Charrette* (1982), 67 C.C.C. (2d) 357 (Ont. C.A.); *R. v. Koffman* (1985), 20 C.C.C. (3d) 232 (Ont. C.A.); *R. v. Musitano* (1986), 24 C.C.C. (3d) 65 (Ont. C.A.); *R. v. Rooke* (1988), 40 C.C.C. (3d) 484 (B.C.C.A.); *R. v. Gallagher*, [1974] 3 All E.R. 118 (C.A.).

be quite improper to draw an adverse inference from the mere failure of a witness to testify. Thus, a trial judge should exercise caution before commenting adversely on the failure to call a witness.

In *R. v. Koffman*,[33] the Ontario Court of Appeal reviewed the law respecting judicial comment on the failure to call a witness to support the defence theory. The propositions that flow from that case may be summarized as follows:[34]

1. Comment on the failure to call a witness is permissible in certain cases, but should be exercised with caution.
2. If the trial judge does comment on the failure to call a witness, the trial judge is further bound to instruct the jury that there is no obligation on the defence to call any witness and there may be a perfectly valid reason for declining to call the witness.
3. Where comment is appropriate, the failure to call a witness should not be given undue prominence in the jury charge and comment should only be made where the witness is of some importance to the case.
4. In respect of a witness whom neither the Crown nor the accused might wish to call, the jury should be advised that there may be a good reason for this and no adverse inference should be drawn against the accused.
5. The charge should not place on the defence any onus to produce corroborative testimony.
5. Where comment on the failure to call a witness is appropriate, the jury should be instructed that an inference may be drawn that the testimony would have been unfavourable; it is not permissible to draw an inference of guilt from the failure to call a witness.

R. v. Gallagher[35] is an example of a case where the Criminal Court of Appeal indicated that it was appropriate to tell the jury that they were entitled to draw an adverse inference from the failure to call a potential witness that might reasonably be expected to have been called. The accused, charged with possession of ammunition, testified that he had left the suitcase, in which the

---

33   *Ibid.*
34   See the judgment of Esson J.A., in *R. v. Rooke, supra,* note 32 at 517, 518.
35   *Supra,* note 32.

ammunition was later found, with three persons whom he named. He testified that the ammunition must have been added at a later date. He did not call any of the three potentially corroborating witnesses. These witnesses were known only to the defence and in such circumstances the court determined that an adverse inference could be drawn. The court added, however, that fairness dictated that the jury also be told that there may be some perfectly good and valid reason why the witnesses had not testified.

Judicial comment on the failure of the defence to call a witness is only appropriate if a possible inference is that the testimony would be unfavourable to the accused. If this is not a natural assumption, then no comment should be made.[36] *R. v. Zehr*[37] is an example of a case where the Ontario Court of Appeal determined that the decision not to call certain witnesses did not lead to any negative inference. The accused, charged with rape, swore that he had gone to a party and then to a restaurant in the company of another person who testified on his behalf. He did not call other people from the party or from the restaurant. The party was earlier in the evening and the people at the party could not testify to the accused's whereabouts at the time of the rape. There was no evidence that anyone at the restaurant knew the accused or would have remembered him. The court reasoned that since no adverse inference was open to the jury, no instruction should have been given. If any instruction was appropriate it was one favourable to the accused, explaining that there was no obligation to call any other witnesses and no adverse inference should be drawn. The Ontario Court of Appeal explained the need for caution:[38]

> While permissible in some cases, comment on the failure to call a witness should only be used with great caution . . . There are many reasons why counsel may choose not to call a witness, and our Courts will rarely question the decision of counsel, for the system proceeds on the basis that counsel conducts the case. Often a witness is not called, and if the reason was known it would not justify an instruction that an adverse inference might be drawn from the witness not being called. Of importance under our system, counsel is not called upon, or indeed permitted, to explain his conduct of a case.

This certainly allows some flexibility in the preparation of an alibi defence. The more critical a witness is to the defence theory though, the more likely the court will sanction an adverse comment. This will not apply to the accused or the spouse of the

---

36   *R. v. Zehr, supra,* note 32.
37   *Ibid.*
38   *Ibid.,* at 68, 69.

accused, who are saved from adverse comment by s. 4(6) of the Canada Evidence Act. The statutory prohibition, of course, does not prevent the trier of fact from viewing an alibi unsupported by the most knowledgeable witness with the greatest of scepticism.

(3) Alibi Supported by Friends and Relatives

People spend time with their relatives and friends and it is only fortuitous if an accused can support an alibi through disinterested witnesses. Since a person's interest in the outcome is relevant to credibility it is entirely proper to instruct a jury to consider the witnesses' interest and relationship to the accused.[39] However, fairness dictates that this instruction should be accompanied by a statement to the effect that these are the people one would expect to be in the company of the accused and that the jury should not consider it unusual that friends and family members have testified in support of the alibi.[40]

Since an individual is often with the same people, it may also arise on occasion that the accused will call on these same friends and relatives to provide an alibi in more than one prosecution. For example, in *R. v. Belanger*,[41] the Crown sought to cross-examine the accused's wife on the fact that she had provided alibi testimony for her husband at a previous trial. The Ontario Court of Appeal determined that this factor alone did not detract from the wife's credibility and therefore the cross-examination was improper. The fact that the witness provided alibi testimony on a previous occasion would only be relevant, said the court, if there was a clear nexus to credibility. This would arise for example, if it could be shown that the evidence on the previous occasion was fabricated or that the testimony proffered on the previous occasion was so similar to that now being advanced as to raise a question of the improbability of both being true. An example of the latter is to be found in the House of Lords decision in *Jones v. D.P.P.*[42] The accused provided alibis, first for a rape and then for a murder, that were so similar that Crown Counsel was led to ask whether the accused and his wife were, "in the habit of going through the same act word for word, the same conversation, at intervals".[43] Not

---

39   *R. v. Paradis* (1976), 38 C.C.C. (2d) 455 (Que. C.A.).
40   *R. v. Sparrow* (1979), 51 C.C.C. (2d) 443 (Ont. C.A.); *R. v. Andrade* (1985), 18 C.C.C. (3d) 41 (Ont. C.A.).
41   (1975), 24 C.C.C. (2d) 10 (Ont. C.A.).
42   (1962), 46 Cr. App. R. 129 (H.L.).
43   *Ibid.*, at 171.

surprisingly the House of Lords determined that the cross-examination was proper even though it disclosed a previous offence, as it was crucial to the issue of credibility.

(4) The Test of Relevance

One of the difficulties with an alibi defence is that witnesses are often asked to cast their minds back to insignificant events. It is difficult enough to remember details of an important event such as witnessing a crime, but an alibi witness is often asked to remember something seemingly unimportant such as seeing the accused at a public place or visiting the accused at his or her home. An alibi witness who can be precise as to the details of an insignificant meeting may be disbelieved as a result of the precision. We do not expect people to have an accurate recall of insignificant events.[44]

This difficulty may lead to a question as to whether evidence to be tendered in support of an alibi meets the first hurdle of admissibility which is relevance. The issue arose in *R. v. Sophonow (No. 2)*,[45] where the accused wished to call witnesses to say that, sometime around Christmas, a man they could not identify came to the hospital where each worked to deliver Christmas stockings to children. The accused's alibi was that he was that man and that he had delivered the stockings at a time coincident with the murder. The trial judge rejected the prospective evidence on the ground that it was irrelevant as being too imprecise in that it could not be directly connected to the accused. The Manitoba Court of Appeal ruled that the evidence should have been allowed. It was for the jury to determine the weight of the evidence but it was certainly open to the jury to find that the accused was the man seen by the witnesses and that the date and time coincided with the murder. To be relevant therefore, alibi evidence need not be directly connected to the accused. It is sufficient if it allows a possible inference in favour of the accused to be drawn.

---

44   *R. v. Beresford* (1971), 56 Cr. App. R. 143 (C.A.).
45   (1986), 25 C.C.C. (3d) 415, leave to appeal to S.C.C. refused 67 N.R. 158 [Man.].

3. JURY INSRUCTIONS

(1) Duty to put the Defence Fairly

Where the defence is alibi there is a responsibility on the trial judge to place the defence fairly and clearly before the jury.[46] Fairness in this regard means putting the matters before the jury in such a manner so as not to denigrate the defence and to allow the jury to make the required factual decisions.[47] Though this obligation does not differ from other defences, alibi itself, as distinct from the evidence in support, has sometimes been the subject of disparaging remarks by the court. For example, in *R. v. Bassnett*,[48] the trial judge instructed the jury, "to be very careful of alibis", and stated that the alibi should be scrutinized "with almost microscopic care".[49] The Criminal Court of Appeal quashed the conviction stating that there was no foundation whatsoever for such comments.[50]

The defence of alibi must be placed before the jury if there is some evidence in support. This is true whether the evidence arises through the Crown's case, the defence case, or both.[51]

The fact that alibi is raised does not preclude other defences being left with the jury. Counsel may be ill-advised to take contrary positions, "my client wasn't there, but if he was he acted in self-defence"; but if the conflicting defences arise on the evidence, the trial judge is duty bound to put both to the jury. This, however, should only be done if the evidence in support of the "secondary" defence is sufficiently strong to raise a *prima facie* case.[52] As the Criminal Court of Appeal stated in *R. v. Bonnick*:[53]

> It is plain that there may be evidence of self-defence even though a defendant asserts that he was not present, and in so far as the judge told the jury the contrary, he was in error; but in the nature of things it

---

46   *R. v. Clarke* (1979), 48 C.C.C. (2d) 440 (N.S.C.A.); *R. v. Corbett* (1984), 17 C.C.C. (3d) 129, affirmed 41 C.C.C. (3d) 385 (S.C.C.) [B.C.]; *R. v. Dyck* (1956), 116 C.C.C. 392 (Sask. C.A.); *R. v. Andrade, supra,* note 40; *R. v. O'Leary* (1982), 1 C.C.C. (3d) 182 (N.B.C.A.); *R. v. Sophonow (No. 1)* (1984), 12 C.C.C. (3d) 272, affirmed 17 C.C.C. (3d) 128n (S.C.C.)[Man.].
47   *R. v. Andrade, ibid.; R. v. Sophonow (No. 1), ibid.*
48   [1961] Crim. L.R. 559 (C.A.).
49   *Ibid.*
50   *Supra,* note 48 at 560.
51   *R. v. Burdick* (1975), 27 C.C.C. (2d) 497 at 504 (Ont. C.A.); *R. v. Foll* (1957), 118 C.C.C. 43 (Man. C.A.); *R. v. Mickey* (1988), 46 C.C.C. (3d) 278 (B.C.C.A.).
52   *R. v. Bonnick* (1977), 66 Cr. App. R. 266 (C.A.); *R. v. MacGregor* (1981), 64 C.C.C. (2d) 353, leave to appeal to S.C.C. refused N.R. 349 [Ont.].
53   *Ibid.,* at 269.

would require fairly cogent evidence, when the best available witness disables himself by his alibi from supporting it.

(2) Burden of Proof

An accused need never prove an alibi. The Crown at all times retains the obligation to prove guilt beyond a reasonable doubt.[54] An alibi is a denial of one element of the Crown's case; the identity of the offender. There is no onus on the defence to prove that the accused was not at the scene of the crime. If, however, the accused challenges the Crown's case with a positive assertion that he or she was elsewhere, then the defence retains the burden of bringing forward some evidence in support of that assertion. The defence thus has an evidentiary burden, but no legal burden.

The instructions to be given the jury with respect to burden of proof were succinctly summarized by the Ontario Court of Appeal in *R. v. Parrington*.[55] The court suggested that the jury be instructed:[56]

(1) that if they believed the alibi testimony given then, of course, they must acquit;
(2) that if they did not believe such testimony, but were left in reasonable doubt by it, once again they must acquit the accused;
(3) that even if they were not left in reasonable doubt by this testimony, then on the basis of all the evidence they must determine whether they were convinced beyond a reasonable doubt of the guilt of the accused.

This last instruction to the jury is important and if missed may be sufficient to render the verdict unsafe.[57] The instruction refocuses the jury's attention on the central issue which is whether the Crown has proved its case. The ultimate issue is not whether the defence has proved the alibi.

4. TIMELY DISCLOSURE OF THE ALIBI

Several Commonwealth jurisdictions have statutes requiring formal notice of an alibi defence, including the names and

54 *Steinberg v. R.* [1931] 4 D.L.R. 8 at 43 (S.C.C.); *Lizotte v. R.* (1950), 99 C.C.C. 113 (S.C.C.).
55 (1985), 20 C.C.C. (3d) 184 (Ont. C.A.). See, in addition, *R. v. Cachia* (1953), 107 C.C.C. 272 (Ont. C.A.); *R. v. O'Leary, supra,* note 46; *R. v. Burdick, supra,* note 51; *R. v. Corbett, supra,* note 46.
56 *Ibid.,* at 187.
57 *R. v. Burdick, supra,* note 51.

addresses of the alibi witnesses.[58] Although Canada has no equivalent statute, the credibility of the alibi may be affected by failure to make a timely disclosure. An alibi not disclosed till late in the day may suffer from an inference of recent fabrication.

Some of the language used in the reported judgments directs an inquiry into whether the alibi was disclosed "at the first, or earliest, opportunity".[59] This language is misleading. It presumes that an innocent person will provide the details of an alibi immediately upon being confronted. First, this conflicts with the right to remain silent,[60] and secondly, it ignores that an innocent person would be well advised to present the alibi after due deliberation. The credibility of the alibi will be greatly affected if errors made in haste and while under stress must be corrected at a later date.

The principle that is consistent with the right to remain silent is that failure to disclose an alibi at a sufficiently early time to permit it to be investigated by the police is a factor to be considered in determining the weight to be afforded the alibi evidence.[61] If the alibi is first disclosed at trial then it is quite reasonable to question why, if there was nothing to hide, the police were not given a reasonable opportunity to investigate.

Late disclosure of the alibi does not automatically lead to an inference that it has been concocted. The jury is entitled to consider any explanation offered in determining what, if any, inference to draw from late disclosure. This presumably could include an error on the part of counsel in failing to provide timely disclosure.[62]

If details of the alibi have been given to the authorities sufficiently in advance of the trial to permit it to be investigated by the police, then it is improper to cross-examine the accused on why disclosure was not made earlier.[63] It is certainly improper to cross-examine on why the alibi was not disclosed to the police on arrest.

58   Criminal Justice Act, 1967 (Eng.), c. 80, s. 11; Criminal Procedure (Scotland) Act, 1975 (Eng.), c. 21, s. 82; Queensland Criminal Code, s. 590A; N.S.W. Crimes Act, 1900, s. 405A [en. Crimes and Other Acts (Amendment) Act, 1974, No. 50, s. 8]; Victoria Crimes Act, 1958, No. 6231, s. 399; N.Z. Crimes Act, 1961, No. 43, s. 367A [en. Crimes Amendment Act, 1973, No. 118, s. 11(1)].

59   *R. v. Clarke* (1979), 48 C.C.C. (2d) 440 at 448 (N.S. C.A.); *R. v. Beaubien* (1979), 16 A.R. 398 (Dist. Ct.); *R. v. Rafferty* (1983), 6 C.C.C. (3d) 72 at 80 (Alta. C.A.).

60   *R. v. Hoare*, [1966] 2 All E.R. 846 (C.A.); *R. v. Machado* (1989), 50 C.C.C. (3d) 133 (B.C.C.A.).

61   *R. v. Dunbar* (1982), 28 C.R. (3d) 324 (Ont. C.A.); *R. v. Parrington, supra*, note 55; *R. v. Paradis*, (1976), 38 C.C.C. (2d) 455 (Que. C.A.); *R. v. Speid* (1988), 42 C.C.C. (3d) 12, leave to appeal to S.C.C. refused 36 O.A.C. 320n.

62   *R. v. Paradis, supra*, note 61.

63   *R. v. Parrington, supra*, note 55.

This would be a gross violation of the right to remain silent.[64] As long as there has been timely disclosure any such cross-examination would be irrelevant as it would not impinge on credibility. If there has not been timely disclosure, then this is clearly something that is properly canvassed in cross-examination.

If the authorities have been given sufficient opportunity to investigate the alibi there is no need to include an instruction on timely disclosure in the charge to the jury since no adverse inference is available.[65] If evidence implying some delay is somehow put before the jury, then it would seem reasonable that the trial judge should clarify for the jury that there is no obligation to disclose at the first opportunity and no adverse inference is available. If timely disclosure has been made then it is open to the trial judge to give a direction favourable to the accused, suggesting that the credibility of the alibi is enhanced by early disclosure.[66]

There is no law in Canada setting out any particular method of providing disclosure.The only criterion would appear to be that the police be given sufficient detail to make an adequate investigation.[67] This may come informally through the accused's statement or by formal notice, given sufficiently in advance of trial to allow the alibi to be investigated. The notice should include the names and addresses of potential witnesses, if known. It is common practice in England to indicate on the alibi notice whether counsel wishes to be present during any police interviews of an alibi witness. This practice is certainly open to a Canadian solicitor.

Care should be taken in preparing an alibi notice since arguably it is a statement of the accused given through an agent. Some counsel may choose to give details of the alibi at the conclusion of the preliminary hearing where any statement made is specifically stated to be available as evidence at trial.[68] The English statutory provisions provide that the alibi notice shall be deemed to be that of the accused, unless the contrary is proved.[69] By virtue of the statutory regime, the Criminal Court of Appeal ruled in *R. v. Rossborough*,[70] that the Crown could put the alibi notice into evi-

64   *Ibid.* See also, *R. v. Hoare, supra,* note 60.
65   *R. v. Parrington, supra,* note 55.
66   *R. v. Tzimopoulos* (1986), 54 C.R. (3d) 1 at 44, leave to appeal to S.C.C. refused 54 C.R. (3d) xxvii [Ont.].
67   *R. v. Mahoney* (1979), 50 C.C.C. (2d) 380, affirmed 67 C.C.C. (2d) 197 (S.C.C.)[Ont.]; *R. v. Hogan* (1982), 2 C.C.C. (3d) 557 (Ont. C.A.).
68   Criminal Code, R.S.C. 1985, c. C-46, s. 541.
69   Criminal Justice Act, 1967(Eng.), c. 80, s. 11(5).
70   (1985), 81 Cr. App. R. 139 (C.A.).

dence as part of its case and could seek to rebut it. Logically the same is true in Canada since there is no difference between the accused telling the police directly as to his or her whereabouts and providing instructions to an agent to do the same thing. Both are statements which the Crown could tender and seek to disprove. If the accused testifies, the Crown would be free to cross-examine on the alibi notice (voluntariness assumed).

Canada has chosen not to adopt a statutory regime governing alibi notice. This may be a wise decision since a review of jurisprudence from jurisdictions with statutes suggests that a great deal of judicial energy is expended on deciding when the statute applies and the remedy for violation. The common law, as it has developed in Canada, appears to create a sensible alternative. There is a benefit to be gained by timely disclosure. Failure to provide disclosure will affect the credibility of the alibi but will not deprive the accused of the right to mount the defence.

5. DISBELIEVED VERSUS FABRICATED ALIBIS

If an alibi might reasonably be true, then the trier of fact will have a reasonable doubt as to the Crown's case and will acquit.[71] The other option is that the alibi is rejected. An alibi may be rejected because there is insufficient evidence in support or the evidence given is not deemed to be credible. An alibi may also be rejected on a finding that it is false, having been procured through lies and perjured testimony.

The use to be made of the alibi evidence differs if there is a finding by the jury of fabrication as opposed to mere disbelief.[72] The Ontario Court of Appeal explained the difference in *R. v. Davison*:[73]

> The learned trial Judge did not ... make clear to the jury the distinction between *proof* that the alibi advanced is false in the sense of being concocted and the mere rejection by the jury of the evidence of alibi because they believe that evidence to be untruthful, although not proved to be false. *Proof* of the falsity of the alibi may constitute affirmative evidence of guilt. The mere rejection of the evidence of alibi because it is disbelieved is not affirmative evidence of guilt and

---

71   See Burden of Proof, *supra*, this chapter, part 3(2).

72   *R. v. Davison* (1974), 20 C.C.C. (2d) 424, leave to appeal to S.C.C. refused 6 O.R. (2d) 103n; *R. v. Mahoney* (1979), 50 C.C.C. (2d) 380, affirmed 67 C.C.C. (2d) 197 (S.C.C.)[Ont.]; *R. v. Kies* (1987), 48 Man. R. (2d) 30 (C.A.); *R. v. MacDonald* (1989), 48 C.C.C. (3d) 230, leave to appeal to S.C.C. refused 94 N.S.R. (2d) 55.

73   *Ibid.*, at 430.

has only the effect of removing it from consideration as a barrier to the acceptance of the case for the prosecution.

Mere disbelief of an alibi does not give rise to an inference of guilt. There are many reasons why an accused might be unable to prove the alibi. The witnesses in support may have a poor memory of the event or be of disreputable character. If an alibi is fabricated, however, one possible inference is that this was done to escape criminal liability.[74] There are other possible inferences as was explained by the Criminal Court of Appeal in *R. v. Turnbull:*[75]

> False alibis may be put forward for many reasons: an accused, for example, who has only his own truthful evidence to rely on may stupidly fabricate an alibi and get lying witnesses to support it out of fear that his own evidence will not be enough. Further, alibi witnesses can make genuine mistakes about dates and occasions like any other witnesses can. It is only when the jury are satisfied that the sole reason for the fabrication was to deceive them and there is no other explanation for its being put forward, that fabrication can provide any support for identification evidence. The jury should be reminded that proving the accused has told lies about where he was at the material time does not by itself prove that he was where the identifying witness says he was.

The result is that only if the Crown can first prove beyond a reasonable doubt that the alibi was fabricated, and can then prove beyond a reasonable doubt that the reason for the fabrication was to obscure guilt, will the evidence be capable of corroborating identification. In all other situations an unproved alibi is simply neutral.[76] In *R. v. Kies,* the Manitoba Court of Appeal suggested that the jury be instructed to approach the issue in three sequential steps:[77]

> A trial judge sitting with a jury must explain to the jury the several questions which it should consider with respect to an alibi defence and the sequence in which the jury should consider them. The first question is, of course, whether the alibi may be true. If the alibi is disbelieved, it is to be disregarded unless the jury is satisfied that it was a concoction. No adverse inference can be drawn from the fact that the alibi was concocted unless the jury is also satisfied that it was given to obscure guilt or the accuracy of other evidence. Only when the jury is satisfied on this last point is the falsity of the alibi capable of adding weight to the case for the prosecution.

---

74   *Mawaz Khan v. R.*, [1967] 1 All E.R. 80 at 83 (P.C.).
75   [1976] 3 All E.R. 549 at 553 (C.A.). See also, *R. v. Burdick* (1975), 27 C.C.C. (2d) 497 at 506 (Ont. C.A.); *R. v. Kies, supra,* note 72.
76   *R. v. Jones* (1971), 3 C.C.C. (2d) 153 (Ont. C.A.); *R. v. Burdick, supra,* note 75; *R. v. MacDonald, supra,* note 72; *R. v. Kies, supra,* note 72 ; *R. v. Tzimopoulos, supra,* note 66; *R. v. Keane* (1977), 65 Cr. App. R. 247 (C.A.).
77   *R. v. Kies, supra,* note 72 at 33.

A practice has developed over the years whereby judges routinely give instructions with respect to fabricated alibi in all cases where the defence is raised. In *R. v. Mahoney*,[78] the Ontario Court of Appeal suggested that this practice is wrong and that the instruction should only be given if there is some evidence on which a jury could find fabrication.[79]

> If the jury accepted the evidence of the Crown witnesses that the appellant was the killer, disbelief of the appellant's denial was inevitable, but that disbelief could not be treated as an additional item of circumstantial evidence to prove guilt. In my view, the jury ought not, routinely, to be instructed with respect to the inferences which may be drawn from the fabrication of a false alibi in the absence of a proper basis for that instruction, as for example, where there is extrinsic evidence of fabrication, or where the appellant has given different versions as to his whereabouts, one of which must be concocted.

R. v. Andrade[80] is an example of a case where it was held proper to instruct on fabrication. When first questioned the accused indicated that he had been at home. He later advised that he had been in error and gave a different account of his whereabouts. The Ontario Court of Appeal approved the instructions on fabrication on the basis that the different versions were capable of being evidence of fabrication, although it could merely have been the result of honest error. It was for the jury to determine what if any inference to draw.

6. REBUTTAL EVIDENCE

The basic principles with respect to the admissibility of rebuttal evidence were set out by the Supreme Court of Canada in *R. v. Krause*:[81]

> The general rule is that the Crown, or in civil matters the plaintiff, will not be allowed to split its case. The Crown or the plaintiff must produce and enter in its own case all the clearly relevant evidence that it has, or it intends to rely upon, to establish its case with respect to all the issues raised in the pleadings; in a criminal case, the indictment and any particulars [authorities omitted].This rule prevents unfair surprise, prejudice and confusion which could result if the Crown or the plaintiff were allowed to split its case, that is, to put in part of its evidence - as much as it deemed necessary at the outset - then to close

---

78   *R. v. Mahoney, supra,* note 72. See also, *R. v. O'Leary* (1982), 1 C.C.C. (3d) 182 (N.B.C.A.); *R. v. Andrade,* (1985), 18 C.C.C. (3d) 41 (Ont. C.A.).
79   *Ibid.,* at 389.
80   *Supra,* note 78.
81   (1986), 54 C.R. (3d) 294 at 300 (S.C.C.).

the case and after the defence is complete to add further evidence to bolster the position originally advanced. The underlying reason for this rule is that the defendant or the accused is entitled at the close of the Crown's case to have before it the full case for the Crown so that it is known from the outset what must be met in response.

The plaintiff or the Crown may be allowed to call evidence in rebuttal after completion of the defence case where the defence has raised some new matter or defence which the Crown has had no opportunity to deal with and which the Crown or the plaintiff could not reasonably have anticipated. But rebuttal will not be permitted regarding matters which merely confirm or reinforce earlier evidence adduced in the Crown's case which could have been brought before the defence was made. It will be permitted only when it is necessary to ensure that at the end of the day each party will have had an equal opportunity to hear and respond to the full submissions of the other.

The right of the Crown to call rebuttal evidence in reply to a defence of alibi has been described by the Supreme Court as "unquestionable".[82] However, the mere fact that an alibi has been advanced does not give the Crown unlimited latitude to call any new evidence. The evidence must be directed to a material point of the alibi and cannot be directed to a collateral matter.[83] The case of *Latour v. R.*[84] illustrates the difference. The accused testified as to his whereabouts on the date of the robbery. The accused was cross-examined as to whether he had ever been at a particular store in a different town. The accused denied this and the Crown called the store clerk in rebuttal to prove that the accused had robbed this store several months after the robbery for which he was on trial. The question was collateral to the main issue which was the accused's whereabouts on the date of the offence before the court. The proposed rebuttal evidence went to the issue of credibility; the Crown wishing to show that the accused had lied under oath. The Supreme Court ruled that the rebuttal evidence was improper as it did not relate to a material point but to the collateral issue of credibility. The Crown was bound by the answer it received to a collateral question.[85]

The "most material" aspect of any alibi is the evidence relating to the accused's whereabouts. There are many examples of cases permitting rebuttal evidence to counter the accused's assertions as to whereabouts. For example, in *R. v. Flynn,*[86] the defence

---

82   *Latour v. R.* (1977), 33 C.C.C. (2d) 377 at 381 (S.C.C.).
83   *Ibid.*
84   *Ibid.*
85   See, in addition, *R. v. Krause, supra,* note 81; *R. v. Gottschall* (1983), 10 C.C.C. (3d) 447 (N.S.C.A.); *R. v. Waite* (1980), 57 C.C.C. (2d) 34 (N.S.C.A.).
86   (1957), 42 Cr. App. R. 15 (C.A.).

witness testified that she saw the accused at a swimming pool at the time of the alleged offence. The Crown was permitted to call rebuttal evidence that she was at work. In *R. v. Blick*,[87] the accused explained his presence near the scene of the crime by explaining he had been using a public lavatory. A juror alerted the court to the fact that the lavatory was closed and the Crown was permitted to call evidence in rebuttal to substantiate this fact.

Rebuttal evidence is also admissible to contradict those portions of the defence that seek to explain allegedly incriminating evidence tendered by the Crown. For example, in *R. v. Andrews*,[88] the accused offered an alibi on a charge of murder. The Crown proved that the accused had a cut to his hand, consistent with an injury obtained from a knife cut. The accused explained the injury as having occured when he fell, a day prior to the murder. The British Columbia Court of Appeal agreed that rebuttal evidence was proper to contradict this portion of the alibi. Simillarly, in *R. v. Sparrow*,[89] the Ontario Court of Appeal upheld the Crown's right to call rebuttal evidence to contradict the accused's version as to how blood matching that of the deceased had got on his car. The defence evidence in both cases was material to the alibi and the explanation offered could not have been anticipated by the Crown.

Although it is often difficult to determine what is material and what is collateral, it is often equally difficult to determine if the proposed evidence, in the words of *Krause*, relates to a matter that the Crown "could not reasonably have anticipated".[90] Rebuttal evidence is designed to allow new matters raised in the defence to be fairly canvassed. If the evidence was always relevant it should be proffered at first instance and not in rebuttal.

R. v. Jackson[91] is an example where rebuttal evidence was refused on the ground that it was at all times relevant and should have been called by the Crown in its case in chief. The accused was charged with a murder that occured inside a federal penitentiary. The Crown alleged that the accused stabbed the victim sometime between 5:30 and 6:00 p.m., when both were locked in their unit. The accused, supported by several other witnesses, testified that he was not in the unit at the relevant time but was elsewhere in the institution. The Crown sought to call evidence in rebuttal to

---

87   (1966), 50 Cr. App. R. 280 (C.A.).
88   (1979), 8 C.R. (3d) 1 at 24, leave to appeal to S.C.C. dismissed 28 N.R. 537 [B.C.].
89   (1979), 51 C.C.C. (2d) 443 (Ont. C.A.).
90   *Supra*, note 81.
91   (1987), 38 C.C.C. (3d) 91 (B.C.C.A.).

contradict this and to bolster the original evidence that the accused was in the unit. The trial judge refused the evidence, the accused was acquitted, and the Crown appealed. The Court of Appeal for British Columbia agreed with the trial judge. The Crown at all times had to prove that the accused was in the unit at the material time. The evidence sought to be introduced would simply buttress the evidence already called that had attempted to place the accused at the scene. The court reasoned that the Crown should have called all of the evidence related to the accused's whereabouts at first instance.

This case can be contrasted with *R. v. McRitchie.*[92] Three police witnesses testified that they had staked out a particular location where they had earlier ascertained a cache of heroin had been placed. The officers identified that accused as the person who came for the drugs. The accused testified that it was a case of mistaken identity and that he had been home with his mother at the material time. The Crown then called in rebuttal another police witness who testified that he had followed a car away from the stake-out location and he identified the accused as a passenger in the car. The British Columbia Court of Appeal ruled that the rebuttal evidence was admissible. It could however be argued that the Crown at all times had to prove identification. The Crown therefore should have called all witnesses who purported to identify the accused. The alibi did not make identity a new issue. It was the primary issue from the beginning of the case to the end. The fact that an alibi is offered should not open the door to any and all evidence in rebuttal. Evidence is only properly received in rebuttal if it relates to an issue that could not be anticipated. This prerequisite to admissibility does not appear to have been addressed in *McRitchie*.

As discussed above, it may often be advantageous to the accused to provide notice to the Crown of an alibi sufficiently in advance of trial to allow it to be investigated.[93] This may allow the Crown to deal with some issues in its case at first instance and may on occasion influence a judge to exercise his or her discretion against admitting the rebuttal evidence. However, for the most part, a reply to an alibi is still properly given in rebuttal even if the Crown has notice of the intended defence. The reason for this, is that the Crown's evidence must comply with the most basic evidentiary principle and that is that the evidence must be relevant to

---

92   36 C.C.C. (2d) 39, affirmed [1977] 2 S.C.R. 600 [B.C.].
93   See, *supra*, this chapter, part 4.

a fact in issue. The Crown should not be expected, nor allowed, to call evidence not yet relevant. As Kerans J.A. stated in dissent in *R. v. Rafferty*:[94]

> ... the rule in Canada is that the Crown should not call evidence unless and until it is relevant; it is not sufficient merely that one foresees that it might later become relevant. Evidence that the accused was not present at a place is not relevant unless first somebody says he was present at that place at some relevant time. Evidence, then, which is relevant only to disprove a defence such as an alibi can properly be called in rebuttal even though the Crown knows perfectly well that an alibi is coming.

The law in England is different from that in Canada by virtue of s. 11(4) of the Criminal Justice Act, 1967, c. 80. That section allows the Crown to disprove an alibi either before or after the defence case. Based on the statute, the Criminal Court of Appeal, in *R. v. Rossborough*,[95] approved the right of the Crown to attack the credibility of the witnesses named in the alibi notice during its case in chief. The result is that the credibility of a witness, who may never testify, may be called into question. This is not only a waste of court time but can obviously lead to great confusion. The basic evidentiary rule of relevance would appear to dictate that the evidence remain inadmissible until such time as the witness testifies.

7. FRESH EVIDENCE OF ALIBI ON APPEAL

An application to admit fresh evidence of alibi on appeal is subject to the general principles enunciated by the Supreme Court in *Palmer v. R.*[96] The first of these principles is that the evidence should not generally be admitted if, by due diligence, it could have been adduced at trial. The need to exercise diligence must necessarily include the responsibility of the accused to play an active role in the preperation of the defence. In the words of Lord Justice Sachs, "Nowhere is that more important than in the case of an alibi, a defence raising facts which are most particularly within the knowledge of the accused".[97] There is thus a reluctance on the part of the court to allow fresh evidence on appeal in support of an alibi from relatives and close friends since these are people that could

---

94   (1983), 6 C.C.C. (3d) 72 at 83 (Alta. C.A.).
95   (1985), 81 Cr. App. R. 139 (C.A.).
96   (1980), 14 C.R. (3d) 22 (S.C.C.). See, *supra*, Chapter 2, part 7(2).
97   *R. v. Beresford* (1972), 56 Cr. App. R. 143 at 149 (C.A.).

easily have been produced at trial.[98] Similarly, on the issue of the credibility of the fresh evidence, which is another factor articulated in *Palmer*, the court will scrutinize with care the evidence from relatives and close friends as their partiality is certainly relevant to their credibility.[99]

Many of the applications for fresh evidence turn on the final factor articulated in *Palmer* which directs an inquiry into whether the fresh evidence might reasonably be expected to affect the trial verdict. If it could affect the verdict the Court of Appeal should grant the motion and order a new trial. The court should not encroach upon the jury's role and weigh the evidence itself.[100] If the fresh evidence does not bring anything new to the case then it would appear quite proper to reject the application. For example, in *R. v. Thatcher*,[101] the accused had put forward a defence of alibi supported by several witnesses. The jury obviously disbelieved the alibi. The motion for fresh evidence related to a new witness who wished to give evidence identical to that already rejected by the jury. The Saskatchewan Court of Appeal, applying *Palmer*, determined that the fresh evidence would not have affected the verdict and dismissed the motion. On the other hand, if the fresh evidence would provide something new, it would seem appropriate to grant the motion in such a situation if the other criteria in *Palmer* are met.[102] Fresh evidence motions to supplement an alibi, however, should never be taken for granted and will never substitute for proper investigation and preparation of the alibi defence before trial.

---

98   *Ibid.* See, however, *R. v. Taylor* (1975), 22 C.C.C. (2d) 321 (Alta. C.A.), where the court granted the motion for fresh evidence from a friend of the accused since the 16-year-old accused did not appreciate the significance of the friend's evidence.

99   *Ibid.*

100   *Stolar v. R.* (1988), 40 C.C.C. (3d) 1 (S.C.C.).

101   (1986), 24 C.C.C. (3d) 449 at 522, affirmed on other grounds 32 C.C.C. (3d) 481 (S.C.C.)[Sask.].

102   *Stolar v. R., supra,* note 100.

Appendix A

Code of Practice for the Identification of Persons by Police Officers*

Commencement – Transitional Arrangements

This code has effect in relation to any identification carried out after midnight on 31 March 1991.

1. General

1.1   This code of practice must be readily available at all police stations for consultation by police officers, detained persons and members of the public.

1.2   The notes for guidance included are not provisions of this code, but are guidance to police officers and others about its application and interpretation. Provisions in the Annexes to the code are provisions of this code.

1.3   If an officer has any suspicion, or is told in good faith, that a person of any age may be suffering from mental disorder or mentally handicapped, or mentally incapable of understanding the significance of questions put to him or his replies, then that person shall be treated as a mentally disordered or mentally handicapped person for the purposes of this code.

1.4   If anyone appears to be under the age of 17 then he shall be treated as a juvenile for the purposes of this code in the absence of clear evidence to show that he is older.

1.5   If a person appears to be blind or seriously visually handicapped, deaf, unable to read, unable to speak or has difficulty orally because of a speech impediment, he should be treated as such for purposes of this code in the absence of clear evidence to the contrary.

1.6   In this code "the appropriate adult" means:

(a)   in the case of a juvenile:

(i)   his parent or guardian (or, if he is in care, the care authority or organisation);
(ii)   a social worker; or

---

* Code D of the Police and Criminal Evidence Act, 1984 (Eng.), Codes of Practice, reproduced with the permission of the Controller of Her Majesty's Stationery Office.

        (iii) failing either of the above, another responsible adult aged 18 or over who is not a police officer or employed by the police.

  (b) in the case of a person who is mentally disordered or mentally handicapped

        (i) a relative, guardian or some other person responsible for his care or custody; or

        (ii) someone who has experience of dealing with mentally disordered or mentally handicapped persons but is not a police officer or employed by the police (such as an approved social worker as defined by the Mental Health Act 1983 or a specialist social worker); or

        (iii) failing either of the above, some other responsible adult aged 18 or over who is not a police officer or employed by the police.

1.7   Any reference to a custody officer in this code includes an officer who is performing the functions of a custody officer. Any reference to a solicitor in this code includes a clerk or legal executive except in Annex D, paragraph 7.

1.8   Where a record is made under this code of any action requiring the authority of an officer of specified rank, his name (except in the case of enquiries linked to the investigation of terrorism, in which case the officer's warrant number should be given) and rank must be included in the record.

1.9   All records must be timed and signed by the maker. Warrant numbers should be used rather than names in the case of detention under the Prevention of Terrorism (Temporary Provision) Act 1989.

1.10   In the case of a detained person records are to be made in his custody record unless otherwise specified.

1.11   In the case of any procedure requiring a suspect's consent, the consent of a person who is mentally disordered or mentally handicapped is only valid if given in the presence of the appropriate adult; and in the case of a juvenile the consent of his parent or guardian is required as well as his own (unless he is under 14, in which case the consent of his parent or guardian is sufficient in its own right).

1.12   In the case of a person who is blind or seriously visually handicapped or unable to read, the custody officer should ensure that his solicitor, relative, the appropriate adult or some other person likely to take an interest in him (and not involved in the investigation) is available to help in checking any documentation. Where this code requires written consent or signification, then the person who is assisting may be asked to sign instead if the detained person so wishes.

1.13   In the case of any procedure requiring information to be given to or sought from a suspect, it must be given or sought in the presence of the appropriate adult if the suspect is mentally disordered, mentally handicapped or a juvenile. If the appropriate adult is not present when the information is first given or sought, the procedure must be repeated in his presence when he arrives. If the suspect appears to be deaf or there is doubt about his hearing or speaking ability or ability to understand English, and the officer cannot establish effective communication, the information must be given or sought through an interpreter.

1.14   Any procedure in this code involving the participation of a person (whether as a suspect or a witness) who is mentally disordered, mentally handicapped or a juvenile must take place in the presence of the appropriate adult; but the adult must not be allowed to prompt any identification of a suspect by a witness.

1.15 Subject to paragraph 1.16 below, nothing in this code affects any procedure under:

> (i) Sections 4 to 11 of the Road Traffic Act 1988 or sections 15 and 16 of the Road Traffic Offenders Act 1988; or,
> (ii) paragraph 18 of Schedule 2 to the Immigration Act 1971; or
> (iii) the Prevention of Terrorism (Temporary Provisions) Act 1989: section 15(9), paragraph 8(5) of Schedule 2, and paragraph 7(5) of Schedule 5.

1.16 Notwithstanding paragraph 1.15, the provisions of section 3 below on the taking of fingerprints, and of section 5 below on the taking of body samples, do apply to persons detained under section 14 of, or paragraph 6 of Schedule 5 to, the Prevention of Terrorism (Temporary Provisions) Act 1989. (In the case of fingerprints, section 61 of PACE is modified by section 15(10) of, and paragraph 7(6) of Schedule 5 to, the 1989 Act.) There is, however, no statutory requirement (and, therefore, no requirement under paragraph 3.4 below) to destroy fingerprints or body samples taken in terrorist cases, no requirement to tell the persons from whom these were taken that they will be destroyed, and no statutory requirement to offer such persons an opportunity to witness the destruction of their fingerprints.

1.17 In this code references to photographs include optical disc computer printouts.

2. Identification by witness

(a) Cases where the suspect is known

2.1 In a case which involves disputed identification evidence, and where the identity of the suspect is known to the police, the methods of identification by witnesses which may be used are:

> (i) a parade;
>
> (ii) a group identification;
>
> (iii) a video film
>
> (iv) a confrontation.

2.2 The arrangements for, and conduct of, these types of identification shall be the responsibility of an officer in uniform not below the rank of inspector who is not involved with the investigation ("the identification officer"). No officer involved with the investigation of the case against the suspect may take any part in these procedures.

Identification Parade

2.3 In a case which involves disputed identification evidence a parade must be held if the suspect asks for one and it is practicable to hold one. A parade may also be held if the officer in charge of the investigation considers that it would be useful, and the suspect consents.

2.4   A parade need not be held if the identification officer considers that, whether by reason of the unusual appearance of the suspect or for some other reason, it would not be practicable to assemble sufficient people who resembled him to make a parade fair.

2.5   Any parade must be carried out in accordance with Annex A.

Group Identification

2.6   If a suspect refuses or, having agreed, fails to attend an identification parade or the holding of a parade is impracticable, arrangements must if practicable be made to allow the witness an opportunity of seeing him in a group of people.

2.7   A group identification may also be arranged if the officer in charge of the investigation considers, whether because of fear on the part of the witness or for some other reason, that it is, in the circumstances, more satisfactory than a parade.

2.8   The suspect should be asked for his consent to a group identification and advised in accordance with paragraphs 2.15 and 2.16. However, where consent is refused the identification officer has the discretion to procede with a group identification if it is practicable to do so.

2.9   A group identification should, if practicable, be held in a place other than a police station (for example, in an underground station or a shopping center). It may be held in a police station if the identification officer considers, whether for security reasons or on other grounds, that it would not be practicable to hold it elsewhere. In either case the group identification should, as far as possible, follow the principles and procedures for a parade as set out in Annex A.

Video Film Identification

2.10   The identification officer may show a witness a video film of a suspect if the investigating officer considers, whether because of the refusal of the suspect to take part in an identification parade or group identification or other reasons, that this would in the circumstances be the most satisfactory course of action.

2.11   The suspect should be asked for his consent to a video identification and advised in accordance with paragraph 2.15 and 2.16. However, where such consent is refused the identification officer has the discretion to proceed with a video identification if it is practicable to do so.

2.12   A video identification must be carried out in accordance with Annex B.

Confrontation

2.13   If neither a parade, a group identification nor a video identification procedure is arranged, the suspect may be confronted by the witness. Such a confrontation does not require the suspect's consent, but may not take place unless none of the other procedures are practicable.

2.14   A confrontation must be carried out in accordance with Annex C.

Notice to Suspect

2.15   Before a parade takes place or a group identification or video identification is arranged, the identification officer shall explain to the suspect:

(i) the purposes of the parade or group identification or video identification;

(ii) the fact that he is entitled to free legal advice;

(iii) the procedures for holding it (including his right to have a solicitor or friend present);

(iv) where appropriate the special arrangements for juveniles;

(v) where appropriate the special arrangements for mentally disordered and mentally handicapped persons;

(vi) the fact that he does not have to take part in a parade, or co-operate in a group identification, or with the making of a video film and, if it is proposed to hold a group identificaiton or video identification, his entitlement to a parade if this can practicably be arranged;

(vii) the fact that, if he does not consent to take part in a parade or co-operate in a group identification or with the making of a video film, his refusal may be given in evidence in any subsequent trial and police may proceed covertly without his consent or make other arrangements to test whether a witness identifies him.

(viii) whether the witness had been shown photographs, photofit, identikit or similar pictures by the police during the investigation before the identity of the suspect became known.

2.16 This information must also be contained in a written notice which must be handed to the suspect. The identification officer shall give the suspect a reasonable opportunity to read the notice after which he shall be asked to sign a second copy of the notice to indicate whether or not he is willing to take part in a parade or group identification or co-operate with the making of a video film. The signed copy shall be retained by the identification officer.

(b) Cases where the identity of the suspect is not known

2.17 A police officer may take a witness to a particular neighbourhood or place to see whether he can identify the person whom he said he saw on the relevant occasion. Care should be taken however not to direct the witness's attention to any individual.

2.18 A witness must not be shown photographs or photofit, identikit or similar pictures for identification purposes if the identity of the suspect is known to the police and he is available to stand on an identification parade. If the identity of the suspect is not known, the showing of such pictures to a witness must be done in accordance with Annex D.

(c) Documentation

2.19 The identification officer shall make a record of the parade, group identification or video identification on the forms provided.

2.20 If the identification officer considers that it is not practicable to hold a parade, he shall tell the suspect why and record the reason.

2.21 A record shall be made of a person's refusal to co-operate in a parade, group identification or video identificaion.

3. Identification by fingerprints

(a) Action

3.1   A person's fingerprints may be taken only with his consent or if paragraph 3.2 applies. If he is at a police station consent must be in writing. In either case the person must be informed of the reason before they are taken and that they will be destroyed as soon as practicable if paragraph 3.4 applies. He must be told that he may witness their destruction if he asks to do so within five days of being cleared or informed that he will not be prosecuted.

3.2   Powers to take fingerprints without consent from any person over the age of ten years are provided by section 61 of the Police and Criminal Evidence Act 1984. Reasonable force may be used if necessary.

3.3   Section 27 of the Police and Criminal Evidence Act 1984 describes the circumstances in which a constable may require a person convicted of a recordable offence to attend at a police station in order that his fingerprints may be taken.

3.4   The fingerprints of a person and all copies of them taken in that case must be destroyed as soon as practicable if:

(a)   he is prosecuted for the offence concerned and cleared; or

(b)   he is not prosecuted (unless he admits the offence and is cautioned for it).

An opportunity of witnessing the destruction must be given to him if he wishes and if, in accordance with paragraph 3.1, he applies within five days of being cleared or informed that he will not be prosecuted.

3.5   When fingerprints are destroyed, access to relevant computer data shall be made impossible as soon as it is practicable to do so.

3.6   References to fingerprints include palm prints.

(b) Documentation

3.7   A record must be made as soon as possible of the reason for taking a person's fingerprints without consent and of their destruction. If force is used a record shall be made of the circumstances and those present.

4. Identification by photographs

(a) Action

4.1   The photograph of a person who has been arrested may be taken at a police station only with his written consent or if paragraph 4.2 applies. In either case he must be informed of the reason for taking it and that the photograph will be destroyed if paragraph 4.4 applies. He must be told that he may witness the destruction of the photograph or be provided with a certificate confirming its destruction if he applies within five days of being cleared or informed that he will not be prosecuted.

4.2   The photograph of a person who has been arrested may be taken without consent if:

(i)   he is arrested at the same time as other persons, or at a time when it is likely that other persons will be arrested, and a photograph is necessary to establish who was arrested, at what time and at what place; or

(ii) he has been charged with, or reported for a recordable offence and has not yet been released or brought before a court; or

(iii) he is convicted of such an offence and his photograph is not already on record as a result of (i) or (ii). There is no power of arrest to take a photograph in pursuance of this provision which applies only where the person is in custody as a result of the exercise of another power (e.g. arrest for fingerprinting under section 27 of the Police and Criminal Evidence Act 1984).

4.3 Force may not be used to take a photograph.

4.4 Where a person's photograph has been taken in accordance with this section, the photograph, negatives and all copies taken in that particular case must be destroyed if:

(a) he is prosecuted for the offence and cleared; or

(b) he is not prosecuted (unless he admits the offence and is cautioned for it).

An opportunity of witnessing the destruction or a certification confirming the destruction must be given to him if he so requests provided that, in accordance with paragraph 4.1, he applies within five days of being cleared or informed that he will not be prosecuted.

(b) Documentation

4.5 A record must be made as soon as possible of the reason for taking a person's photograph under this section without consent and of the destruction of any photographs.

5. Identification by body samples, swabs and impressions

(a) Action

5.1 Dental impressions and intimate samples may be taken from a person in police detention only:

(i) if an officer of the rank of superintendent or above considers that the offence concerned is a serious arrestable offence; and

(ii) if that officer has reasonable grounds to believe that such an impression or sample will tend to confirm or disprove the suspect's involvement in it; and

(iii) with the suspect's written consent.

5.2 Before a person is asked to provide an intimate sample he must be warned that a refusal may be treated, in any proceedings against him, as corroborating relevant prosecution evidence. He must also be reminded of his entitled to have free legal advice and the reminder must be noted in the custody record.

5.3 Except for samples of urine or saliva, intimate samples may be taken only by a registered medical or dental practitioner as appropriate.

5.4 A non-intimate sample, as defined in paragraph 5.11, may be taken from a detained suspect only with his written consent or if paragraph 5.5 applies. Even if he consents, an officer of the rank of inspector or above must have reasonable grounds for believing that such a sample will tend to confirm or disprove the suspect's involvement in a particular offence.

5.5   A non-intimate sample may be taken without consent if an officer of the rank of superintendent or above has reasonable grounds for suspecting that the offence in connection with which the suspect is detained is a serious arrestable offence and for believing that the sample will tend to confirm or disprove his involvement in it.

5.6   Where paragraph 5.5 applies, reasonable force may be used if necessary to take non-intimate samples.

5.7   The suspect must be informed, before the intimate or non-intimate sample or dental impression is taken, of the grounds on which the relevant authority has been given, including the nature of the suspected offence, and that the sample will be destroyed if paragraph 5.8 applies.

5.8   Where a sample or impression has been taken in accordance with this section, it and all copies of it taken in that particular case must be destroyed as soon a practicable if:

(a)   the suspect is prosecuted for the offence concerned and cleared; or

(b)   he is not prosecuted (unless he admits the offence and is cautioned for it).

(b) Documentation

5.9   A record must be made as soon as practicable of the reason for taking a sample or impression and of its destruction. If force is used a record shall be made of the circumstances and those present. If written consent is given to the taking of a sample or impression, the fact must be recorded in writing.

5.10   A record must be made of the giving of a warning required by paragraph 5.2 above.

(c) General

5.11   The following terms are defined in section 65 of the Police and Criminal Evidence Act 1984 as follows:

(a)   "intimate sample" means a sample of blood, semen or any other tissue fluid, urine, saliva or pubic hair or a swab taken from a person's body orifice;

(b)   "non-intimate sample" means:
(i)   a sample of hair other than pubic hair;
(ii)   a sample taken from a nail or from under a nail;
(iii)   a swab taken from any part of a person's body other than a body orifice;
(iv)   a footprint or a similar impression of any part of a person's body other than a part of his hand.

5.12   Where clothing needs to be removed in circumstances likely to cause embarrassment to the person, no person of the opposite sex, who is not a medical practitioner or nurse shall be present, (unless in the case of a juvenile, that juvenile specifically requests the presence of a particular adult of the opposite sex who is readily available) nor shall anyone whose presence is unnecessary. However, in the case of a juvenile this is subject to the overriding proviso that such a removal of clothing may take place in the absence of the appropriate adult only if the juvenile signifies in the presence of the appropriate adult that he prefers the search to be done in his absence and the appropriate adult agrees.

ANNEX A
IDENTIFICATION PARADES

(a) General

1. A suspect must be given a reasonable opportunity to have a solicitor or friend present, and the identification officer shall ask him to indicate on a second copy of the notice whether or not he so wishes.

2. A parade may take place either in a normal room or in one equipped with a screen permitting witnesses to see members of the parade without being seen. The procedures for the composition and conduct of the parade are the same in both cases, subject to paragraph 7 below (except that a parade involving a screen may take place only when the suspect's solicitor, friend or appropriate adult is present or the parade is recorded on video).

(b) Parades involving prison inmates

3. If an inmate is required for identification, and there are no security problems about his leaving the establishment, he may be asked to participate in a parade or video identification. (A group identification, however, may not be arranged other than in the establishment or inside a police station.)

4. A parade may be held in a Prison Department establishment, but shall be conducted as far as practicable under normal parade rules. Members of the public shall make up the parade unless there are serious security or control objections to their admission to the establishment. In such cases, or if a group or video identification is arranged within the establishment, other inmates may participate. If an inmate is the suspect, he should not be required to wear prison uniform for the parade unless the other persons taking part are other inmates in uniform or are members of the public who are prepared to wear prison uniform for the occasion.

(c) Conduct of a parade

5. Immediately before the parade, the identification officer must remind the suspect of the procedures governing its conduct and caution him in the terms of paragraph 10.4 of the code of practice for the detention, treatment and questioning of persons by police officers.

6. All unauthorised persons must be excluded from the place where the parade is held.

7. Once the parade has been formed, everything afterwards in respect of it shall take place in the presence and hearing of the suspect and of any interpreter, solicitor, friend or appropriate adult who is present (unless the parade involves a screen, in which case everything said to or by any witness at the place where the

parade is held must be said in the hearing and presence of the suspect's solicitor, friend or appropriate adult or be recorded on video).

8.   The parade shall consist of at least eight persons (in addition to the suspect) who so far as possible resemble the suspect in age, height, general appearance and position in life. One suspect only shall be included in a parade unless there are two suspects of roughly similar appearance in which case they may be paraded together with at least twelve other persons. In no circumstances shall more than two suspects be included in one parade and where there are separate parades they shall be made up of different persons.

9.   Where all members of a similar group are possible suspects, separate parades shall be held for each member of the group unless there are two suspects of similar appearance when they may appear on the same parade with at least twelve other members of the group who are not suspects. Where police officers in uniform form an identification parade, any numerals or other identifying badges shall be concealed.

10.   When the suspect is brought to the place where the parade is to be held, he shall be asked by the identification officer whether he has any objection to the arrangements for the parade or to any of the other participants in it. The suspect may obtain advice from his solicitor or friend, if present, before the parade proceeds. Where practicable, steps shall be taken to remove the grounds of objection. Where it is not practicable to do so, the officer shall explain to the suspect why his objections cannot be met.

11.   The suspect may select his own position in the line. Where there is more than one witness, the identification officer must tell the suspect, after each witness has left the room, that he can if he wishes change position in the line. Each position in the line must be clearly numbered, whether by means of a numeral laid on the floor in front of each parade member or by other means.

12.   The identification officer is responsible for ensuring that, before they attend the parade, witnesses are not able to:

(i)   communicate with each other about the case or overhear a witness who has already seen the parade;

(ii) see any member of the parade;

(iii) on that occasion see or be reminded of any photograph or description of the suspect or be given any other indication of his identity; or

(iv) see the suspect either before or after the parade.

13.   The officer conducting a witness to a parade must not discuss with him the composition of the parade, and in particular he must not disclose whether a previous witness has made any identification.

14.   Witnesses shall be brought in one at a time. Immediately before the witness inspects the parade, the identification officer shall tell him that the person he saw may or may not be on the parade and if he cannot make a positive identification he should say so. The officer shall then ask him to walk along the parade at least twice, taking as much care and time as he wishes. When he has done so the officer

shall ask him whether the person he saw in person on an earlier relevant occasion is on the parade.

15.   The witness should make an identification by indicating the number of the person concerned.

16.   If the witness makes an identification after the parade has ended the suspect and, if present, his solicitor, interpreter, or friend shall be informed. Where this occurs, consideration should be given to allowing the witness a second opportunity to identify the suspect.

17.   If a witness wishes to hear any parade member speak, adopt any specified posture or see him move, the identification officer shall first ask whether he can identify any persons on the parade on the basis of appearance only. When the request is to hear members of the parade speak, the witness shall be reminded that the participants in the parade have been chosen on the basis of physical appearance only. Members of the parade may then be asked to comply with the witness's request to hear them speak, to see them move or to adopt any specified posture.

18.   When the last witness has left, the identifcation officer shall ask the suspect whether he wishes to make any comments on the conduct of the parade.

(d) Documentation

19.   If a parade is held without a solicitor or a friend of the suspect being present a colour photograph or video film of the parade shall be taken. A copy of the photograph shall be supplied on request to the suspect or his solicitor within a reasonable time.

20.   Where a photograph or video film is taken in accordance with paragraph 19, it shall be destroyed or wiped clean at the conclusion of the proceedings unless the person concerned is convicted or admits the offence and is cautioned for it.

21.   If the identification officer asks any person to leave a parade because he is interfering with its conduct the circumstances shall be recorded.

22.   A record must be made of all those present at a parade or group identification whose names are known to the police.

23.   If prison inmates make up a parade the circumstances must be recorded.

24.   A record of the conduct of any parade or must be made on the forms provided.

ANNEX B
VIDEO IDENTIFICATION

(a) General

1.   Where a video parade is to be arranged the following procedures must be followed.

2.   Arranging, supervising and directing the making and showing of a video film to be used in a video identification must be the responsibility of an identification officer or identification officers who have no direct involvement with the relevant case.

3.   The film must include the suspect and at least eight other people who so far as possible resemble the suspect in age, height, general appearance and position in life. Only one suspect shall appear on any film unless there are two suspects of roughly similar appearance in which case they may be shown together with at least twelve other persons.

4.   The suspect and other persons shall as far as possible be filmed in the same positions or carrying out the same activity and under identical conditions.

5.   Provision must be made for each peson filmed to be identified by number.

6   If police officers are filmed, any numerals or other identifying badges must be concealed. If a prison inmate is filmed either as a suspect or not, then either all or none of the persons filmed should be in prison uniform.

7.   The suspect and his solicitor, friend, or appropriate adult must be given a reasonable opportunity to see the complete film before it is shown to witnesses. If he has a reasonable objection to the video film or any of its participants, steps should, if practicable be taken to remove the grounds for objection. If this is not practicable the identification officer shall explain to the suspect and/or his representative why his objections cannot be met and record both the objection and the reason on the forms provided.

8.   The suspect's solicitor, or where one is not instructed the suspect himself, where practicable should be given reasonable notification of the time and place that it is intended to conduct the video identification in order that a representative may attend on behalf of the suspect. The suspect himself may not be present when the film is shown to the witness(es). In the absence of a person representing the suspect the viewing itself shall be recorded on video. No unauthorised persons may be present.

(b) Conducting the Video Identification

9.   The identification officer is responsible for ensuring that, before they see the film, witnesses are not able to communicate with each other about the case or overhear a witness who has seen the film. He must not discuss with the witness the composition of the film and must not disclose whether a previous witness has made any identification.

10.   Only one witness may see the film at a time. Immediately before the video identification takes place the identification officer shall tell the witness that the person he saw may or may not be on the video film. The witness should be advised that at any point he may ask to see a particular part of the tape again or to have a particular picture frozen for him to study. Furthermore, it should be pointed out that there is no limit on how many times he can view the whole tape or any part of it. However, he should be asked to refrain from making a positive identification or saying that he cannot make a positive identification until he has seen the entire film at least twice.

11.   Once the witness has seen the whole film at least twice and has indicated that he does not want to view it or any part of it again, the identification officer shall ask the witness to say whether the individual he saw in person on an earlier occasion has been shown on the film and, if so, to identify him by number. The

identification officer will then show the film of the person identified again to confirm the identification with the witness.

12.   The identification officer must take care not to direct the witness's attention to any one individual on the video film, or give any other indication of the suspect's identity. Where a witness has previously made an identification by photographs, or a photofit, identikit or similar picture has been made, the witness must not be reminded of such a photograph or picture once a suspect is available for identification by other means in accordance with this code. Neither must he be reminded of any description of the suspect.

(c) Tape Security and Destruction

13.   It shall be the responsibility of the identification officer to ensure that all relevant tapes are kept securely and their movements accounted for. In particular, no officer involved in the investigation against the suspect shall be permitted to view the video film prior to it being shown to any witness.

14.   Where a video film has been made in accordance with this section all copies of it must be destroyed if the suspect:

(a)   is prosecuted for the offence and cleared; or

(b)   is not prosecuted (unless he admits the offence and is cautioned for it).

An opportunity of witnessing the destruction must be given to him if he so requests within five days of being cleared or informed that he will not be prosecuted.

(d) Documentation

15.   A record must be made of all those participating in or seeing the video whose names are known to the police.

16.   A record of the conduct of the video identification must be made on the forms provided.

ANNEX C

CONFRONTATION BY A WITNESS

1.   The identification officer is responsible for the conduct of any confrontation of a suspect by a witness.

2.   Before the confrontation takes place, the identification officer must tell the witness that the person he saw may or may not be the person he is to confront and that if he cannot make a positive identification he should say so.

3.   The suspect shall be confronted independently by each witness, who shall be asked "Is this the person?". Confrontation must take place in the presence of the suspect's solicitor, interpreter or friend, where he has one, unless this would cause unreasonable delay.

4.   Confrontation may take place either in a normal room or one equipped with a screen permitting a witness to see the suspect without being seen. In both cases the procedures are the same except that a room equipped with a screen may be used only when the suspect's solicitor, friend or appropriate adult is present or the confrontation is recorded on video.

ANNEX D
SHOWING OF PHOTOGRAPHS

(a) Action

1.   An officer of the rank of sergeant or above shall be responsible for supervising and directing the showing of photographs. The actual showing may be done by a constable or a civilian police employee.

2.   Only one witness shall be shown photographs at any one time. He shall he given as much privacy as practicable and shall not be allowed to communicate with any other witness in the case.

3.   The witness shall be shown not less than twelve photographs at a time. These photographs shall either be in an album or loose photographs mounted in a frame or a sequence of not less than twelve photographs on optical disc, and shall, as far as possible, all be of a similar type.

4.   When the witness is shown the photographs, he shall be told that the photograph of the person he saw may or may not be amongst them. He shall not be prompted or guided in any way but shall be left to make any selection without help.

5.   If a witness makes a positive identification from photographs, then, unless the person identified is otherwise eliminated from enquiries, other witnesses shall not be shown photographs. But both they and the witness who has made the identification shall be asked to attend an identification parade or group or video identification if practicable unless there is no dispute about the identification of the suspect.

6.   Where the use of a photofit, identikit or similar picture has led to there being a suspect available who can be asked to appear on a parade, or participate in a group or video identification, the picture shall not be shown to other potential witnesses.

7.   Where a witness attending an identification parade has previously been shown photographs or photofit, identikit or similar pictures (and it is the responsibility of the the officer in charge of the investigation to make the identification officer aware that this is the case) then the suspect and his solicitor must be informed of this fact before the identity parade takes place.

8.   None of the photographs (or optical discs) used shall be destroyed, whether or not an identification is made, since they may be required for production in court. The photographs should be numbered and a separate photograph taken of the frame or part of the album from which the witness made an identification as an aid to reconstituting it.

(b) Documentation

9.   Whether or not an identification is made, a record shall be kept of the showing of photographs and of any comment made by the witness.

Appendix B

Ontario Model Jury Charge

ONTARIO MODEL JURY CHARGE

"The case against the accused depends wholly [or in large part] on the correctness of his identification by [the witness or witnesses]. I must therefore warn you that there is a very special need for caution before convicting in reliance on the correctness of that identification.

"The reason for that need for caution is that all identification evidence suffers from an inherent frailty - human observation and recollections are notoriously unreliable in this area.

"Most cases of miscarriage of justice have been due to mistaken identity. I am sure you have no doubt that [the witness] is convinced in his own mind that he has identified the right man; and his evidence is convincing. But a convincing witness, though perfectly honest, may also be mistaken, and several such witnesses may also be mistaken.

"You must therefore examine closely the circumstances in which the identification was made in this case, and I now propose to review that evidence with you.

"[then discuss the following aspects of the evidence]

"1. *Original observation* – how long did the witness have the accused under observation? At what distance? In what light? Was the observation impeded in any way, e.g. by passing traffic or a press of people? Had the witness ever seen the accused before? How long a time elapsed between the original observation and the subsequent identification to the police? Did the accused have any special distinguishing features, either physical or in his speech or dress?

"2. *Subsequent identification* – was the identification wholly independent and not induced by any suggestion? If photographs were shown to witness, were they representative? If witness identified accused in court after being picked out of a photograph, is he merely identifying the accused with the photograph, rather than with the man originally observed? Was the subsequent identification made by reference to features not mentioned to police when the witness was first seen by them?

"3. *Identification parade* – has it been shown that nothing whatever was done to indicate the accused to the witness, either by showing a photograph or by description, or an indication of his place in the line-up? Was the accused conspicuously different from others in the line-up in age, build, colour, complexion, dress or otherwise?

"4.   Remind jury of any specific weaknesses in the identification evidence; e.g. any material discrepancy between the description given to the police in the first instance, and his actual appearance; contradictory descriptions; failure of another witness with equal opportunity to recognize accused.

"5.   Remind the jury that even though recognition by the witness of someone previously known to him is usually stronger than identification of a stranger, mistakes are sometimes made in recognition of close relatives and friends.

"6.   Identify for the jury the evidence which is capable of supporting this identification, e.g.:

"(a) fingerprints or other tell-tales at the scene of the crime;
"(b) incriminatory evidence found on person or premises of accused, including gunpowder residue;
"(c) accused seen going into a building, or getting into a car with which he can be identified;
"(d) accused has given an alibi which is not only disbelieved, but which jury are satisfied was given to deceive police.

"7.   If the quality of the identification evidence is poor, e.g. based on a fleeting glance or is a mere impression, with no description of the characteristics which distinguish the accused from any other person, e.g. 'That's the man', then unless there is supporting evidence, the jury should be clearly instructed that in the view of the judge, the identification does not provide a safe basis for conviction.

"Finally

"Instruct the jury that if, after careful examination of the evidence in the light of the circumstances, and with due regard to all the other evidence in the case, they feel satisfied beyond reasonable doubt of the correctness of the identification, they are at liberty to act upon it."

Appendix C

Sample Cross-examination

INTRODUCTION

The following cross-examination examples are based up on several elementary principles of advocacy. The first of these principles is that the purpose of cross-examination (for that matter any examination) is to provide information that can later be used in argument before the finder of fact. The second principle is that points to be made in cross-examination ought to be made as efficiently as possible. The premise being that the fewer the number of questions asked the less chance there is of the examiner getting into trouble. The third principle is that of "safety first", so the questions in cross-examination should be in such a form as to attempt to limit the responses available to the witness. In the result, if at all possible, only highly leading questions ought to be used.

THE SCENARIO

The accused is charged with the armed robbery of a convenience store. The only clerk in the store says the robber came into the store, walked around the aisles until the two other customers in the store left, came up to the counter, pulled out a knife and demanded the money in the till. The clerk gave him the money and the robber then immediately turned around and ran out of the store.

The clerk described the robber as being 5'10" tall, of medium build, with a dark complexion and long hair. He was dressed in blue jeans and a cowboy shirt. She described the knife as being 3"- 4" long, with an ivory handle.

Ten days after the robbery the police asked the clerk to come down to the police station in order to look at some pictures. At that time, she was shown eight pictures, one at a time. She then identified the accused from those pictures. She subsequently identified the accused at the preliminary hearing and at the trial.

OBJECTIVES

The cross-examination of this witness should have two major objectives. The first is to show that the conditions at the event were such that her subsequent identification cannot be relied upon. The second is to cast doubt on the validity of the subsequent identification procedure.

The Event

There are several lines of cross-examination that can be pursued.

One objective would be to demonstrate that until he pulled the knife the robber was just another customer. As a result the clerk had no reason to note him. This cross-examination could encompass factors such as the fact that she was busy with other customers during the time he was in the store and that her view of the robber was obstructed by the store shelving.

Q. You'll agree with me, will you not, that until he pulled out the knife, the robber was just another customer?
A. Yes.

Q. One of many who would come into the store during your shift?
A. Yes.

Q. In fact, while this person was in the store, there were two other customers present?
A   Yes.

Q. And you were busy serving them, were you not?
A. Yes.

Q. And as a good employee, you would be devoting your full attention to those customers when they were at the counter?
A. I suppose so.

Q. As well, there are a number of shelves in the store, are they not?
A. Yes.

Q. And during the time the robber was in the store, he was walking along the aisles between the shelving wasn't he?
A. I think so.

Q. And you'd agree with me, would you not, that the shelving would prevent you from getting a clear view of someone in the aisles?
A. Sometimes, it would depend where he was.

As well, one would try to show that the event was of short duration in order to argue that the witness did not have a long time to observe the robber.

Q. When the robber came up to the counter, he immediately pulled out the knife, didn't he?
A. Not immediately.

Q. But within a matter of seconds?
A. Yes.

Q. And at the same time, he demanded the money from the till?
A. Yes.

Q. And you complied with that demand right away didn't you?
A. Yes.
Q. And as soon as you gave him the money, he turned around and ran out the door?
A. Yes.
Q. So you'll agree with me that the whole incident from the beginning to end happened very quickly didn't it?
A. Yes, but it seemed like an eternity to me.

In addition, one would attempt to point out that because of the presence of the knife, the clerk was frightened. This cross-examination would also try and point out that the clerk was fixated on the knife. It would therefore permit counsel to argue that due to the stress of the situation, the witness would be unable to make a reliable identification. As well, the fact that the witness was focused on the weapon would decrease the amount of time in which the robber's face could be viewed.

Q. You testified that the person who robbed you had a knife?
A. Yes.
Q. And I take it the knife was pointed directly at you?
A. Yes.
Q. That frightened you, didn't it?
A. Yes.
Q. You've described the knife in some detail haven't you?
A. I got a good look at it.
Q. And the reason you got a good look at it was that you wanted to keep an eye on it during the robbery?
A. I guess.
Q. And the reason you kept an eye on the knife was to give you the ability to avoid it, if the man made a move towards you?
A. Yes.

The subsequent identification

The objective in this cross-examination is to demonstrate that in this process the witness was, in effect, given a multiple choice examination where none of the above was not one of the choices. This is done by showing that the witness expected to identify someone and, as a result, through a process of elimination identified the person closest in appearance to that of the robber. This type of cross-examination can be utilized whether a photo spread or a lineup was utilized.

Q. The police didn't ask you to come look at some pictures until ten days after the robbery did they?
A. Right.
Q. And during these ten days did you see the robber again?

A. No.

Q. And I take it you went to work during this period?

A. Yes.

Q. And, of course, being in the retail business, you dealt with many other customers during this time?

A. Yes.

Q. And, the first time you saw the robber was on the night of the robbery?

A. Yes.

Q. When the police called you they said they wanted you to look at some pictures to see if you could identify the robber?

A. Yes.

Q. I suggest to you that it made you think that the police had somebody in mind.

A. I wasn't really sure.

Q. But it crossed your mind. Didn't it?

A. Yes.

Q. At the police station you were presented with only eight pictures by the police weren't you?

A. Yes.

Q. You weren't asked to look at any books or other large collection of pictures, were you?

A. No, I wasn't.

Q. And you were shown these pictures one at a time?

A. Yes.

Q. You'll agree with me will you not that these pictures don't show you the height and weight of the individuals in those pictures?

A. No, they don't.

Q. And you stated the robber was the man in picture number 5?

A. Yes.

Q. I suggest that once you saw the robber in picture, you didn't look that carefully at pictures 6,7, and 8?

A. I thought I did.

Q. In any event, looking at numbers 6 and 7, the men in them both had light coloured hair, didn't they?

A. Yes.

Q. And that's why you eliminated them wasn't it?

A. Yes.

Q. Number 8, here, seems to be a very heavy set individual doesn't he?

A. Yes.

Q. And that's why you eliminated him, wasn't it?

A. Yes.

Q. Numbers 1 and 4 have fair complexion, don't they?

A. I guess.

Q. And that's why you eliminated them, right?
A. Yes.

Q. And if we look at number 2, he has a rather prominent nose, doesn't he?
A. Yes, he does.

Q. And that's why you eliminated him.
A. Yes.

Q. And lastly number 3's eyebrows are bushy aren't they?
A. Yes.

Q. And the robber didn't have bushy eyebrows, did he?
A. No.

Q. And that's why you eliminated him?
A. Yes.

Contradictory Testimony

In the event that the witness's testimony does not conform to her initial description, either by virtue of the fact that the witness mentions a feature that was not included in her initial description or where a feature in the initial description is left out, these contradictions ought to be brought out in cross-examination. In these instances it is important not to ask the witness why her testimony did not conform to the original description. This will only permit the witness to wriggle out of the contradiction. It is best simply to point out the contradiction and argue that the witness's credibility is affected by contradictions. Where the witness omits a detail, the argument would be that the witness's ability to recollect must be questioned. This lack of ability to recollect should be taken into account by the fact finder when assessing the reliability of her subsequent identification.

Where the witness adds a new detail, the argument would be that the witness is describing the person she saw in the subsequent identification procedure. As a result, the identification made at that time has coloured her recollection of the robber and therefore the accuracy of her identification of the accused must be put into doubt.

Q. When you gave your initial description to the police, you stated that the robber had long hair, didn't you?
A. Now that you mention it, I did.

Q. However, you made no mention of long hair in your testimony today, did you?
A. I guess I forgot.

Q. As well, today you stated that the robber had bushy eyebrows, right?
A. Yes.

Q. However, you didn't tell the police that the robber had bushy eyebrows did you?
A. I guess I forgot to mention it to them.

INDEX